D1610485

GRANDPARENTING PRACTICES AROUND THE WORLD

Edited by

Virpi Timonen

First published in Great Britain in 2019 by

Policy Press
University of Bristol
1-9 Old Park Hill
Bristol
BS2 8BB
UK
t: +44 (0)117 954 5940
pp-info@bristol.ac.uk
www.policypress.co.uk

North America office:
Policy Press
c/o The University of Chicago Press
1427 East 60th Street
Chicago, IL 60637, USA
t: +1 773 702 7700
f: +1 773-702-9756
sales@press.uchicago.edu
www.press.uchicago.edu

British Library Cataloguing in Publication Data
A catalogue record for this book is available from the British Library

Library of Congress Cataloging-in-Publication Data
A catalog record for this book has been requested

ISBN 978-1-4473-4064-5 hardback
ISBN 978-1-4473-4066-9 ePdf
ISBN 978-1-4473-4067-6 ePub
ISBN 978-1-4473-4068-3 Mobi

Cover design by Jess Augarde
Front cover image: shutterstock

Contents

iv

List of figures and tables

List of abbreviations

AgenDA	Ageing and Generational Dynamics in Africa
CREW	Care, Retirement & Wellbeing of Older People Across Different Welfare Regimes
ELSA	English Longitudinal Study of Ageing
ESS	European Social Survey
EU	European Union
GGS	Generations and Gender Survey
HAI	HelpAge International
HDRSS	Heads & Deanery Research Support Scheme
ICT	information and communication technologies
ILC	International Longevity Centre
LGBTQ	lesbian, gay, bisexual, transgender and queer
LMM	Latent Markov Model
LSOG	Longitudinal Study of Generations
MAS	Myanmar Ageing Survey
MICRA	Manchester Institute for Collaborative Research on Ageing
NIH	National Institutes of Health
NSO	National Statistical Office
OAP	Old Age Pension
OECD	Organisation for Economic Co-operation and Development
OPA	Older Persons Act 13 of 2006 (South Africa)
PRC	People's Republic of China
SHARE	Survey of Health, Ageing and Retirement in Europe
SOPT	Survey of Older Persons in Thailand
SRT	social relational theory
SSA	Sub-Saharan Africa
TANF	Temporary Assistance to Needy Families
TUS	Time Use Survey
UCT	University of Cape Town
UPF	Universitat Pompeu Fabra
VNAS	Vietnam Ageing Survey
WHO	World Health Organization

Notes on contributors

Bruno Arpino is an Associate Professor at the Department of Political and Social Sciences, Universitat Pompeu Fabra (UPF), Spain, where he is also Co-Director of the Research and Expertise Centre on Survey Methodology (RECSM). His research interests are in the areas of social demography and applied statistics. He is particularly interested in studying intergenerational relationships, ageing and health, fertility and immigrants' assimilation. He coordinates a three-year international project titled Care, Retirement & Wellbeing of Older People Across Different Welfare Regimes (CREW). For more information, please see his personal website: https://sites.google.com/site/brunoarpino/.

Vern L. Bengtson is Research Professor in the Roybal Institute on Aging at the Suzanne Dworak-Peck School of Social Work, University of Southern California (USC), CA, and AARP (American Association of Retired Persons)/University Professor of Gerontology Emeritus. A past president of the Gerontological Society of America, he has published 19 books and 260 research articles on ageing, families and intergenerational relationships. Over his 50-year scholarly career, Bengtson's research contributions have been recognised in the form of Distinguished Scholar awards from four major professional associations. Among his recent books are *How Families Still Matter: A Longitudinal Study of Youth in Two Generations*, *The Handbook of Theories of Aging* and *Families and Faith: How Religion Is Passed Down across Generations*.

Judith E. Brown is a Research Officer at the University of New South Wales, Australia. She specialises in applied social statistical analysis and has considerable expertise in time-use analysis. She has published in the fields of social policy, sociology, psycho-oncology and health psychology.

Lyn Craig is Professor of Sociology and Social Policy and Australian Research Council Future Fellow at the University of Melbourne, Australia. Her research interests include time use and gender, workforce participation, intersections between the family and the economy, intergenerational connections over the life course, and comparative family and social policy.

Giorgio Di Gessa is a lecturer in Global Ageing at King's College London, UK. He completed his PhD in Demography at the London School of Hygiene and Tropical Medicine, UK. He has a longstanding interest in the field of social gerontology, particularly in the demographic and social determinants of health and wellbeing in later life in Europe. He has a particular interest in associations between social engagement (such as caring, volunteering and paid work) and mental and physical health at older ages. Much of his work involves cross-national comparisons of the complex relationships between ageing and health using longitudinal secondary data and a life-course perspective. Dr Di Gessa has a keen interest and expertise in quantitative methodologies, including hierarchical modelling and causal inference.

Megan L. Dolbin-MacNab is Associate Professor of Human Development and Family Science and Director of the Marriage and Family Therapy Doctoral Program at Virginia Tech, VA. She is also a faculty affiliate of Virginia Tech's Center for Gerontology. Her research on grandfamilies has explored grandchild experiences and wellbeing, parenting and family dynamics, and best practices for community-based interventions. Dr Dolbin-MacNab is the author of numerous journal articles and book chapters about grandfamilies, as well as resources for practitioners. She also consults with local and state support programmes on delivering effective services to grandfamilies.

April L. Few-Demo is Professor of Family Studies in the Department of Human Development and Family Science at Virginia Tech, VA. Her research interests include the topics of intimate violence, adolescent sexuality, qualitative methodologies, rural women's re-entry and LGBTQ+ family issues. Few-Demo's scholarship highlights the utility of Black feminism, intersectionality and critical race theories in family science. She has contributed to *Sourcebook of Family Theory and Research*, *Violence in The Lives of Black Women* and *Written/Unwritten: Tenure and Race in the Humanities* and has co-edited *The Handbook of Feminist Family Studies* and the *Sourcebook of Family Theories and Methodologies*.

Lucie Galčanová works as a Researcher in the Office for Population Research at Masaryk University, Brno, Czech Republic. Her theoretical and research interests in sociology include the cultural and spatial aspects of population ageing and housing as well as urban studies, with a focus on home and domesticity. She lectures on the sociology of space and architecture, social gerontology and qualitative research methods.

Karen Glaser is a Professor of Gerontology at King's College London, UK. She has three main research interests: family care from a comparative perspective, life-course research focusing on the relationship between work and family histories and later life health, and the impact of lifelong disorders and disabilities on the health of affected individuals and their families. Since 2010, Karen has worked on a project investigating grandparenting in Europe. Funded by the Calouste Gulbenkian Foundation and in partnership with the Beth Johnson Foundation and the Institute of Gerontology, the study examines variations in grandparental care across 12 European countries.

Esther C.L. Goh is Associate Professor and Head of the Department of Social Work at the National University of Singapore. Her research centres on championing the need to utilise a more dynamic theory to examine childrearing and parent–child relationships. Adopting a bilateral lens that conceptualises both children and parents (including adult caregivers) as agentic beings influencing each other, this line of research diverges from the conventional unilateral model, which sees influence as only from parents (antecedents) to children (outcomes). To discover the complexities of bilateral influences between these agentic beings, she utilises qualitative methodologies, including ethnographic and a range of in-depth qualitative methods.

Myra Hamilton, PhD, is a Senior Research Fellow at the Social Policy Research Centre at the University of New South Wales, Australia. She is a sociologist and social policy researcher whose work explores how formal and informal care is organised in societies and the inequalities produced as a consequence. The focus of her research program is unpaid care provision at different stages of the life course and its impact on work, retirement, incomes and wellbeing, and the ways in which policies and services can support individuals and families to meet their care needs.

Jaco Hoffman, DPhil (Oxon), is Professor of Socio-Gerontology and Leader of the Optentia Research Focus subprogramme, Ageing and Generational Dynamics in Africa (AgenDA), at North-West University (Vaal Triangle Campus), South Africa, and James Martin Senior Research Fellow in the Oxford Institute of Population Ageing at the University of Oxford, UK. He is also an Honorary Professor in the Institute of Ageing in Africa, Department of Medicine, Faculty of Health Sciences, University of Cape Town (UCT), South Africa. Dr Hoffman co-directs, with Professor Sebastiana Kalula of UCT, the International Longevity Centre (ILC), South Africa.

John Knodel is Research Professor Emeritus at the University of Michigan, MI, and International Affiliate of the College of Population Studies at Chulalongkorn University, Thailand. He has conducted comparative quantitative and qualitative research with Professor Sebastiana Kalula (UCT) since 1971 on social demographic topics in South East Asia, especially Thailand but also Cambodia, Vietnam and Myanmar. Recent research involves how adult migration affects older-age parents, intergenerational family support exchanges, long-term care of older persons and grandparental care of children left behind by migrants from Myanmar to Thailand. Virtually all his work is undertaken in collaboration with colleagues in the region.

Rachel Margolis is an Associate Professor of Sociology at the University of Western Ontario, Canada. Her research addresses how family dynamics shape social inequality and population change in developed countries. Current projects address thinning kinship networks in North America and Europe, the demography of grandparenthood, and parental wellbeing and low fertility.

Hanna Ojala, PhD, is University Lecturer in Gender Studies at University of Tampere, Finland. Her research has focused on intersections of age, gender and class in the various contexts of men's ageing, such as health, retirement, anti-ageing, sports and communities. She has published in *Ageing & Society*, *Journal of Aging Studies*, *The Gerontologist*, *International Journal of Men's Health* and *Health Psychology*.

Ilkka Pietilä, PhD, is Assistant Professor of Social Gerontology at the Faculty of Social Sciences, University of Helsinki, Finland. His research interests relate to age and gender, covering themes such as retirement, ageing bodies, ageism, masculinities, consumption and health. His articles have appeared in several journals, including *The Gerontologist*, *Ageing & Society*, *Sociology of Health and Illness*, *Journal of Aging Studies*, *International Journal of Men's Health*, *Health Psychology* and *Social Science and Medicine*.

Debora Price is a Professor of Social Gerontology at the University of Manchester and Director of the Manchester Institute for Collaborative Research on Ageing (MICRA), UK. She initially qualified as a barrister, specialising in family law, before moving to academia. She retains a strong interest in how policy influences and interacts with family change, especially the implications for women, mothers and grandmothers. Her research centres on finance over the life course, pensions and poverty in later life, financial services for an ageing society, household money and the financial consequences of cohabitation and separation.

Eloi Ribe received his PhD in sociology from the University of Edinburgh, UK, in 2018. His current research interests include intergenerational intimate and care practices, poverty and exclusion of elderly people and transforming social care arrangements for elderly dependent individuals. He has authored and coauthored reports and articles on a variety of topics, including a cross–country research project on grandparental care arrangements, alternative forms of long-term care for dependent elderly people, and the effects of gender, lineage and re-partnering on intimate grandparent–grandchild relationships.

Merril Silverstein, is inaugural holder of the Marjorie Cantor Chair in Aging Studies in the Department of Sociology and the Department of Human Development and Family Science at Syracuse University, NY. He received his doctorate in sociology from Columbia University, NY, after which he served on the faculty of the Leonard Davis School of Gerontology at the University of Southern California, CA. In over 170 research publications, he has focused on ageing in the context of family life, with an emphasis on intergenerational relations in international perspective. He serves as Principal Investigator of the Longitudinal Study of Generations and was an originator of the Longitudinal Study of Older Adults in Anhui Province, China. He is a Brookdale Fellow and a Fulbright Senior Scholar and, between 2010–14, served as Editor-in-Chief of *Journal of Gerontology: Social Sciences.*

Bussarawan Teerawichitchainan is Associate Professor of Sociology, School of Social Sciences, Singapore Management University. Her areas of interest include family demography, the life course and ageing, population health and social inequality. Her current research addresses topics related to ageing, intergenerational relationships and the wellbeing of older persons in the context of South East Asia and from a comparative, cross-national perspective. She is presently a Co-Principal Investigator of an NIH (National Institutes of Health)-funded project titled Vietnam Health and Aging Study, which examines the long-term impacts of war on older-aged Vietnamese survivors in northern Vietnam.

Virpi Timonen is Professor in Social Policy and Ageing at Trinity College, Dublin, Ireland. A Finnish national who earned her doctorate at the University of Oxford, UK, her work focuses on the sociology of ageing and social policies as they are unfolding in ageing societies. She has an interest in the life course from youth to old age, especially in the context of intergenerational relations within families and societies, and expertise in the grounded theory method. This is her second edited book on grandparenting.

Lucie Vidovićová, PhD, is a Sociologist. Her long-term research interests include the sociology of ageing, age discrimination, active ageing and social exclusion. She is also involved in research projects in the fields of environmental gerontology, social policy, labour markets, family and lifelong learning. She conducts research for national as well as European bodies and works as a consultant on a number of implementation projects. She sees ageing as a fun topic, loves to challenge the myths and embraces the unexpected futures of ageing. Find her at: www.ageismus.cz

Dovile Vildaite, PhD, earned her doctorate in Child and Youth Research from the School of Social Work and Social Policy at Trinity College, Dublin, Ireland, in 2016. Her research interests include transnational family migration, extended family ties and grandparent–grandchild relationships, sociocultural influences on child and youth development, and mixed-methods research.

Sheng-li Wang is a Lecturer in Sociology at Fuzhou University, China, and PhD student of Sociology at Sun Yat-sen University, China. Her research interests include social work practice and medical sociology. She utilises qualitative methodologies including case studies and a range of in-depth qualitative methods. Xiamen and Guangdong are her main research sites.

Yanqiu Rachel Zhou is a Professor at the School of Social Work and the Institute on Globalization and the Human Condition, McMaster University, Canada. Her major research interests include transnationalism, social policy, temporalities and global health. She has published widely in various peer-reviewed journals, including *Globalizations*; *Journal of Aging Studies*; *Health; Time and Society* and *Social Science and Medicine*. She is also a co-editor of two books: *Time, Globalization, and Human Experiences: Interdisciplinary explorations* (Routledge, 2016) and *Time and Globalization: An interdisciplinary dialogue* (Routledge, 2017), and a special issue on time and globalization (*Globalizations*, 2016) and the lead editor of a symposium on transnationalism, sexuality and HIV risk (*Culture, Health & Sexuality*, 2017).

ONE

Introduction: widening the lens on grandparenting

Virpi Timonen

Introduction

This book is a sequel to *Contemporary grandparenting*, published in 2012 (Arber and Timonen, 2012). In the first chapter of *Contemporary grandparenting*, we noted that the existing literature on grandparenting heavily focused on exploring the factors – such as age, gender, geographical proximity, marital status and lineage – that influence the frequency of contact and quality of relationships between grandparents and grandchildren. While the purpose of this introduction is not to provide a review of literature published since 2012, I note that several recent studies have continued to probe into these aspects of grandparenting – for instance, Dunifon and Bajracharia (2012), Danielsbacka and Tanskanen (2012) and Kolk (2017). Another long-established line of enquiry pertains to the extent and circumstances of intergenerational transfers of time, money and accommodation. In the 2012 book, we argued that while it is important that patterns of contact and transfers of time and material resources between generations continue to receive attention, it is also essential to broaden the enquiry to examine the evolving nature and meanings of these transfers, and changes in intergenerational relationships more generally. We were also motivated by the absence of book-length accounts of grandparenting, with the exception of some outdated volumes that focused on grandparenting in a single-country context.

Contemporary grandparenting explored the extent to which, under different welfare contexts and family circumstances, grandparents (especially grandmothers) perform the roles of 'child savers' and 'mother savers' and act as a 'reserve army' or 'family savers' in situations where their adult children(-in-law) are strained or unable to look after their children (Arber and Timonen, 2012). But we also noted that alongside these functions, grandparents are increasingly important in many cultures as 'family maximisers' (Baker and Silverstein, 2012), making important inputs to enable younger family generations to succeed in realms such as the labour market and education. In other words, the **functions** of grandparents – as sources of help, care and support to younger family generations – have been a central focus in the literature. Other key conceptual frameworks discussed in *Contemporary grandparenting* included the **norm of non-interference** and the **norm of obligation** – the expectation that grandparents offer help and support to younger generations without interfering in their decisions regarding, in particular, key choices surrounding the upbringing of children (May et al., 2012). Theorising on intergenerational solidarity, the book used **conflict** and **ambivalence** to illustrate how frameworks that apply to grandparents are characterised by not only 'opposites' but also a recognition that intergenerational relationships are inherently complex and evolving – as illustrated, for instance, by the experiences of grandparents co-residing with their adult children and grandchildren in Hong Kong, a context where such co-residence has generally declined (Ko, 2012).

This book will continue to emphasise that grandparenting takes many diverse forms and cannot be reduced to a small number of 'types'. Grandparenting has evolved considerably, and continues to evolve, as a result of both sociodemographic and economic influences and grandparents' own agency. While studies that pertain to one context are of course valuable, it is important to take a comparative approach to the study of grandparenting to tease out the impacts of context (culture and welfare states) on grandparents and the families they relate to. Chapters in this book represent a global outlook: they arise from research on grandparenting in Europe, America, Asia, Africa and Australia. Despite the extensive cultural, economic and social differences between these diverse contexts, they have one thing in common: grandparents are increasing in number, and they are becoming more important and influential within both families and the societies they live in. We need up-to-date accounts of evolving grandparenting practices around the world (a wealth of these is illuminated in Shwalb and Hossain, 2017), but we also need more and better conceptual and theoretical frameworks that help to make sense of these. The book at hand hopes to both illustrate the cultural variety of everyday grandparenting practices and work towards constructing the lenses that enable us to theorise and conceptualise grandparenting.

This book is therefore in many ways a further, deeper exploration of the topics that were discussed in *Contemporary grandparenting*, but it also addresses a number of new topic areas. In the remainder of this chapter, I will outline how this book builds on the insights brought to light in what I have come to think of as '*Grandparenting I*' (Arber and Timonen, 2012). The broad thematic areas covered here in '*Grandparenting II*' are in many ways overlapping, but in each case add new dimensions and angles to the topic. The demographic and welfare state contexts of grandparenting have certainly retained their central importance, and evince some intriguing developments, not in the least the postponement in the age of becoming a grandparent in some contexts. While one section could not possibly do justice to the diversity of grandparents in developing countries, I nonetheless considered it important to include chapters on grandparenting in countries that are undergoing rapid economic and social development. Gender and intersectionalities, while extensively referenced in the earlier book, are here brought into particularly close focus. This volume also provides an opportunity to delve into the topic of transnational grandparenting, something that received only cursory treatment in *Contemporary grandparenting*. Grandparental roles, agency and influence deserve more attention, and hence the last section of the book is devoted to these topics.

Demographic contexts of grandparenting

Contemporary grandparenting addressed the implications of key demographic and societal changes in the context of grandparenting roles, and how diverse cultural contexts and welfare states are mediating grandparents' and their families' responses to these changes. The book noted that demographic change, in particular the ageing of populations across the world, has led to a prolongation of the period of their lives that grandparents and grandchildren share. This in turn has opened up the opportunity for grandparents and grandchildren to develop both longer-lasting and qualitatively different relationships than in the past. In many ways, therefore, demography underpins – but certainly does not determine – the nature and extent of social interactions and transfers between family generations. For instance, while the increase in the number and longevity of grandparents is a near-universal phenomenon, the time use of grandparents varies, so that in some countries they are a lot more involved in intensive time-consuming childcare than in others (Herlofson and Hagestad, 2012).

Demography shapes grandparenting at a fundamental level: births, deaths, family formation and dissolution, and their timing, generate the 'frame' within which grandparenthood comes about and is practised. The longer people live (assuming reasonably stable fertility-related behaviours in the younger generations), the longer they spend in the grandparent role. However, fertility patterns might exert a contravening force: the later people reproduce, the later the entry into the grandparent role, and the greater the proportion of the childless among those coming to the end of their reproductive age, the greater the proportion of those who never enter the grandparent role. This exclusion from the role of a grandparent is of growing concern in regions where childlessness is on the rise, including many Central, Eastern and Southern European countries as well as parts of Asia.

Taking Canada as an exemplar of these increasingly shared demographic trends, Margolis (2016) demonstrated that, between 1985 and 2011, the share of Canadian women in their early 50s (age 50–54) who were grandmothers dropped significantly, from about 60% to less than 30%. Among men in this age group, the proportion of those who were grandfathers also halved, from 44% to 22% (Margolis 2016, p 617). Postponement of childbearing among the currently middle-aged cohorts' children is the main driver of these declines, but childlessness plays a small role, too. It is worth nothing that these delays detected in Canada are considerably greater than those identified in Germany in a study of cohorts born in 1929–58 (Leopold and Skopek, 2015). Despite postponement in the transition into the grandparent role, gains in longevity (especially among men) mean that the time spent in this role is generally increasing for men. However, through the striking discovery of a small decline in the total time period spent in the grandmother role in Canada (from 1985 to 2011), Margolis (2016) demonstrated that the long-term trend towards longer periods of time spent in the grandparent role is being in some cases reversed, and therefore cannot be taken for granted. Margolis and Arpino further interrogate these important demographic developments in Chapter Two.

Although postponed childbearing means that prospective grandparents have to wait longer for this role transition, it also means the transition might come at a more propitious time, namely around or after retirement from paid work. In principle, this increases the chances that grandparents can spend time with grandchildren instead of experiencing potential conflict between the worker and grandparent roles (whereby the difficulties working parents face in striking a work–life balance might also become prevalent among working grandparents). Moreover, today's grandparents are, at least in some contexts (see Margolis and Iciaszczyk, 2015), healthier than grandparents of similar age in the past, which means they are (again, in principle) better able to engage in activities with their grandchildren. Nonetheless, it is important to note that this does not apply across all contexts or all subgroups among grandparents; a remarkable portrayal of grandmothers juggling – and, in some cases, struggling to reconcile – work and grandchild care in the United States can be found in Harrington Meyer (2012).

Welfare state and cultural contexts of grandparenting

Demographic developments therefore exert a fundamental impact on the timing, prevalence and duration of grandparenting. However, there is much more to grandparenting from a sociological perspective. What does grandparenting mean for the grandparents and their children and grandchildren? What is the societal significance of grandparenting? What are some of the key social and economic forces that are shaping grandparenting practices? And what are some of the other megatrends that coincide with population ageing and lower fertility rates, with implications for grandparenting practices?

Growth in the labour market participation of women is one key trend that was discussed in *Contemporary grandparenting*. Some welfare states have responded to this with extensive provision or subsidisation of childcare; others continue to regard childcare as largely a private family responsibility (Sun, 2012). As a consequence, grandparents have come to play diverse roles in childcare provision to support working families. At the same time, the policy drive towards longer working lives has made the assumption that grandparents (and grandmothers in particular) are available to provide childcare increasingly problematic (Harrington Meyer, 2012). The lives of younger family generations are evolving, but one certainly should not assume that the lives of the older generations have remained static. On the contrary, gerontological research has brought to light the many ways in which old age is not what it used to be, and we need to be aware of how, for instance, preferences for paid work or leisure pursuits might be shaping grandparenting practices (as illustrated in McGarrigle et al., 2018).

Grandparents as a source of childcare, and the significance of this provision at societal level, continues to receive a lot of scholarly attention. Di Gessa and colleagues (2016) studied the associations between intensive grandparental childcare and contextual structural and cultural factors in Europe. They discovered higher levels of intensive grandparental childcare in countries with low labour force participation among women and low formal childcare provision, where mothers in paid work largely have to rely on grandparental childcare. This finding is in line with the argument put forward by Herlofson and Hagestad (2012), who use different data but also arriving at the conclusion that grandparental childcare is strongly associated with the level of public provision and support of childcare (see also Bordone et al., 2017). In this book, Price and coauthors further elaborate on the interconnection between welfare state regimes and grandparental childcare, leading to the development of family policy regimes that are underpinned by grandparents, and in particular by the negotiation of care and work roles among grandmothers and mothers (Chapter Three).

Notwithstanding the call for a broader lens in the scholarship on grandparents, the research energies devoted to the issue of grandchild care are justified, as the amount of grandparental childcare is extensive and increasing in some contexts. In a cohort study using data from the Netherlands, Geurts and colleagues (2015) discovered that the likelihood of grandparents providing care for their daughter's children increased between 1992 and 2006. The main factors behind this increase were higher maternal employment rates, growth in lone motherhood, reduced travel time and a decline in the number of adult children. The increase in grandparental childcare in a European welfare state such as the Netherlands is remarkable – and even surprising, because the availability of formal childcare has increased over time. As a response to this, the Netherlands has recently introduced a new policy where grandparents can receive up to €6 per hour for providing childcare. Even more strikingly, a study by Thomese and Liefbroer (2013) suggests that the involvement of both paternal and maternal grandparents in grandchild care is associated with a greater number of births, and that grandparental childcare might be part of an emerging reproductive strategy for Dutch parents.

There is a large and growing literature that examines the health (physical, cognitive and mental) impacts of grandchild care (Hilbrand et al., 2017). Recent studies have discovered positive associations between grandchild care and self-rated physical health in diverse contexts (for instance, in rural China: Zhou et al., 2017; and in various European countries: Di Gessa et al., 2016). However, most studies also seem to point to differential impacts of looking after grandchildren, contingent on factors such as the educational level of the grandparent, familial relationships, social supports and types of care provided (for a systematic review of research on the effects of grandchild care provision on the psychological wellbeing of grandparents, see Kim et al., 2017). To take just one example from this burgeoning literature, a study of the cognitive functioning of grandmothers caring for grandchildren in South Korea found that childcare was both instantaneously and longitudinally beneficial to cognition for grandmothers with higher education (Jun, 2015). In contrast, for less-educated grandmothers, childcare had neither immediate nor lagged effects on cognition. The perception of childcare as a burden moderated the association between caregiving and depressive symptoms among Chinese American grandparents in a study by Xu and coauthors (2017), suggesting that while caregiving generally has a positive impact on grandparents' wellbeing, role strain can interfere with this. The findings about the impact of grandchild care evince considerable variability in outcomes for grandparents, not least on the basis of cultural and economic circumstances, which vary greatly between regions of the world and countries within those regions.

Socioeconomic development and transnational grandparenting

Knodel and Teerawichitchainan address grandparenting in developing South East Asia in Chapter Four. Their analysis not only drives home the (often neglected) importance of economic development for family practices but also demonstrates considerable intercountry differences in grandparenting practices within the region. In Chapter Five, Hoffman outlines the challenges faced by South African grandparents who find themselves battling poverty and HIV/AIDS in tandem with extensive grandchild care duties. However, grandparents facing great challenges should never be viewed as lacking agency – a viewpoint Hoffman shares with Dolbin-MacNab and colleagues (2016), who also demonstrated resilient behaviours among grandmothers raising grandchildren in South Africa.

The topic of grandparenting in contexts of economic and social development is linked to transnational grandparenting because economically motivated migration, whether within-country or international, gives rise to families where members live at considerable distance from each other. Furthermore, the topic links with the aforementioned demographics, welfare states and provision of childcare; for instance, Vega's (2017) research with immigrant grandmothers shows that older recent immigrant women are more intensively involved in childcare provision than their native-born and more established immigrant counterparts.

Transnational grandparents can find themselves at different points along a continuum: from intensive round-the-clock intergenerational coexistence during visits abroad (or family members' visits from abroad) to a situation where any face-to-face contact becomes impossible or very infrequent. This volume seeks to deepen insights into transnational grandparenting by including two chapters on this topic. Chapter Six by Zhou interrogates the experiences of Chinese grandparents who have engaged in extensive circular migration, or even emigrated, to contribute to raising the children of their immigrant adult children in Canada. In Chapter Seven, Vildaite outlines her research on the 'left behind' grandmothers of the one-and-a-half generation Lithuanian immigrants to Ireland (that is, teenagers and young adults who arrived in Ireland as children). In other words, these chapters analyse two contrasting **turns to transnationalism**: one in which grandparents relocate (temporarily or permanently) to the 'destination' country, the other in which grandparents remain in the country of origin.

The grandparents that 'stay behind' have been studied by (among others) Sigad and Eisikovits (2013), who considered the impact of transnational migration on the extended family in the US–Israel context. They argued that the 'left behind' struggle with redefining their roles as grandparents and with the sense of being deprived of the roles they had expected to play. Further, they posited that grandparenting children who are geographically distant and raised in a foreign culture necessitates the development of new ways of maintaining relationships with grandchildren. While we therefore have some insights into the experiences of grandparents who remain in the country of origin and seek to maintain family relationships from there, as Vildaite points out, to date we have known very little about the experiences of their grandchildren, let alone the views of both generations. Chapter Seven sheds light on how both the Lithuanian grandmothers and their grandchildren who emigrated in childhood or youth view their relationship.

As a result of extensive social, economic and demographic changes framed by a wide variety of welfare state and cultural contexts, as well as the increase in transnational grandparenting, the role of grandparents in 21st-century families is more multidimensional, complex and dynamic than it has been in earlier periods in history. At the micro level of grandparents' identities, attitudes and behaviours, we noted in *Contemporary grandparenting* that several changes were taking place. The changing nature of masculinities is influencing grandfathering practices. These comprise both new generations of grandfathers, who take a greater role in their own children's care, and grandfathers who draw on new channels such as information technology to communicate with their grandchildren (Tarrant, 2012). Generational changes at societal level, including the ageing of baby boomers, also affect grandparenting. Changing social norms have led to more informal and interactive relationships between many grandparents and their grandchildren. The underresearched areas we noted in *Contemporary grandparenting* included (older) grandchildren's influence on grandparents and the longer-lasting relationships with older/adult grandchildren that become possible with increased life expectancies, which are very different from interactions with young grandchildren (see Delerue Matos and Borges Neves, 2012). There are, of course, many other poorly understood topics, and the field of research on grandparents is constantly expanding. In particular, we now have a better understanding of how gender shapes grandparenting.

Gender, family status and intersectionalities

In *Contemporary grandparenting*, we argued that grandparenting is often a euphemism for grand*mothering* (Arber and Timonen, 2012). Available research evinces persistence of a highly gendered division of labour among most grandparents. Grandfathers tend to be more involved with grandchildren when they are married or partnered, suggesting that grandfathers' involvement is strongly mediated by grandmothers (Knudsen, 2012). However, recent research on grandfathers indicates some changes in this regard as grandfathers are recognised as having agency, including the ability and inclination to become more involved in grandchildren's care and lives (Buchanan and Rotkirch, 2016).

In the European context, the gender gap in grandparenting is smallest in the north and largest in the south, consonant with differences in the family–state division of caring responsibilities and the more general cultural framing of gender roles (Leopold and Skopek, 2014). Horsfall and Dempsey (2015) examined the gendered organisation of grandchild care in Australia: a context that they characterise as highly maternalist and reliant on grandparents for informal care of children. Their mixed-method study revealed that gendered inequalities associated with providing childcare significantly influenced the lives of grandmothers. Grandmothers experienced greater dissatisfaction with free time and undertook considerably more domestic labour compared to grandfathers. Grandmothers were positioned as nurturing and as coordinators of care, while grandfathers engaged in children's recreational activities but were relatively free to opt in or out of grandchild care (Horsfall and Dempsey, 2015). In Chapter Eight, Craig and colleagues extend and deepen this line of analysis by examining the gendered divisions of grandchild care in Australia, Korea, Italy and France, and show how maternal and grandmaternal caregiver roles are closely intertwined as a result of welfare state structures (see also Chapter Three).

Mann et al. (2016) argued that men make sense of their grandfatherhood by connecting the role to **hegemonic masculinities**. Notwithstanding their emotionally close and affectionate relationships with grandchildren, grandfathers seek to maintain or forge connections to what they perceive as masculine roles. Examples of how continuity with traditional forms of masculinity is achieved include undertaking sporting activities with grandchildren, advising on school work and career choices and adopting the role of a father figure in the grandchild's life. Hence, Mann and colleagues (2016) posited that grandfatherhood can be seen as a form of **capital** for older men: a conduit to resources and opportunities to enact masculinity by being fit and active, a significant role model and a source of support. They advocated the extension of the hegemonic masculinities framework through recognition that traditional masculinities can coexist with greater involvement in the lives of grandchildren and with the adoption of caring roles. However, the impact of other intersecting variables on grandfathering has to date remained underinvestigated. In this volume, Ojala and Pietilä also interrogate grandfathering practices, taking a close look at how social class shapes such practices in the Nordic context (Chapter Nine).

Contemporary grandparenting noted that changes in patterns of partnership formation and increases in family breakdown and family reconstitution have implications for grandparenting. Divorce in the older generation impacts on their contact with the younger generations; for instance, divorced men tend to have less contact with adult children and grandchildren than their married counterparts. Dissolution of their adult children's relationships also influences older adults' intergenerational contacts; grandparents' experiences range from intensive co-parenting alongside their divorced son or daughter to a drastic reduction, or complete withdrawal, of contact with grandchildren (Timonen and Doyle, 2012). Nonetheless, grandparents have agency and can take action to deepen relationships with grandchildren, which might combat the negative impacts of, for instance, geographical distance and divorce (Mahne and Huxhold, 2012). However, the influence of the 'middle generation' persists in both 'intact' and 'reconstituted' families; Chapman et al. (2016) argued that stepgrandchildren who perceived stepgrandparents as fulfilling traditional grandparent roles, and whose parents modelled and facilitated warm, close relationships with stepgrandparents, were most likely to perceive these intergenerational relationships as important.

At the high end of the spectrum of contact with and proximity to grandchildren, the topic of **custodial grandparents** – also referred to as **grandparent-headed families** and, increasingly, **grandfamilies** – continues to receive a lot of scholarly attention, especially in the United States where a journal has recently been established that specifically focuses on this group of grandparents (*GrandFamilies: The Contemporary Journal of Research, Practice and Policy*). Recent literature provides further analysis of earlier findings concerning the relatively disadvantaged position of most custodial grandparents and the outcomes that are, for the most part, attributable to social and economic disadvantage rather than grandparenting per se (Hadfield, 2014; Harris, 2013). It is also important to pay attention to how ethnicity and marginalisation influence and motivate the cultural practices of grandparental caregiving; for instance, see Henderson et al. (2017) for a study of Native Alaskan custodial grandparents and Hill (2016) for a study of Six Nations grandmothers in North America. The literature on custodial grandparents continues to call for access to a comprehensive array of services – financial, psychological, medical and legal – for this group of grandparents (Du Preez et al., 2017). In addition to these services, grandparent caregivers should be empowered to engage in activities that encourage support and self-care – a scenario that has not been fulfilled to date (Harris 2013). As the reliance on grandfamilies continues and extends, it is crucial, as Dolbin-MacNab and Few-Demo argue in Chapter Six, to grasp and address the complex intersectionalities that predispose some grandparents to become the main or sole caregivers of their grandchildren.

Among the other important intersectionalities we had to omit from *Contemporary grandparenting* (due to difficulty finding available authors) was lesbian, gay, bisexual, transgender and queer (LGBTQ) grandparenting, a topic that Orel and Fruhauf researched, leading to a publication in the same year (2012). There is now a small literature on LGBTQ grandparents. Tornello and Patterson (2016) found that gay grandfathers who had disclosed their sexual orientation to their grandchildren reported closer relationships with them. Conversely, Scherrer (2016) studied grandchildren's experiences of disclosing their sexual identities to their grandparents and concluded that having a close relationship with grandparents, especially where the grandparents have less conservative values, is conducive to grandchildren's disclosure of LGBTQ identity. Grandparenting by people across the range of sexual orientations is a topic of growing importance – not least because many countries have now legislated for marriage equality – and there are growing numbers of same-sex parents, most of whom are likely to become grandparents.

Grandparenting, where it is not experienced as excessively onerous, can be seen as a position of privilege; a role and status that can go hand in hand with other active and valued roles in society. This is certainly the perception of most grandparents in the small but significant minority who have no contact with their grandchildren – a phenomenon that is more common among paternal than maternal grandparents (largely due to the norm of maternal custody of children in the event of divorce or separation), and that has been argued to be rooted in a cultural bias towards the nuclear family form (Sims and Rofail, 2013). Gair's (2017) investigation of grandparents who had experienced disrupted, lost or denied contact with grandchildren revealed that such experiences were very distressing and impacted negatively on grandparents' self-assessed health. The situation of grandparents who are denied contact with grandchildren calls for further research and policy development, including careful attention to extending grandparents' rights.

Grandparental roles, agency and influence

The experiences of the majority of grandparents, who *do* have the opportunity to negotiate their roles and involvement within the extended family, continue to provide rich material for research. As illustrated in *Contemporary grandparenting* (Arber and Timonen, 2012) and several chapters in this volume, policy makers and researchers often construe grandparents as sources of functional support (particularly childcare) and potential sources of financial or material transfers. However, grandparents are also holders and transmitters of less tangible resources, including emotional, social, educational and cultural capital (Noriega et al., 2017). In many ways, these forms of capital are more significant and longer-lasting than the (usually relatively short-term) assistance with childcare, yet the literature on grandparents as caregivers dwarfs the literature on grandparents as holders of cultural capital.

Grandparents' positive influences on the cognitive development, academic achievements, health and wellbeing of their grandchildren have been documented (see, for instance, Fergusson et al., 2008; Modin and Fritzell, 2009), and these are among the reasons why grandparents are popular sources of childcare from both parents' and welfare states' perspectives. Analysing data from Denmark, Miallegaard and Jaeger (2015) argue that grandparents' cultural capital has a positive effect on the likelihood that their grandchildren choose the academic track in upper-secondary education. Hällsten and Pfeffer (2017) also discovered substantial associations between grandparents' wealth and their grandchildren's grade-point averages in secondary school in Sweden. These results suggest that, even in the relatively egalitarian Scandinavian context, grandparents affect grandchildren's educational success via transmission of noneconomic resources. In most European countries, grandparents' effect on grandchildren's educational careers is quite modest (Deindl and Tieben, 2017). However, the significance of such intergenerational transmission is considerably greater in more unequal societies, such as the United Kingdom, where Chan and Boliver (2013) discovered that (net of parents' social class) the odds of grandchildren entering the professional-managerial rather than unskilled-manual class were at least 2.5 times better if the grandparents were themselves in professional-managerial rather than unskilled-manual positions. This **grandparent effect** in social mobility persists even when parents' education, income and wealth are taken into account.

These findings indicate that resource transmission by grandparents is becoming a powerful conduit of intragenerational inequalities in some countries. Research on the extended family's impact on children's educational achievements in the case of the United States indicates that grandparents' resources are particularly important for children's educational outcomes in families with lower socioeconomic status (Jaeger, 2012). In other words, grandparental resources constitute a compensatory mechanism that alleviates the negative consequences of living in a nuclear family of low socioeconomic status. Also pertaining to the US context, Chapter Eleven by Silverstein and Bengtson sheds light on another form of intergenerational influence, namely the transmission of religiosity. In increasingly secular and generationally segregated western societies, the idea that grandparents might play a significant role in the religious socialisation of their grandchildren seems counterintuitive, yet Silverstein and Bengtson present findings that evince continued salience of grandparents for the religious orientations of many youth.

The relationship between the grandparent role and other 'active ageing' roles has been examined by several researchers, and there is evidence of both conflict and consonance in these roles. Arpino and Bordone (2017), using data from the European Survey of Health, Ageing and Retirement Study (SHARE), found that provision of grandchild care had no effect on participation in at least one social activity. However, they did find a negative effect on the number of social activities that care-providing grandmothers engage in. In their analysis of the types of social activities that are reduced as a consequence of grandchild care, Arpino and Bordone (2017) found that volunteering, educational and political/community-organisational activities were particularly likely to be 'pruned back'. Bulanda and Jendrek (2016), in a study of the relationship between grandparenting roles and volunteer activity, found that grandparents who provide nonresidential grandchild care are more likely to volunteer than grandparents not providing grandchild care and those raising a co-residing grandchild. This finding, they argue, is in accordance with resource theory and the accumulation of roles, whereby the 'best resourced' grandparents are more likely to provide relatively light childcare – a position that is also conducive to adopting the volunteer role (because it is not as demanding and time-consuming as full-time childcare/co-residence). In contrast, less well-resourced grandparents are more likely to shoulder extensive grandchild care, which in turn might close off other opportunities and roles such as volunteering. In Chapter Twelve, Goh and Wang interrogate the choices that Chinese grandparents are able to make, and the extent to which some are able to orient themselves to other activities, while others end up agreeing to extensive childcare duties.

In many cultural contexts, entry into the grandparent role is seen as a major transition for the individual (and the grandparent couple). Various assumptions surround the significance of this transition for the individual, among these the idea that grandparenthood might lead to a reordering of priorities in the grandparent's life. In a study that probed this assumption, Wiese et al. (2016) reported that the transition to grandparenthood can alter older adults' priorities. Their longitudinal, quasi-experimental study compared a grandparent group (who were surveyed shortly before and after the birth of their first grandchild) with a control group (who did not become grandparents during the study). The new grandparent group reported less psychological involvement in their jobs and fewer concerns about retirement; in other words, their priorities appeared to have shifted as a result of becoming grandparents. The altered priorities were greater among maternal grandparents, who also expressed fewest worries about uselessness and unproductiveness in retirement. A connection between early retirement (especially around the ages of 55–60) and becoming a grandparent – but only among women – was discovered by Van Bavel and De Winter (2013) in a study drawing on the European Social Survey. These studies suggest that some grandparents become less oriented to paid work and less concerned with their perceived usefulness; instead, they discover new purpose, meaning and ways of occupying themselves in the grandparent role. However, as Chapter Thirteen by Vidovićová and Galčanová highlights, it is important to take a closer look at how grandparents themselves socially construct, experience and portray their roles, and in some cases actively distance themselves from what they see as dominant archetypes, such as a strong orientation to nurturing grandchildren in the Czech social imaginary of ideal–typical grandmotherhood.

Conclusion

The chapters that follow address both theoretical issues and novel research findings. Conceptual models and new theorising are illustrated by drawing on recent empirical studies from a range of countries. The empirical materials are drawn from a wide range of cultural and welfare contexts, spanning both Organisation for Economic Co-operation and Development and developing countries. Both macro- and micro-level issues are covered, with a particular focus on gender, welfare states, economic development and grandparental agency; this ensures the book covers many topic areas of greatest relevance and interest. The chapters therefore combine up-to-date empirical findings with new theorising that will be relevant to academics, researchers, students and experts working in the realms of family and old-age policy and practice.

However, the impetus for another book on grandparenting is not just academic. Since the publication of *Contemporary grandparenting* (Arber and Timonen, 2012), the societal significance of grandparenting and general interest in the topic have grown further. There are more people who are actively engaged with grandparenting, in a variety of ways: as grandparents, as professionals and volunteers working with grandparents, as policy makers or analysts and as researchers and teachers. Policy makers at both national and international levels are more interested than ever in how they can incentivise and support the involvement of grandparents in the lives of the younger family generations. Despite this growing interest and enthusiasm, the contributors to this book are very aware of the importance of not presenting a simplistic 'grandparenting is great' narrative; rather, the aim is to highlight how grandparenting practices are socially structured and constructed, yet also influenced by individual grandparents as they seek to make choices about higher or lower levels of involvement in the lives of younger family generations.

References
Arber, S. and Timonen, V. (eds) (2012) *Grandparenting: Changing family relationships and global contexts*, Bristol: Policy Press

Arpino, B. and Bordone, V. (2017) 'Regular provision of grandchild care and participation in social activities', *Review of Economics of the Household*, 15(1): 135–174

Baker, L. and Silverstein, M. (2012) 'The well-being of grandparents caring for grandchildren in China and the United States', in S. Arber and V. Timonen (eds) *Grandparenting: Changing family relationships and global contexts*, Bristol: Policy Press, pp 51–70.

Bordone, V. Arpino, B. and Arnstein, A. (2017) 'Patterns of grandparental childcare across Europe: The role of the policy context and working mothers' need', *Ageing & Society*, 37(4): 845–873.

Buchanan, A. and Rotkirch, A. (2016) *Grandfathers: Global perspectives*. London: Palgrave Macmillan.

Bulanda, J. and Jendrek, M. (2016) 'Grandparenting roles and volunteer activity', *Journals of Gerontology Series B – Psychological Sciences and Social Sciences*, 71(1): 129–140.

Chan, T. and Boliver, V. (2013) 'The grandparents effect in social mobility: Evidence from British Cohort Studies', *American Sociological Review*, 78(4): 662–678.

Chapman, A., Coleman, M. and Ganong, L. (2016) '"Like my grandparent, but not: A qualitative investigation of skip-generation stepgrandchild–stepgrandparent relationships', *Journal of Marriage and Family*, 78(3): 634–643.

Danielsbacka, M. and Tanskanen, A. (2012) 'Adolescent grandchildren's perceptions of grandparents' involvement in the UK: An interpretation from life course and evolutionary theory perspective', *European Journal of Ageing*, 9(4): 329–341.

Deindl, C. and Tieben, N. (2017) 'Resources of grandparents: Educational outcomes across three generations in Europe and Israel', *Journal of Marriage and the Family*, 79(3): 769–783.

Delerue Matos, A. and Borges Neves, R. (2012) 'Understanding adolescent grandchildren's influence on their grandparents', in S. Arber and V. Timonen (eds) *Contemporary grandparenting: Changing family relationships in global contexts*, Bristol: Policy Press, pp 203–224.

Di Gessa, G., Glaser, K., Price, D., Ribe, E. and Tinker, A. (2016) 'What drives national differences in intensive grandparental childcare in Europe?', *Journals of Gerontology Series B – Psychological Sciences and Social Sciences*, 71(1): 141–153.

Di Gessa, G., Glaser, K. and Tinker, A. (2016) 'The health impact of intensive and nonintensive grandchild care in Europe: New evidence from SHARE', *Journals of Gerontology (Psychological and Social Sciences)*, 71(5): 867–879.

Dolbin-MacNab, M., Jarrott, S., Moore, L., O'Hara, K., Vrugt, M. and Erasmus, M. (2016) 'Dumela Mma: An examination of resilience among South African grandmothers raising grandchildren', *Ageing & Society*, 36(10): 2182–2212.

Dunifon, R. and Bajracharia, A. (2012) 'The role of grandparents in the lives of youth', *Journal of Family Issues*, 33(9): 1168–1194.

Du Preez, J., Richmond, J. and Marquis, R. (2017) 'Issues affecting Australian grandparents who are primary caregivers of grandchildren: A review', *Journal of Family Studies*, 23(1): 142–159.

Fergusson, E., Maugham, B. and Golding, J. (2008) 'Which children receive grandparental care and what effect does it have?', *Journal of Child Psychology and Psychiatry*, 49: 161–169.

Gair, S. (2017) 'Missing grandchildren: Grandparents' lost contact and implications for social work', *Australian Social Work*, 70(3): 263–275.

Geurts, T., van Tilburg, T., Poortman, A.-R. and Dykstra, P. (2015) 'Childcare by grandparents: Changes between 1992 and 2006', *Ageing & Society*, 35: 1318–1334.

Hadfield, J. (2014) 'The health of grandparents raising grandchildren: A literature review', *Journal of Gerontological Nursing*, 40(4): 32–42.

Hällsten, M. and Pfeffer, F. (2017) 'Grand advantage: Family wealth and grandchildren's educational achievement in Sweden', *American Sociological Review*, 82(2): 328–360.

Harrington Meyer, M. (2012) 'Grandmothers juggling work and grandchildren in the United States', in S. Arber and V. Timonen (eds) *Contemporary grandparenting: Changing family relationships in global contexts*, Bristol: Policy Press, pp 71–89.

Harris, D. (2013) 'Grandma's hands rocked the cradle', *Children and Youth Services Review*, 35(12): 2072–2079.

Henderson, T., Dinh, D., Morgan, K. and Lewis, J. (2017) 'Alaska native grandparents rearing grandchildren: A rural community story', *Journal of Family Issues*, 38(4): 547–572.

Herlofson, K. and Hagestad, G. (2012) 'Transformations in the role of grandparents across welfare states', in S. Arber and V. Timonen (eds) *Contemporary grandparenting: Changing family relationships in global contexts*, Bristol: Policy Press, pp 27–49.

Hilbrand, S., Coall, D. and Meyer, A. (2017) 'A prospective study of associations between helping, health and longevity', *Social Science & Medicine*, 187: 109–117.

Hill, L. (2016) 'Haudenosaunee grandmothers caring for their grandchildren: The process of assuming the caregiving role', *Journal of Gerontological Social Work*, 59(4): 281–295.

Horsfall, B. and Dempsey, D. (2015) 'Grandparents doing gender: Experiences of grandmothers and grandfathers caring for grandchildren in Australia', *Journal of Sociology*, 51(4): 1070–1084.

Jaeger, M. (2012) 'The extended family and children's educational success', *American Sociological Review*, 77(6): 903–922.

Jun, H. (2015) 'Educational differences in the cognitive functioning of grandmothers caring for grandchildren in South Korea', *Research on Aging*, 37(5): 500–523.

Kim, H., Kang, H. and Johnson-Motoyama, M. (2017) 'The psychological wellbeing of grandparents who provide supplementary grandchild care: A systematic review', *Journal of Family Studies*, 23(1): 118–141.

Knudsen, K. (2012) 'European grandparents' solicitude: Why older men can be relatively good grandfathers', *Acta Sociologica*, 55(3): 231–250.

Ko, L. (2012) 'Solidarity, ambivalence and multigenerational co-residence in Hong Kong', in S. Arber and V. Timonen (eds) *Contemporary grandparenting: Changing family relationships in global contexts*, Bristol: Policy Press, pp 91–111.

Kolk, M. (2017) 'A life-course analysis of geographical distance to siblings, parents and grandparents in Sweden', *Population Space and Place*, 23(3): e2020.

Leopold, T. and Skopek, J. (2014) 'Gender and the division of labor in older couples: How European grandparents share market word and childcare', *Social Forces*, 93(1): 63–91.

Leopold, T. and Skopek, J. (2015) 'The delay of grandparenthood: A cohort comparison of East and West Germany', *Journal of Marriage and Family*, 77: 441–460.

Mahne, K. and Huxhold, O. (2012) 'Social contact between grandparents and older grandchildren: a three-generation perspective', in S. Arber and V. Timonen (eds) *Contemporary grandparenting: Changing family relationships in global contexts*, Bristol: Policy Press, pp 225–246.

Mann, R., Tarrant, A. and Leeson, G. (2016) 'Grandfatherhood: Shifting masculinities in later life', *Sociology*, 50(3): 594–610.

Margolis, R. (2016) 'The changing demography of grandparenthood', *Journal of Marriage and Family*, 78(3): 610–622.

Margolis, R. and Iciaszczyk, N. (2015) 'The changing health of Canadian grandparents', *Canadian Studies in Population*, 42(3–4): 63–76.

May, V., Mason, J. and Clarke, L. (2012) 'Being there, yet not interfering: the paradoxes of grandparenting', in S. Arber and V. Timonen (eds) *Contemporary grandparenting: Changing family relationships in global contexts*, Bristol: Policy Press, pp 139–158.

McGarrigle, C., Timonen, V. and Layte, R. (2018) 'Choice and constraint in the negotiation of the grandparent role: A mixed-methods study', *Gerontology and Geriatric Medicine*. DOI: 10.1177/2333721417750944.

Miallegaard, S. and Jaeger, M. (2015) 'The effect of grandparents' economic, social and cultural capital on grandchildren's educational success', *Research in Social Stratification and Mobility*, 42: 11–19.

Modin, B. and Fritzell, J. (2009) 'The long arm of the family: Are parental and grandparental earnings related to young men's body mass index and cognitive ability?', *International Journal of Epidemiology*, 38: 724–732.

Noriega, C., Lopez, J. and Dominguez, R. (2017) 'Perceptions of grandparents who provide auxiliary care: Value transmission and child-rearing practices', *Child & Family Social Work*, 22(3): 1227–1236.

Orel, N. and Fruhauf, C. (2012) 'Lesbian, gay, bisexual and transgender grandparents', in A. Goldberg and K. Allen (eds) *LGBT parent families: Possibilities for new research and implications for practice*, New York: Springer, pp 177–192.

Scherrer, K. (2016) 'Gay, lesbian, bisexual and queer grandchildren's disclosure process with grandparents', *Journal of Family Issues*, 37(6): 739–764.

Shwalb, D. and Hossain, Z. (2017) *Grandparents in cultural context*. New York & London: Routledge.

Sigad, L. and Eisikovits, R. (2013) 'Grandparenting across borders: American grandparents and their Israeli grandchildren in a transnational reality', *Journal of Aging Studies*, 27(4): 308–316.

Sims, M. and Rofail, M. (2013) 'The experiences of grandparents who have limited or no contact with their grandchildren', *Journal of Aging Studies*, 27(4): 377–386.

Sun, S. (2012) 'Grandparenting in the context of care for grandchildren by foreign domestic workers', in S. Arber and V. Timonen (eds) *Contemporary grandparenting: Changing family relationships in global contexts*, Bristol: Policy Press, pp 113–136.

Tarrant, A. (2012) 'Grandfathering: the construction of new identities and masculinities', in S. Arber and V. Timonen (eds) *Contemporary grandparenting: Changing family relationships in global contexts*, Bristol: Policy Press, pp 181–201.

Thomese, F. and Liefbroer, A. (2013) 'Child care and child births: The role of grandparents in the Netherlands', *Journal of Marriage and Family*, 75(2): 403–421.

Timonen, V. and Doyle, M. (2012) 'Grandparental agency after adult children's divorce', in S. Arber and V. Timonen (eds) *Contemporary grandparenting: Changing family relationships in global contexts*, Bristol: Policy Press, pp 159–180.

Tornello, S. and Patterson, C. (2016) 'Gay grandfathers: Intergenerational relationships and mental health', *Journal of Family Psychology* 30(5): 543–551.

Van Bavel, J. and De Winter, T. (2013) 'Becoming a grandparent and early retirement in Europe', *European Sociological Review*, 29(6): 1295–1308.

Vega, A. (2017) 'The time intensity of childcare provided by older immigrant women in the United States', *Research on Aging* 39(7): 823–848.

Wiese, B., Burk, C. and Jaeckel, D. (2016) 'Transition to grandparenthood and job-related attitudes: Do grandparental sex and lineage matter?', *Journal of Marriage and Family*, 78(3): 830–847.

Xu, L., Tang, F., Li, L. and Dong, X. (2017) 'Grandparent caregiving and psychological well-being among Chinese American older adults: The roles of caregiving burden and pressure', *Journals of Gerontology: Biological and Medical Sciences*, 72(1): S56–S62.

Zhou, J., Mao, W., Lee, Y. et al. (2017) 'The impact of caring for grandchildren on grandparents' physical health outcomes: The role of intergenerational support', *Research on Aging*, 39(5): 612–634.

PART 1
The demographic and welfare-state contexts of grandparenting

TWO

The demography of grandparenthood in 16 European countries and two North American countries

Rachel Margolis and Bruno Arpino

Introduction

Intergenerational relationships between grandparents and grandchildren can offer tremendous benefits to family members of each generation. For grandparents, grandchildren are often important sources of emotional meaning and support (Silverstein and Long, 1998), and can have positive effects on physical and mental health and cognitive functioning (Arpino and Bordone, 2014; Di Gessa et al., 2016; Szinovacz and Davey, 2006). For grandchildren, grandparents can offer important inputs for social development or economic wellbeing (Chan and Bolivar, 2013; Knugge, 2016; Silverstein and Ruiz, 2006). The middle generation also often benefits from grandparents and grandchildren spending time together and receives important support with childrearing (Aassve et al., 2012; Arpino et al., 2014; Igel and Szydlik, 2011).

When grandparenthood begins and how long it lasts are determined by the demography of the family (Arpino et al., 2017; Margolis, 2016). The transition to grandparenthood occurs when one's child becomes a parent for the first time. Unlike becoming a parent and many other life-course events, the transition to grandparenthood has been labelled a **countertransition** (Hagestad and Neugarten, 1985) because its occurrence and timing are not determined by the persons themselves but rather by their adult children and their partners' transition to parenthood. The length of grandparenthood is the period of time that begins at the birth of one's first grandchild until the end of the grandparent's life (Margolis, 2016). At the population level, a variety of social and demographic factors affect when grandparenthood generally starts, how long it lasts and the demographic characteristics of the population of grandparents. The demography of grandparenthood – the timing, length and population characteristics – shape the extent to which young children have grandparents available, how many grandparents are alive and the duration of overlap with grandparents (Leopold and Skopek, 2015a, 2015b; Margolis, 2016). Kin availability is important to understand because it is a necessary condition for having close intergenerational relationships and garnering the benefits that they can offer.

In this chapter, we examine how the demography of grandparenthood varies across 16 countries in Europe and two countries in North America, and why it is changing. These countries represent great variation in contexts with different grandparenting norms, labour-force participation patterns and demographics. Next, we examine variation in two key determinants of intergenerational relationships: the labour-force participation and health of grandparents. Last, we comment on some important changes in the demography of grandparenthood that may occur in the future. To examine changes in these important patterns in the demography of grandparenthood across contexts and over time, we rely on multiple data sources. We use the fourth wave of the Survey of Health, Ageing and Retirement in Europe (SHARE) (Börsch-Supan, 2017; Börsch-Supan et al., 2013), the Health and Retirement Study for the United States (2010) and the General Social Survey (2011) in Canada for information about the prevalence and characteristics of grandparents. We also use data from the Human Fertility Database (2017) and the Human Mortality Database (2017) to set the demographic scene for the changes that are occurring.

The demographic context of grandparenthood

Not all older adults have or will eventually have grandchildren. How common grandparenthood is among older adults varies greatly across countries. Figure 2.1 shows the percentage of adults aged 50 and above with grandchildren. To construct this, we used the Survey of Health Aging and Retirement in Europe, the General Social Survey in Canada and the Health and Retirement Study (US), including both men and women. Switzerland is the country where the smallest share of older adults has grandchildren, with fewer than half being grandparents (49%). Almost six in ten have grandchildren in Austria, Germany, the Netherlands, Spain, Italy and Canada. Being a grandparent is much more common in Northern Europe, with 69% of Swedes, 67% of Danes and more than three quarters of older adults in the East–Central

Figure 2.1: Weighted per cent of adults aged 50 and above with grandchildren, 2010–11

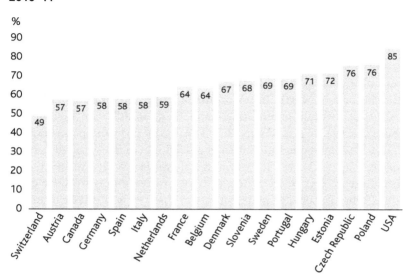

Note: Countries are arranged in ascending order of the per cent of grandparents.

European countries of the Czech Republic and Poland. The United States has the greatest share of grandparents among older adults, with 85% of all older adults in the US having grandchildren.

Why is there so much variation in the prevalence of grandparenthood among older adults? Three factors determine this. The first is the age distribution of the population; older populations with higher median ages will, on average, have greater proportions that are grandparents. The second is the level of childlessness, both historical and current, because this determines what proportion of the population cannot become grandparents. This may be because they do not have any children or because all their children are childless. Levels of childlessness vary greatly across contexts. In most European countries, childlessness has been increasing rapidly (Kreyenfeld and Konietzka, 2017). This trend is led by Germany, Switzerland and Austria, where about 20% of women are finishing their reproductive years without children (Sobotka, 2017). England, Wales, the Netherlands and Finland also have relatively high levels of childlessness for recent cohorts (of the 1968 birth cohort, 18% in England and Wales and 17% in the Netherlands, and 20% of the 1967 birth cohort in Finland) (Sobotka, 2017). Although childlessness was quite low until recently in Eastern and Southern Europe, these countries are also seeing steady increases in childlessness. There is divergence within North America. Canada's childlessness rate reached 20% of the 1965 birth cohort after steadily increasing since the 1946 birth cohort (Human Fertility Database, 2017). However, in the US, after an increase from 10% in 1976 to 20% in 2006, there has been a recent decline to 15% in 2012 (Frejka, 2017).

The third factor that influences the share of older adults that are grandparents is the timing of fertility. Fertility postponement over multiple generations has led to grandparenthood occurring later than ever before in North America and Europe. To examine how the transition to grandparenthood happens in middle age in different countries, we turn to Figure 2.2. This figure plots the percentage of men and women combined with grandchildren in five-year age groups, between ages 50 and 74, by country. Countries with a relatively low mean age at first birth generally have greater proportions of older adults who are already grandparents in their early 50s. For example, in the US, the mean age at first birth is relatively low compared to most European countries (26.8 in 2014) and 61% of US adults aged 50–54 have grandchildren. The Eastern European countries also have relatively early childbearing; here, 3–5 in 10 adults aged 50–54 have

Figure 2.2: Weighted per cent of adults aged 50–74 with grandchildren, by age group and country

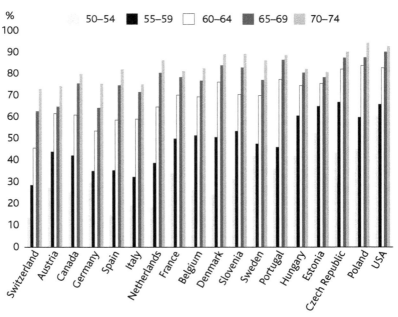

Note: Countries are arranged in ascending order of the per cent of grandparents ages 50 and above.

grandchildren, as do 5–7 in 10 adults aged 55–59. In countries with a higher mean age at first birth, it is less common to have grandchildren before age 60. Central European countries such as Switzerland, Austria and Germany, as well as Canada, have much later transitions to grandparenthood because of later parenthood. As shown in Figure 2.2, fewer than one quarter of adults in Switzerland and Canada aged 50–54 have grandchildren, and the transition in these countries usually happens in the later 50s and 60s.

The length of grandparenthood

The length of grandparenthood is important for contextualising intergenerational relationships because it represents the time available for intergenerational interactions and transfers. Prospective grandparents may want to know their expected time as a grandparent; if they look forward to it, they might make positive health behavioural or lifestyle changes to remain active and alive during this period.

At first glance, the length of grandparenthood is a simple concept. At the individual level, it is the time between the transition to grandparenthood and the respondent's end of life. However, surveys rarely collect data on the age at which transition to grandparenthood occurs; much more often, they only collect current grandparent status. At the population level, one could create a measure for the average length of grandparenthood for a particular cohort. However, for recent cohorts we would have to wait until mortality is realised for the whole group. Therefore, we can only construct cohort measures of the length of grandparenthood for cohorts that have already died. It is much more useful to draw on demographic measures to get a sense of how the length of grandparenthood is changing over time. Recent research has used the Sullivan (1971) method (Jagger et al., 2006) to estimate the number of remaining years at each age that adults in a population will spend as a grandparent, and also without grandchildren. This measure can be interpreted in the same way as life expectancy at a certain age: if one experienced all the age-specific rates for grandparenthood and mortality, how long on average would someone at a given age in a certain year spend as a grandparent, and how long would someone spend without grandchildren?

How long, on average, is the period of grandparenthood? Estimates for North America are between 19 and 26 years for the years 2010–11. In 2011, the average length of grandparenthood was 24.3 years for Canadian women and 18.9 years for Canadian men (Margolis, 2016), and 25.5 years for US women and 21.5 years for US men

(Margolis and Wright, 2017). Within the United States, there is great variation in the average length of grandparenthood by ethnicity. For example, Hispanics have a longer period of grandparenthood than their non-Hispanic Black or non-Hispanic white counterparts due to greater longevity and earlier transition to grandparenthood (Margolis and Wright, 2017). There is much less variation in the length of grandparenthood by education due to greater longevity offsetting later entry into grandparenthood among the highly educated (Margolis and Wright, 2017). These studies estimating the length of grandparenthood at the population level are relatively new; we do not yet have comparable estimates for Europe or other parts of the world.

Labour-force participation and health of grandparents

The extent to which grandparents are available to engage in grandchild care and social activities with grandchildren depends in large part on whether grandparents are engaged in the labour force and their health status (Hank and Buber, 2009). Below, we chart patterns of labour-force participation (Figure 2.3) and health status (Figure 2.4) of grandparents across countries in Europe and North America, drawing on survey data from 2010–11.

Figure 2.3 charts the percentage of adults ages 50–69 with grandchildren who reported working at least part time in the last week. We focused on the age range 50–69 because labour-force participation is, in general, very low for people aged 70 and over; for grandfathers ages 70 and over in most countries, labour-force participation is around 2–3% (not shown).

As is evident from Figure 2.3, for both men and women there is a huge degree of variation in the labour-force participation of grandparents ages 50–69 across countries. In North America, about 55% of grandfathers and 45% of grandmothers are working. Similar figures can be observed in Denmark and Estonia. In Southern Europe and parts of Eastern Europe, labour-force participation for grandparents aged 50–69 is much lower; it reaches its lowest levels in Poland and Italy, where around 10% of grandmothers and 12–15% of grandfathers in this age range are working.

This pattern of results is inversely associated with intensive grandparental childcare across countries. Bordone and colleagues (2017), for example, show that the percentage of grandparents providing childcare on a daily basis is highest in Southern European countries and Poland, characterised by **familialism** by default (Saraceno and Keck, 2010): a system of low formal childcare provision and meagre parental leave policies. In other European countries, grandparents are usually less intensively involved in grandchild care. Although the direction of causality between family policies, the provision of grandparental childcare and female labour-force participation is hard to establish, the cross-country variation observed in Figure 2.3 may suggest a potential conflict for grandparents between the roles of childcare provider and worker. Previous studies have also hypothesised competition between the two roles and shown that the arrival of the first (or a new) grandchild accelerates retirement (Lumsdaine and Vermeer, 2015; Van Bavel and De Winter, 2013).

The results in Figure 2.3 complement the analysis by Leopold and Skopek (2015b), who used survival methods to estimate the median age of becoming a grandparent and compared it with the median age of retirement for those who ever worked. They found that in both the United States and European countries grandparenthood preceded retirement by at least five years, and often many more. Grandparents' labour-force participation rates, shown in Figure 2.3, also reflect general dynamics in the labour market – as shown by the lower rates observed for women, which make them more available for grandchild

Figure 2.3: Weighted per cent of grandparents aged 50–69 working, by sex and country

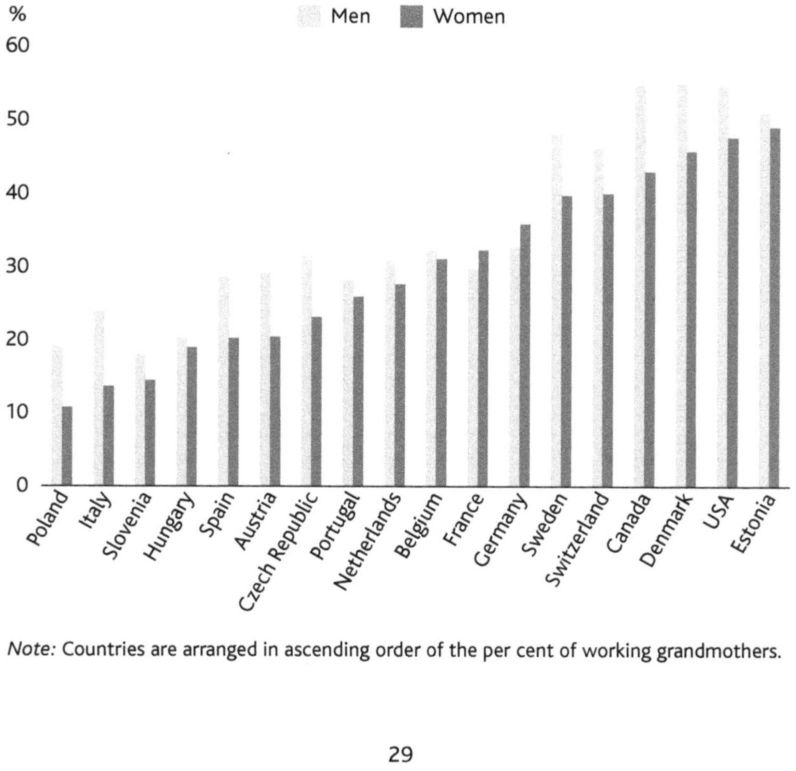

Note: Countries are arranged in ascending order of the per cent of working grandmothers.

care but could also reflect endogenous (early) retirement due to grandmotherhood (Van Bavel and De Winter, 2013). Cross-country variation in grandparents' labour-force participation is also strongly affected by variability in the age distribution of grandparents. For example, the United States has the highest labour-force participation rate for grandfathers (55%) but also the highest percentage of men who are already grandfathers by the age of 54 (62%).

Next, we examine the percentage of grandparents who report being in good, very good or excellent health overall. Figure 2.4 shows these numbers for grandfathers and grandmothers by country. In contrast to the case of labour-force participation, the prevalence of grandparents in good health shows a less clear geographical pattern. Grandparents who report being healthiest are in North America, Denmark and Switzerland. In these countries, more than three quarters of grandfathers and grandmothers report being in good health. On the contrary, in some Eastern European countries (Estonia and Hungary), as well as Portugal, fewer than 40% of grandparents report being in good health. The other countries occupy an intermediate position. In general, grandfathers report being in good health more often than

Figure 2.4: Weighted per cent of grandparents aged 50–69 in good health or better, by sex and country

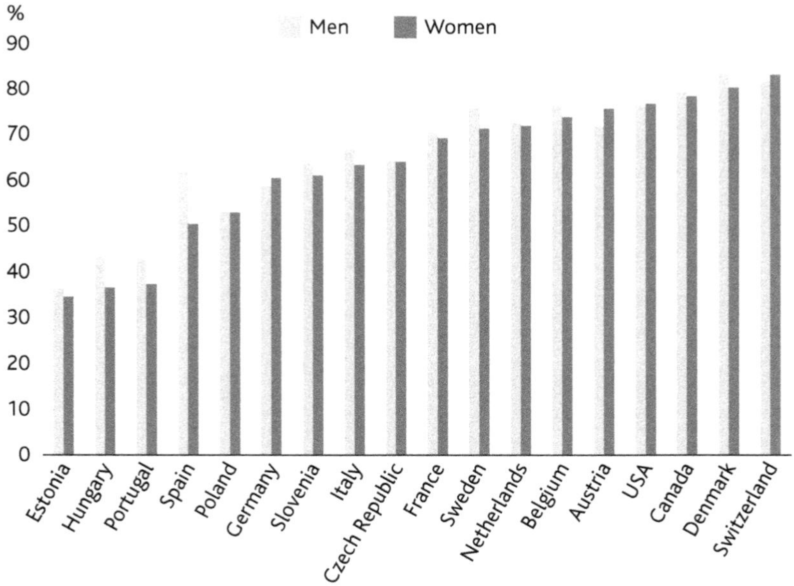

Note: Countries are arranged in ascending order of the per cent of grandmothers in good or better health.

grandmothers, similar to overall population trends. The evidence in Figure 2.4 may suggest that the low percentage of working grandparents observed in most Southern and Eastern European countries is partially due to the poor health conditions of grandparents in those countries. However, as we noticed for labour-force participation, cross–country variations may also be due to age composition effects.

The future of the demography of grandparenthood

What is the future of the demography of grandparenthood? How will current and future demographic and social changes affect grandparenthood at the population level? Changes in fertility will affect grandparenthood in three important ways. First, fertility postponement shows little sign of abating, with the mean age at first birth continuing to increase each year in most European countries. Figure 2.5 shows the mean age at first birth for countries in our analysis using information in the Human Fertility Database (2017). The trend towards later and later parenthood will serve to further postpone grandparenthood in these countries to a later period of the life course. Tomorrow's population of grandparents will be significantly older than today's. Second, increases in childlessness will increase the number of older adults without any grandchildren, and also decrease the mean number of grandchildren among grandparents, if grandparents have some adult children who are childless and others who have children. With the increases in childlessness in most European countries, as well as Canada, we will likely see greater proportions of older adults without grandchildren – and fewer *sets* of grandchildren among those who are grandparents. Childlessness can also mean the extinction of family lines. New research using register data in Sweden has addressed the prevalence of great-grandchildlessness in Northern Sweden (Kolk et al., 2017) – an area of research that will receive more attention in the future. The third way in which changes in fertility will affect grandparenthood in the future is the *level* of fertility, which will affect the number of grandchildren that grandparents have. Across Europe, grandparents have on average between 3.2 and 4.3 grandchildren (not shown; calculations from SHARE data, 2011). Grandparents in Northern Europe tend to have slightly more grandchildren than those in Eastern, Central and Southern Europe, mirroring fertility differentials within Europe.

Even though grandparenthood is being postponed until later in life, the period of grandparenthood may not necessarily be shorter in the future, because increases in life expectancy can offset the

Figure 2.5: Mean age at first birth, 1975–2014

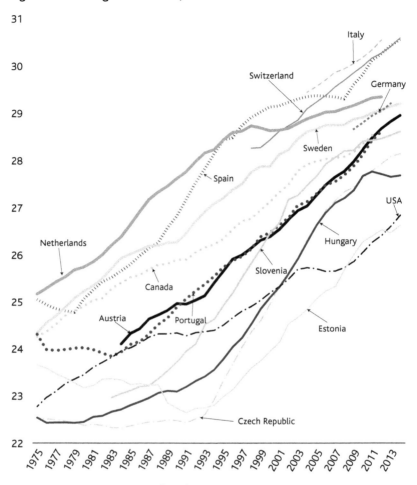

Source: Human Fertility Database (2017)

effects of fertility postponement. Declines in death rates, especially at older ages, have led to more years lived after 65 (Human Mortality Database, 2017). In North America, increases in life expectancy have counterbalanced or even outweighed fertility postponement, serving to stabilise or even increase the length of grandparenthood (Margolis, 2016; Margolis and Wright, 2017). For example, in Canada, from 1985 to 2011 the average number of years of grandparenthood stayed about the same among women – 24.7 and 24.3 years respectively – while it increased from 17.0 to 18.9 years among men (Margolis, 2016). This was due to large decreases in mortality at older ages among

Figure 2.6: Life expectancy at birth, men and women combined, 1985–2014

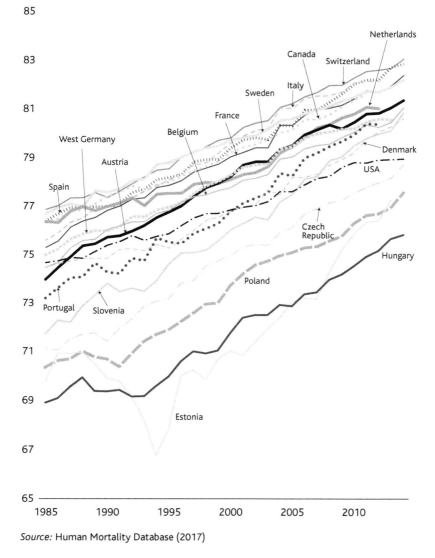

Source: Human Mortality Database (2017)

men during this period. In the US, the period of grandparenthood increased among both women and men, but we see recent increases that were larger among men. The period of grandparenthood was 18.8 years for men in 1998 and 21.5 years in 2010; among women, it increased from 23.8 years to 25.5 years respectively (Margolis and Wright, 2017). In Europe, changes in the length of grandparenthood have not yet been studied. However, current mortality trends imply that the length of grandparenthood will not decrease much, just move to later in life.

What does later grandparenthood mean for the health of the population of future grandparents? The health of grandparents can affect the significance, experience and activities performed during grandparenthood. Therefore, whether older adult years are spent healthy or disabled will have important implications for the health of the grandparent population. Recent trends in the health of the older population provide some evidence for the compression of morbidity at older ages and some evidence for the expansion of poor health. For example, although healthy life expectancy increased among both men and women in Austria from 1978–98 (Doblhammer and Kytir, 2001), the United Kingdom in the 1990s (Jagger et al., 2007), the United States in the 1980s and 1990s (Crimmins, 2004) and France in the 1980s (Cambois et al., 2001), there is also evidence that gains in life expectancy were mostly concentrated in disabled years in the Netherlands from 1983–90 (Van de Water et al., 1996). In other countries, there is evidence of increases in both healthy and disabled years (Crimmins and Beltrán-Sánchez, 2011; Crimmins and Saito, 2001; Mandich and Margolis, 2014; Martel and Bélanger, 2006). Future research should address how these trends are playing out. Healthier, most robust grandparents may have more active interaction with grandchildren. However, grandparents who are older and sicker than in the past may not only have less positive interactions with grandchildren but could also potentially demand care and attention from their adult children.

Another important trend to watch is the extent to which increases in the age at retirement make grandparents less available for intergenerational relationships and transfers. Despite the importance of how transitions in these two life domains (grandparenthood and work) overlap, it is only recently that research has explicitly addressed their overlap. Leopold and Skopek (2015a) examined how the sequencing of these life-course events is changing in East and West Germany. They found that for older birth cohorts, grandparenthood came a good while before retirement, but that among the baby boom cohort the gap between these two life-course events is shrinking – and is even expected to reverse among men, for whom retirement will occur before the transition to grandparenthood among those with children. Using data from 2000–08, Leopold and Skopek (2015b) found that in both the United States and European countries the median age at grandparenthood was about five years lower that the median age at retirement. Future research should examine how the timing of these two important life transitions is related.

Other factors influencing intergenerational relationships

Our focus on the demography of grandparenthood highlights the importance of kin availability, whether older adults have access to grandchildren and whether children have access to grandparents. However, being a grandparent does not necessarily mean there will be close intergenerational relationships with younger kin. Although much literature points to the fact that most grandparents have strong relationships with grandchildren, there are also other important factors that influence these relationships, which we did not consider here (but are considered in other chapters in this book).

The first factor is geographic proximity. Recent research using the SHARE data shows that almost half of grandparents in Europe live within five kilometres of at least one adult child with children, while 55% live more than five kilometres away (Hank and Buber, 2009). Proximity is important in studying these relationships because it influences the frequency of contact and the ability to provide day-to-day care. Indeed, Cherlin and Furstenberg (1986) found that geographical distance alone explained almost two thirds of the variance in frequency of contact with grandchildren.

Second, little research has addressed the extent to which grandparents' inclination to provide a lot of childcare for grandchildren is changing over time. There is anecdotal evidence reported in newspapers that older people today are prioritising social activities, exercise, work or dating over grandchild care (Kaufman, 2009). However, no research that we know of has examined grandparents' attitudes towards grandchild care. This may change a lot in the future.

Another important change in the demography of grandparenthood is the increase in step-grandparents. One becomes a step-grandparent in one of two ways. The first way is that an individual marries a spouse who has becomes a biological grandparent through an adult child from a previous relationship. The second way is that an individual's child marries a partner with a child from a previous relationship (Yahirun et al., 2017). These types of relationships are becoming more common because of increases in divorce and remarriage among both generations. In the US and Europe, divorce rates greatly increased starting in the 1970s, which led to an increase in blended families and thus created a larger group of step-grandparents. These demographic changes are interesting for the study of grandparenthood because types and quality of relationships between step-grandchildren and step-grandparents vary greatly (Chapman et al., 2016). There is much more to learn about the demography of step-grandchild–step-grandparent relationships and how patterns of contact and support differ from biological relationships.

In thinking about the demography of grandparenthood, one cannot forget that grandparents are part of larger kinship networks. Much research on grandparents focuses on grandparent–grandchild relationships and grandparents providing childcare to younger generations. It is easy to forget that other family members may also be part of the picture and may require care. It is not easy to obtain a clear picture of the kin structures of older people (Herlofson and Hagestad, 2011) for a variety of methodological reasons to do with survey data. Our surveys often do not sample those most likely to be in four-generation families, the oldest old and the very youngest. Moreover, we rarely ask about all kin available to a survey respondent, thus missing generations above or below the adjacent generation. Thinking about all the kin and the number of generations that are alive within a lineage is important for studying the intergenerational relationships of grandparents. One important reason for this is that often, today's grandparents still have ageing parents who are alive. For example, in the US is far more it common among those in their 50s and 60s to have three generations of kin available (ageing parents, adult children and grandchildren) than just two. Many of these older adults are transferring resources both upwards (to help older parents) and downwards (providing childcare to grandchildren) (Margolis and Wright, 2016). We see similar generational patterns in Norway, where almost 25% of adults aged 55–59 are part of four-generation lineages (Herlofson and Hagestad, 2011). Our future research examining the predictors or determinants of providing grandchild care also needs to examine whether older kin are alive, and whether grandparents are also transferring resources to the older generation. For this, we need to increasingly examine broader kinship data.

Conclusions

The possibility of assuming the grandparent role, and its content and quality, depend strongly on the demography of grandparenthood. In this chapter, we have examined some key aspects of the demography of grandparenthood: the prevalence of grandparents and their age distribution, working status and health.

Using data from multiple data sources (SHARE, the Health and Retirement Study for the United States and the General Social Survey in Canada), we found considerable heterogeneity across countries. We found, for example, that by the age of 54 fewer than 20% are grandparents in Switzerland while about 60% have at least one grandchild in the US. Striking differences were also found with respect to the labour-force participation of both grandfathers and grandmothers, ranging from as low as 10–20% (in some Eastern and Southern European countries) to about 50% (in Northern Europe, the US and Estonia). Finally, grandparents' health conditions also vary a lot, with grandparents in Southern Europe and some Eastern European countries reporting considerably worse health than grandparents in Switzerland, Northern Europe and North America.

Using data from the Human Fertility Database (2017) and the Human Mortality Database (2017), we also discussed how the demography of grandparenthood may evolve in the future years. Future trends in the demography of grandparenthood will strongly depend on the timing of fertility of multiple generations and mortality and morbidity decline. For example, fertility postponement may imply a higher age at becoming a grandparent but increases in life expectancy may compensate for it, and the length of the grandparenthood phase of life may actually be increasing, albeit shifted towards older ages.

Acknowledgements

This work was supported by the Government of Canada – Canadian Institutes of Health Research (MYB-150262) and Social Sciences and Humanities Research Council (435-2017-0618 and 890-2016-9000). Bruno Arpino acknowledges funding from the Spanish Ministry of Economy, Industry and Competitiveness (PCIN-2016-005) within the second Joint Programming Initiative 'More Years Better Lives'. This chapter uses data from SHARE Wave 4 (DOI: 10.6103/SHARE.w4.600); see Börsch-Supan et al. (2013) for methodological details. The SHARE data collection has been primarily funded by the European Commission through FP5 (QLK6-CT-2001-00360), FP6 (SHARE-I3: RII-CT-2006-062193, COMPARE: CIT5-CT-2005-028857, SHARELIFE: CIT4-CT-2006-028812) and FP7 (SHARE-PREP: N°211909, SHARE-LEAP: N°227822, SHARE M4: N°261982). Additional funding from the German Ministry of Education and Research, the Max Planck Society for the Advancement of Science, the US National Institute on Aging (U01_AG09740-13S2, P01_AG005842, P01_AG08291, P30_AG12815, R21_AG025169, Y1-AG-4553-01, IAG_BSR06-11, OGHA_04-064, HHSN271201300071C) and various national funding sources is gratefully acknowledged (see www.share-project.org).

References

Aassve, A., Meroni, E. and Pronzato, C. (2012) 'Grandparenting and childbearing in the extended family', *European Journal of Population*, 28(4): 499–518.

Arpino, B. and Bordone, V. (2014) 'Does grandparenting pay off? The effect of child care on grandparents' cognitive functioning', *Journal of Marriage and Family*, 76: 337–351.

Arpino B., Gumà, J. and Julià A. (2017) 'The demography of grandparenthood: The role of life histories', *RECSM Working Paper*, 50.

Arpino B., Pronzato, C. and Tavares, L.P. (2014) 'The effect of grandparental support on mothers' labour market participation: An instrumental variable approach', *European Journal of Population*, 30: 369–390.

Bordone V., Arpino, B. and Aassve, A. (2017) 'Patterns of grandparental childcare across Europe: The role of the policy context and working mothers' need', *Ageing and Society*, 37(4): 845–873.

Börsch-Supan, A. (2017) Survey of Health, Ageing and Retirement in Europe (SHARE) Wave 4, release version 6.0.0., SHARE-ERIC, data set. DOI: 10.6103/SHARE.w4.611.

Börsch-Supan, A., Brandt, M., Hunkler, C., Kneip, T., Korbmacher, J., Malter, F., Schaan, B., Stuck, S. and Zuber, S. (2013) 'Data resource profile: The Survey of Health, Ageing and Retirement in Europe (SHARE)', *International Journal of Epidemiology*, 42(4): 992–1001.

Cambois, E., Robine, J.M. and Hayward. M.D. (2001) 'Social inequalities in disability-free life expectancy in the French male population, 1980–1991', *Demography*, 38(4): 513–524.

Chan, T.W. and Boliver, V. (2013) 'The grandparent effect in social mobility: Evidence from British birth cohort studies', *American Sociological Review*, 78(4): 662–678.

Chapman, A., Coleman, M. and Ganong, L. (2016) '"Like my grandparent, but not": A qualitative investigation of skip-generation stepgrandchild–stepgrandparent relationships', *Journal of Marriage and Family*, 78(3): 634–643.

Cherlin, A. and Furstenberg, F.F. (1986) *The new American grandparent.* New York: Basic Books.

Crimmins, E.M. (2004) 'Trends in the health of the elderly', *Annual Review of Public Health*, 25L: 79–98.

Crimmins, E.M. and Beltrán-Sánchez, H. (2011) 'Mortality and morbidity trends: is there compression of morbidity?' *Journals of Gerontology: Social Sciences*, 66(1): 75–86.

Crimmins, E.M. and Saito, Y. (2001) 'Trends in healthy life expectancy in the United States, 1970–1990: Gender, racial, and educational differences', *Social Science and Medicine*, 52: 1629–1641.

Di Gessa, G., Glaser, K. and Tinker, A. (2016) 'The health impact of intensive and nonintensive grandchild care in Europe: New evidence from SHARE', *The Journals of Gerontology Series B: Psychological Sciences and Social Sciences*, 71(5): 867–879.

Doblhammer, G. and Kytir, J. (2001) 'Compression or expansion of morbidity? Trends in healthy life expectancy in the elderly Austrian population between 1978 and 1998', *Social Science and Medicine*, 52: 385–391.

Frejka, T. (2017) 'Childlessness in the United States', in M. Kreyenfeld and D. Konietzka (eds) *Childlessness in Europe: Contexts, causes, and consequences*, Dordrecht: Springer International Publishing, pp 159–179.

Hagestad, G.O. and Neugarten, B.L. (1985) 'Age and the life course', in E. Shanas and R. Binstock (eds) *Handbook of aging and the social sciences*, New York: Van Nostrand and Reinhold, pp 35–55.

Hank, K., and Buber, I. (2009) 'Grandparents caring for their grandchildren: Findings from the 2004 Survey of Health, Ageing, and Retirement in Europe', *Journal of Family Issues*, 30(1): 53–73.

Health and Retirement Study, Public Use Dataset (2010) Produced and distributed by the University of Michigan with funding from the National Institute on Aging (grant number NIA U01AG009740).

Herlofson, K. and Hagestad, G.O. (2011) 'Challenges in moving from macro to micro: Population and family structures in ageing societies', *Demographic Research*, 25(10): 337–370.

Human Fertility Database (2017) Max Planck Institute for Demographic Research (Germany) and Vienna Institute of Demography (Austria). Available at www.humanfertility.org.

Human Mortality Database (2017) University of California, Berkeley (US) and Max Planck Institute for Demographic Research (Germany). Available at www.mortality.org.

Igel, C. and Szydlik, M. (2011) 'Grandchild care and welfare state arrangements in Europe', *Journal of European Social Policy*, 21(3): 210–224.

Jagger, C., Cox, B., Le Roy, S., EHEMU (2006) *Health expectancy calculation by the Sullivan method* (3rd edn), European Health Expectancy Monitoring Unit technical report. Retrieved from: http://maryland.mri.cnrs.fr/ehemu/pdf/Sullivan_guide_final_jun2007.pdf.

Jagger, C., Matthews, R., Matthews, F., Robinson, T., Robine, J.M. and Brayne, C. (2007) 'The burden of diseases on disability-free life expectancy in later life', *The Journals of Gerontology Series A: Biological Sciences and Medical Sciences*, 62(4): 408–414.

Kolk, M., Fieder, M. and Skirbekk, V. (2017) *Extinction of family lines: Great-grandchildlessness in 19th, 20th and 21st century northern Sweden*. Poster presented at PAA 2017, Chicago, IL.

Knugge, A. (2016) 'Beyond the Parental Generation: The influence of grandfathers and great-grandfathers on status attainment', *Demography*, 53(4): 1219–1244.

Kreyenfeld, M. and Konietzka, D. (eds) (2017) *Childlessness in Europe: Contexts, causes, and consequences*. Dordrecht: Springer International Publishing.

Leopold, T. and Skopek, J. (2015a) 'The delay of grandparenthood: A cohort comparison in East and West Germany', *Journal of Marriage and Family*, 77(2): 441–460.

Leopold, T. and Skopek, J. (2015b) 'The demography of grandparenthood: An international profile', *Social Forces*, 94(2): 801–832.

Lumsdaine, R.L. and Vermeer, S.J. (2015) 'Retirement timing of women and the role of care responsibilities for grandchildren', *Demography*, 52(2): 433–454.

Mandich, S. and Margolis, R. (2014) 'Changes in disability-free life expectancy in Canada between 1994 and 2007', *Canadian Studies in Population*, 41(1–2): 192–208.

Margolis, R. (2016) 'The changing demography of grandparenthood', *Journal of Marriage and Family*, 78(3): 610–622.

Margolis, R, and Wright, L. (2016) 'Older adults with three generations of kin: Prevalence, correlates, and transfers', *The Journals of Gerontology Series B: Psychological Sciences and Social Sciences*, 72(6): 1067–1072. DOI: 10.1093/geronb/gbv158.

Margolis, R and L. Wright. (2017) 'Healthy grandparenthood: How long is it and how has it changed?', *Demography*, 54(6): 2073–2099.

Martel, L. and Bélanger, A. (2006) 'An analysis of the change in dependence-free life expectancy in Canada between 1986 and 1996', *Report on the Demographic Situation in Canada, 1998–1999*. Statistics Canada Catalogue, 91-209-XPE.

Kaufman, J. (2009) 'When grandma can't be bothered', *The New York Times*, 4 March. Available at: http://www.nytimes.com/2009/03/05/fashion/05grandparents-1.html?pagewanted=all&_r=0.

Saraceno, C. and Keck, W. (2010) 'Can we identify intergenerational policy regimes in Europe?', *European Societies*, 12(5): 675–696.

Sobotka, T. (2017) 'Childlessness in Europe: Reconstructing long-term trends among women born in 1900–1972', in M. Kreyenfeld and D. Konietzka (eds) *Childlessness in Europe: Contexts, causes, and consequences*, Dordrecht: Springer International Publishing, pp 17–53.

Silverstein, M., and Long, J.D. (1998) 'Trajectories of grandparents' perceived solidarity with adult grandchildren: A growth curve analysis over 23 years', *Journal of Marriage and Family*, 60(4): 912–923.

Silverstein, M., and Ruiz, S. (2006) 'Breaking the chain: How grandparents moderate the transmission of maternal depression to their grandchildren', *Family Relations*, 55(5): 601–612.

Sullivan, D. (1971) 'A single index of mortality and morbidity', *HSMHA Health Reports*, 86(4): 347–354.

Szinovacz, M.E., and Davey, A. (2006) 'Effects of retirement and grandchild care on depressive symptoms', *International Journal of Aging and Human Development*, 62(1): 1–20.

Van de Water, H., Boshuizen, H., Perenboom, R., Mathers, C. and Robine, J.M. (1996) 'Health expectancy: An indicator for change?' *Journal of Epidemiology and Community Health*, 49: 330–332.

Van Bavel, J. and De Winter, T. (2013) 'Becoming a grandparent and early retirement in Europe', *European Sociological Review*, 29(6): 1295–1308.

Yahirun, J., Park, S. and Seltzer, J. (2017) *Step-grandparenthood in the United States*, California Center for Population Research working paper series, PWP-CCPR-2017-008, Los Angeles, CA: University of California.

THREE

Grandparental childcare: a reconceptualisation of family policy regimes

*Debora Price, Eloi Ribe, Giorgio Di Gessa
and Karen Glaser*

Introduction

In recent decades, substantial sociodemographic and economic transformations in western economies have altered family structures as well as relations between the family and the state. New economic relations together with greater civil and social rights have contributed to changing the social division of labour between men and women. These developments have led to substantial changes in the social organisation of childcare. New demands for alternatives to maternal care have become more common and greater demands have been placed on the state to assist and provide support to families with children. In parallel, societies are experiencing increasing longevity, thus increasing possibilities for multigenerational relations, while at the same time posing new challenges in the provision of care for older generations. Policy settings and societal conditions have entered a new phase of relations where gender, age and time interact with welfare states in complex ways.

Within this matrix of new and gendered demands for paid work and care, how are we to understand the role of grandparents in contemporary societies? As a significant body of emerging research (Arber and Timonen, 2012; Bordone et al., 2017; Di Gessa et al., 2016; Glaser et al., 2013) and the chapters in this volume show, amid other complex transfers up and down the generations, grandparents play an essential role in supporting adult children and grandchildren in the provision of childcare. This has been shown to be driven by many demographic and social factors (Albert and Ferring, 2013; Di Gessa et al., 2016a, 2016b; Geurts et al., 2015; Glaser et al., 2010, 2013; Hank and Buber, 2009), with much less attention paid to the political and policy environments (Aassve et al., 2012; Bordone et al., 2017; Herlofson and Hagestad, 2012; Igel and Szydlik, 2011; Saraceno and Keck, 2010).

While we have increasing studies on grandparental care, there has therefore been less analysis of how social policies shape grandparents' role in the organisation of childcare. In this chapter, we propose a new way of conceptualising the public sphere by focusing simultaneously on policy impacts on parents and grandparents, as well as the structural and cultural environment. We ask, when looked at in this way, what difference does the welfare state make to grandparental support for childcare?

We first briefly review existing models for family policy analysis and propose a new conceptualisation for understanding the implications of family policy regimes for grandparenting. We then turn to empirical analysis of policies and outcomes across 11 European countries to illustrate our argument: that we need to conceptualise and analyse policies as impacting on families in two adult generations simultaneously, both in terms of labour market and childcare, and being embedded in gender and generational cultures and expectations. Because childcare is a highly gendered task, with mothers and grandmothers providing the vast bulk of childcare across cultures (Fuller-Thomson and Minkler, 2001; Gray, 2005; Hank and Buber, 2009; Koslowski, 2009; Wheelock and Jones, 2002), we focus our empirical analysis on grandmothers. We close by showing that our proposed model has explanatory power in understanding variation in noncustodial grandmaternal childcare across Europe.

Family policy regime analysis

It is only since the 1980s that family and care issues have taken a more central place in welfare state policies (Mätzke and Ostner, 2010; Wheelock and Jones, 2002) and theoretical approaches have moved away from ideas that regard the family as a functional institution for the socialisation of children (Parsons and Bales, 1955). In more mutable and heterogenous perspectives, it is argued that the family as a social institution changes according to economic and demographic changes, often linked to labour-market restructuring, which in turn exerts pressures on the state to meet new social demands (Hantrais, 2000). This means that family policy analysis has focused heavily on increases in the labour-market participation of women and mothers; gender differences in employment conditions and pay; changes in fertility rates, family formation and dissolution and living arrangements; and the role of public and political institutions in influencing these factors (Daly and Lewis, 2000; Lewis, 1992, 2009; O'Connor et al., 1999; Sainsbury, 1999).

Within these discussions, family policy research has centred its attention almost exclusively on nuclear and lone-parent families (mostly lone mothers) with young children, or adult dyads between adult children and ageing parents. The ways that policy shapes intergenerational relations are usually considered from the perspective of the adult generation caring for *either* children *or* elderly parents (or both), but not how parents and grandparents interact in the provision of childcare. Because care is mostly provided by women, this means existing research has tended to emphasise the role of policy in structuring mothers' care versus formal and informal care, rather than conceptualising family care (mother and grandmother) versus nonfamily care. Furthermore, existing policy-focused research has tended to emphasise mothers in the paid labour market while ignoring grandmothers in the paid labour market. This is despite grandmothers of young children mostly being of working age. This is becoming a more important issue, especially for grandmothers who provide substantial childcare, as we see policies to extend working lives and encourage later retirement around the globe. Finally, existing research has tended to consider structural and institutional factors (especially childcare and gendered labour markets) over cultural factors (attitudes and preferences, acknowledging that these are shaped within normative policy settings).

In an influential article, Leitner (2003) classified welfare states according to whether policies are 'familialising' (encourage care in the family), or 'de-familialising' (assume paid work by individuals of working age and care outside the family through intervention by the state). However, her conceptualisation of care in the family focused on the middle generation providing care to children and/or older parents, with an analysis of legal entitlement to paid parental leave, provision of institutional childcare under the age of three, long-term care leave and formal care services for older people. Saraceno (2010) criticised this approach for failing to appreciate the role of market forces in shaping family care but in this and a later article (Saraceno and Keck, 2011), when seeking to identify intergenerational policy regimes in Europe, Saraceno too looked only for patterns of institutional regulation 'downward (towards children) and upward (towards the old)'. In Lewis's (2009) book *Work–family balance, gender and policy*, the word 'grandparent' appears just seven times and 'grandmother' only twice. Family care in these analyses is therefore generally conceptualised as reflecting relations between the state, market and the middle generation.

On the other hand, a growing body of work emphasises the importance of grandparental support in mothers' decision to return to the paid labour market (Aassve et al., 2012; Arpino et al., 2010; Bordone et al., 2017; Lakomý and Kreidl, 2015; Wheelock and Jones, 2002) and the challenges for grandmothers in juggling work and care (Harrington Meyer, 2014; Lakomý and Kreidl, 2015; Van Bavel and De Winter, 2013). Furthermore, Pfau-Effinger (2005; and Frericks et al., 2014) has long argued that we need to add to these types of analyses the role that cultural expectations play in transforming family and care policies and societies. In the grandparenting context, Herlofson and Hagestad (2012) and Jappens and van Bavel (2012) show that cultural expectations of grandparenting roles in childcare and financial support vary widely across Europe, and Neuberger and Haberkern (2014) have shown that normative contexts for grandparenting influence quality of life among European grandparents providing childcare, such that in countries with high grandparenting obligations, grandparents who did not look after their grandchildren reported a lower quality of life.

However, despite the acknowledged importance of these issues for understanding childcare, very few scholars have introduced policy regime analysis into our understanding of grandparental childcare (Herlofson and Hagestad, 2012). In the first study of its kind, Igel and Szydlik (2011) noted that welfare state arrangements influenced patterns of grandparental care for children under the age of five across Europe. Using multilevel analysis of the Survey of Health, Ageing and Retirement in Europe (SHARE), they showed that whether grandparents helped at all or intensively with looking after children was associated with public expenditure on family support, childcare and maternity/paternity leave. They found that higher public expenditures made grandparents more likely to undertake some childcare but less likely to undertake intensive childcare. Bordone and colleagues (2017), using country-specific analyses, investigated the extent to which grandparental care of children aged 0–2 was influenced by two summary indicators reflecting the policy environment: parental leave (combining length and compensation) and coverage for the provision of public childcare services to children aged 0–2. They, too, showed that less public support is associated with more intensive (daily) childcare by grandparents. In a separate analysis, they further showed that higher rates of women working part time within a country are associated with grandparents providing less-intensive childcare – for instance, weekly rather than daily – and that daily grandparental involvement is driven by mothers' needs for childcare due to work. They noted that national rates of older women (aged 55–65) engaged in the labour market also varied widely across Europe and suggested this could affect availabilities for childcare. In a more complex multilevel analysis of grandparenting in Europe, where the theoretical framework presented in this chapter was used to shape the analysis (and to which we will later turn), Di Gessa and colleagues (2016) showed that policies, structures and attitudes are all important parts of the national-level explanatory matrix.

Extending these recent bodies of work, we therefore conceptualise policies as impacting on families in two generations – both in terms of labour-market opportunities and care provision – and being embedded in gender and generational cultures and expectations. We argue here that we should reposition childcare in policy analysis as two generational, encompassing (in the main) collaboration between mothers and grandmothers (Glaser et al., 2013; Herlofson and Hagestad, 2012). We suggest that family and care policies directly or indirectly operate to strengthen or weaken the role of grandmothers in providing childcare through affecting the availability of mothers to look after children themselves or combine work and care, as well as the potential availability of grandmothers to do the same. This means we hypothesise that a given set of policies may encourage the nuclear family in providing or arranging care at home; or may implicitly or explicitly rely on extended family care. Further to this, family responses to paid work and childcare structures will vary culturally across countries. Taking both aspects into account, we distinguish entitlements and rights, which are part of the **policy logic** of a country, and outcome measures (such as uptake and usage), which are part of the **behavioural response** (cultural, structural) of families.

Variation in grandmaternal care across Europe

We consider these issues across 11 European countries: Italy, Spain, Portugal, Hungary, Romania, Denmark, Sweden, UK, the Netherlands, France and Germany. As others have noted (Glaser et al., 2013; Hank and Buber, 2009), and as shown in Table 3.1, we see widespread variation in both the proportions of non-co-residential grandmothers who look after children at all and those who provide what we call 'intensive childcare', by which we mean daily care or at least 15 hours of childcare a week. Table 3.1 clearly shows (and see also Bordone et al., 2017) that these two dimensions are not obviously related to each other, with Romania scoring highest for both – almost all grandmothers provide some childcare and 30% provide almost daily childcare (more than 20 days a month). Countries such as Sweden and the Netherlands have very low proportions providing intensive childcare but middling proportions providing some childcare. Germany has the lowest proportion who provide some care but a middling proportion providing intensive childcare, and Spain and Italy have among the lowest providing any childcare but among the highest providing intensive childcare. Glaser and colleagues (2013) have shown that the demographic and population structures of these countries vary widely (for instance, in the ages and numbers of grandparents, adult children and grandchildren, and so on), but these factors alone cannot

Table 3.1: Variation in grandmaternal childcare across 11 European countries

	Percentage of grandmothers looking after grandchildren at all[a]	Percentage of grandmothers looking after children intensively[b]
Sweden*	51	2
Netherlands*	57	2
Denmark*	59	2
France*	51	7
Germany*	40	8
UK[c]**	63	8
Hungary[d]***	56	13
Portugal[e]****	Data missing	14
Spain*	42	17
Italy*	42	22
Romania[d]***	93	30

Notes

[a] Data for SHARE: Percentage of respondents who have regularly or occasionally looked after their grandchildren without the parents' presence during the 12 months prior to the interview. Data for English Longitudinal Study of Ageing (ELSA): Percentage of respondents who have looked after a grandchild in the past week. Data for Generations and Gender Survey (GGS): Percentage of respondents who have helped to look after their grandchild(ren) at all.

[b] Data for SHARE: Percentage of individuals who have looked after a grandchild almost daily or almost weekly but for at least 15 hours a week. Data for ELSA: Percentage of respondents who have provided daily care to their grandchild(ren). Data for GGS: Percentage of respondents who have provided help to look after their grandchild(ren) between 20 and 30 days a month. Data for the European Social Survey (ESS): Percentage of respondents with children aged less than 12 (only asked for the youngest child in the household) who report usual childcare provided by a grandparent.

[c] Data is for England only.

[d] Data in these countries is for all grandparents.

[e] Families with children aged younger than 12.

Sources

* SHARE wave 1; ** ELSA wave 1; *** GGS wave 1; **** ESS wave 2.

explain the extent of variation between these European countries (Di Gessa et al., 2016; Glaser et al., 2013).

Grandparenting policy regimes across Europe

We theorise, then, that in addition to being driven by individual-level characteristics, the extent of grandparental childcare – and more specifically childcare by grandmothers – is the result of interactions between labour-market cultures and structures, family and gender cultures and the policy environment, as depicted in Figure 3.1. In reconceptualising how we think about family policy, we approached our analysis with three ideas in mind. First, when considering the policy logics we need to think about the responses and incentives for the whole family, including both grandparent and parent generations. Second, understanding policy regimes is not enough as behavioural responses are important; in particular, we need to reflect on how people participate in labour markets and childcare. Third, we need to consider that cultural factors shape individual responses to both policy regimes and work/care structures. In each case the responses are highly gendered, with women providing most care to children and adults.

To operationalise this theoretical framework, for each country under analysis we collected data across these three distinct dimensions (see Table 3.2) from Eurostat, SHARE, the European Social Survey (ESS) and Eurobarometer.[1] We collected these indicators as at 2008–09 to coincide roughly with the empirical observations of grandmaternal

Figure 3.1: Influences on grandmaternal care

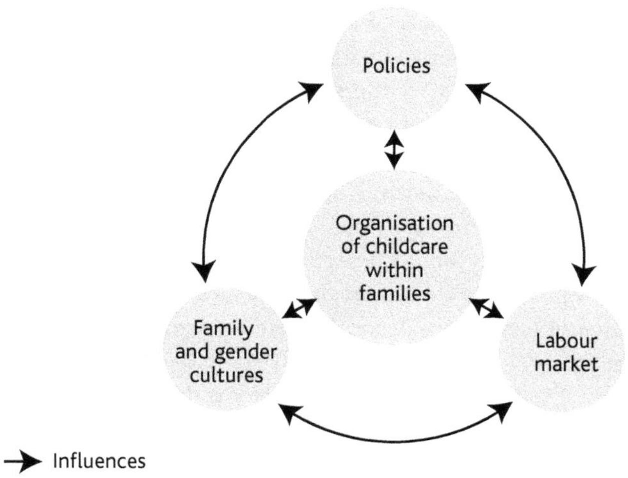

➔ Influences

Table 3.2: Operationalising the theoretical framework

Policies	Family and gender cultures and structures	Labour market cultures and structures
• Maternity, paternity and parental rights • Leave to care for a sick child or adult • 'Family-friendly' labour market policies • Child benefits • Childcare and education entitlements and services • Retirement policies • Long-term care policies	• Attitudes to childcare • Gender role attitudes • Satisfaction with public support for families • Use of childcare services • Use of elder care services	• Working patterns of women and mothers by: – age of children – number of working hours – marital status • Couples in breadwinner-carer/part-time carer and dual-full-time-worker arrangements • Gender pay gap

childcare shown in Table 3.1. In considering the policy environments, we examined maternity, paternity and parental rights; leave to care for a sick child and adults; labour-market policies; child benefits; childcare and educational entitlements and services; and pension and long-term care policies. To capture gendered labour-market structures, we looked at the working patterns of women and mothers by age of children, number of working hours and marital status; the proportions of couples in breadwinner-carer, part-time-carer and dual-full-time-worker arrangements; and the gender pay gap. For cultural indicators, we examined attitudes to childcare, gender role attitudes, satisfaction with public support for families, actual use of childcare services and actual use of elder-care services.

Taking our two-generational approach, we then analysed policies and other indicators according to whether they support mothers providing care (versus work), support grandmothers providing care (versus work) or support market or state models of care (thus supporting work by both mothers and grandmothers). In this conceptualisation, policies that provide strong support for mothers to remain at home (such as high levels of income replacement or low levels of conditionality for leave) will reduce the need for grandmothers to become involved in family care. However, structural and cultural indicators will also play a role. To give some examples, policies that provide little support for mothers to stay at home will have different empirical outcomes depending on whether there is widespread provision and cultural acceptance of formal childcare. If there are strong beliefs that care should remain in the family, then such policies may promote grandmaternal care if mothers wish to work. Lack of financial support for grandmothers to leave work, such as poor pension provision, may however militate against grandmothers providing childcare; similarly, countries with inadequate long-term care provision might make it difficult for grandmothers who are caring for an older generation to provide childcare.

Given the complexity of these interactions, we first proceeded with a qualitative (theory-driven) analysis of what might be expected from varied constellations of policy, attitudes and structures. We then assessed the associations of these with observed grandmaternal care using a constant comparative method. Subsequently, selecting key indicators that resulted from this analysis, we tested our theories in an empirical model.

Policy logics in a two-generational perspective

First, we turn to consider the policy logics of our set of countries in a two-generational perspective along two dimensions: leave policies and provision of services, and the degree of economic autonomy or independence given to women through state subsidy or cash transfers. If leave and services policies strongly support mothers' care for children at home, we term this **nuclearisation**, since this encourages care within the nuclear family without such need for grandmaternal care; similarly, adult care and leave policies may fail to support grandmothers' availability to provide childcare, which also encourages care within the nuclear family. If policies fail to provide strongly for mothers' autonomous financial needs, then they become economically dependent on partners or the state, which we term **economic dependence**. If mothers are strongly incentivised by policy logics to stay at home with children, but wish to work, then there will be few formal childcare alternatives and grandmothers may step in to fill the childcare gap.

The expected outcomes from this analysis are shown in Table 3.3. The top-left corner shows the constellation of policies where both leave and services encourage mothers to remain at home but simultaneously services are expensive and income replacement is low. In such countries we might expect demand for intensive grandparental childcare to be particularly high, since there is no childcare infrastructure for mothers who work yet high economic need for some mothers to work. In these countries we would expect a polarisation between high levels of mothers at home providing childcare, while also showing high levels of grandmothers providing intensive childcare for those mothers who work. However, there will be less need for **reserve army**-type occasional supplemental childcare support from grandparents, given this polarisation. In these countries, we expect mothers and

Table 3.3: How policy logics might impact the wider family

		Nuclearisation: encouraging women to care or work in the nuclear family through leave policies and provision of services	
		High: Care-oriented logic	Low: Work-oriented logic
Economic dependence on the family: encouraging women to care or work through economic support for care by state subsidy or cash transfers	High: Care-oriented logic	Leave for care high Limited state provision of care Limited market provision of care Cash transfers highly conditional Little or no income replacement Low cash transfers Expensive provision of services *Much need for grandparental childcare to replace mothers' daily care if in paid work, as no infrastructure for working mothers with strong care logics and high economic need for some mothers to paid work; little need for grandparents if mothers at home*	Publicly provided care high (or market provided care high) Limited leave for care (conditional) Widely available cash transfers Little or no income replacement Low cash transfers Expensive provision of services *Mothers incentivised to work and organise formal care but will need reserve army support*
	Low: Work-oriented logic	Leave for care high Limited state provision of care Limited market provision of care Cash transfers highly conditional High income replacement High cash transfers Cheap provision of services *Mothers incentivised to look after young children at home; will need grandparents if in paid work but mixed incentives to be in paid work; will need reserve army support with limited formal provision*	Publicly provided care high Market provided care high Limited leave for care Widely available cash transfers High income replacement High cash transfers Cheap provision of services *Little need for grandparental childcare, whether daily or reserve army; grandmothers not expected to be available for childcare*

grandmothers to substitute for each other, and we term this group of countries 'mothers or grandmothers'.

In the bottom-right corner, we show constellations of policies where policies in the leave, services and income-replacement domains all incentivise paid work. Here, public or market provision of childcare is high, there is limited leave for care and cash transfers have wide eligibility. Cash transfers and income replacement are also high, and services are cheap. In these countries, while we expect mothers to be working, we do not expect to see high levels of grandmaternal care, with grandmothers themselves supported to be in the workforce and low demand for their care. We term these 'paid work'.

In the top right and bottom left, we show countries where the policy logics are in contradiction, with high incentives for mothers to care at home in the labour market and services domains but low incentives for mothers to care at home in the economic domains, and vice versa. In the top right, we show a constellation of policies where public or market provision of childcare is high, where there is limited leave for care, where cash transfers have wide eligibility but are low value, where there is little income replacement and where services are expensive. In these countries mothers are incentivised to work and organise formal childcare but need grandparental 'reserve army' supplemental support. We therefore do not expect to see high levels of intensive grandmaternal care, but we do expect to see relatively high levels of grandmothers providing some help. We term these 'reserve army'.

In the bottom-left quadrant, we have a constellation of policies where there are high levels of leave for care but limited state and market provision of care, and cash transfers are highly conditional; but on the other hand, cash transfers and income-replacement levels are relatively high and the provision of services is cheap. In these countries, there are mixed incentives because of the limited levels of formal provision and high conditionality for receipt of any benefits. If mothers undertake any paid work, they will need grandmaternal support for childcare. In these countries we expect levels of both intensive and 'reserve army' support from grandmothers to be high. We term these 'family unsupported'.

The outcomes of mapping our 11 countries to these quadrants are shown in Table 3.4. Italy, Spain and Portugal are mapped to the 'mothers or grandmothers' group. In brackets, we show first the proportion of grandmothers providing any care and then the proportion providing intensive childcare. It can be seen that the distributions in these countries are indeed similar, with among the

Table 3.4: Mapping country groups to patterns of grandparenting

		Nuclearisation: encouraging mothers to care or work through leave policies and provision of services	
		High: Care-oriented logic	Low: Work-oriented logic
Economic dependence: encouraging mothers to care or work through economic support for care by state subsidy or cash transfers	High: Care-oriented logic	*Mothers or grandmothers* Italy (41:22) Spain (42:17) Portugal (nd:14)	*Reserve army* Germany (40:8) Netherlands (57:2) UK (63:8)
	Low: Work-oriented logic	*Family unsupported* Romania (93:30) Hungary (56:13)	*Paid work* France (51:7) Sweden (51:2) Denmark (59:2)

Note: nd = no data for Portugal.

lowest levels of grandmothers providing any care (which suggests high levels of care at home by mothers who do not work) but also high levels of grandmothers providing intensive childcare for those mothers who work. They do indeed appear to be substituting for one another. Germany, the Netherlands and the UK map to the 'reserve army' group. These are countries where mothers are expected to work and find childcare but will likely need support with this, since services are expensive and cash transfers are low. It can be seen that the distributions again look to be a reasonable fit, with relatively high levels of grandmothers providing some care and middling or low levels providing intensive childcare. Romania and Hungary map to the 'family unsupported' group, where we expect to have a high level of grandparental childcare provided both at all and intensively. Once again, the empirical outcome fits this, with Romania showing the highest levels and Hungary among the highest for both measures. France, Sweden and Denmark map to the final quadrant, 'paid work', where we expect to see middling levels of 'reserve army' support and low levels of intensive support, and this is indeed what we observe.

While clearly helpful, this analysis does however show (as we expected) that there must be other factors at play. For example, the Netherlands looks very similar to France, Sweden and Denmark in its distributions. Similarly, Germany and the UK, while grouped together in the 'reserve army' quadrant, have quite different proportions providing any care (40% and 63% respectively). We therefore turn to examine our other pillars: gendered cultures and structures in society and the labour market.

In Figure 3.2, by way of illustration, we present bivariate regression analysis of some of the key variables in these domains that are strongly associated with intensive grandmaternal care.[2] The first two graphs (Figures 3.2a and 3.2b) show the strong association with country-level labour-market structures. Perhaps counterintuitively, there is no association between the proportion of mothers working full time and grandmaternal care, whether daily, weekly or at all (data not shown). However, we observe a strong positive association (r^2=0.48), between the proportion of mothers out of the labour market and the proportion of grandmothers looking after children daily. A nice example of the ecological fallacy, as these are not the same families, this analysis lends support to our hypothesis that in some countries there is a substitution effect between mother-care and grandmother-care. In these countries, while most mothers are at home (needing little childcare support), if mothers are in paid work they rely heavily on grandmothers for intensive childcare.

We next show the importance of also looking at the percentage of women aged 50–64 in paid work and how this relates to grandmaternal provision of intensive childcare (Figure 3.2b). There is a strong association shown between countries that have low employment levels in these age groups for women and the extent to which grandmothers, who are potentially more available to do so with low participation rates in paid work, provide intensive childcare.

The next graph (Figure 3.2c) illustrates the importance of formal childcare usage. As mentioned, there is no apparent relationship between the proportion of women working full time in a country and grandmaternal childcare, whether daily, weekly or at all. However, as the proportion of 0–2-year-olds in formal childcare in a country increases, the proportion of grandmothers providing intensive care drops. This is a strong relationship, with r^2=0.48. This suggests that formal childcare and grandmaternal care are to some extent substitutes for each other, as we would expect from our policy analysis in quadrant four above. However, to be noted (data not shown) and as also found by Bordone et al. (2017), as the proportion of 0–2-year-olds in formal childcare increases, the proportion of grandmothers providing *any* care increases, too. This depicts a 'reserve army' model operating at the same time.

The final two graphs (Figures 3.2d and 3.2e) capture attitudinal domains, and these variables may also capture some elements of the quality of formal childcare on offer. Again, we observe a strong relationship, this time between the proportion in a country who believe preschool children suffer with a working mother and the

Figure 3.2: Selected variables, association at country level with proportion of grandmothers providing intensive childcare

3.2a

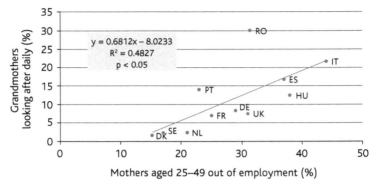

3.2b

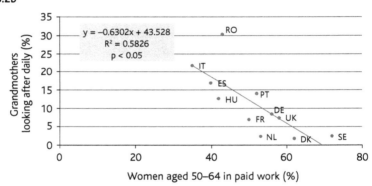

3.2c

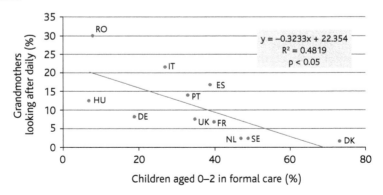

(continued)

Figure 3.2: Selected variables, association at country level with proportion of grandmothers providing intensive childcare (continued)

3.2d

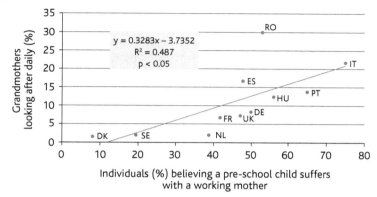

3.2e

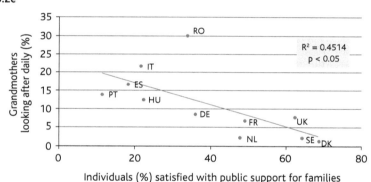

proportion of grandmothers providing intensive childcare. This analysis strongly supports our core hypothesis that we should be conceptualising childcare as something negotiated within the family, including mothers and grandmothers, versus formal care, rather than simply thinking about mothers. It makes sense that if the cultural space normatively suggests that working mothers might not be best for children, grandmothers might be considered a better substitute than formal institutions. This is further enforced by the final graph (Figure 3.2e), which shows that the more people are dissatisfied with institutional support for families, the higher the proportions of grandmothers providing intensive childcare.

Explanatory potential

We therefore suggest that to explain the extent of noncustodial grandmaternal childcare across countries, it is important to include not only a family policy regime framework but also analysis of labour-market structures and cultural indicators, indicating availabilities to provide childcare as well as normative environments. We tested this model in Di Gessa et al. (2016), investigating the drivers of national differences in intensive grandparental care across Europe. The purpose of this research was to use multilevel models to test the relative importance in explaining variation in grandparental care of demographic and socioeconomic variation, including grandparent, adult child and grandchild characteristics, as compared with policy regimes, contextual-structural factors (such as labour markets and childcare provision) and cultural attitudes to family versus institutional care.

We found that, even controlling for cross-national differences in demographic and socioeconomic distributions, policy regimes and contextual-structural factors play an important role in explaining grandparental childcare variations in Europe. In particular, higher levels of intensive grandparental childcare are found in countries with low labour-force participation among younger and older women and low formal childcare provision, where those mothers who are in paid work largely rely on grandparental support on an almost daily basis.

More particularly in terms of the factors examined in this chapter, when we considered only sociodemographic characteristics in accounting for the prevalence of intensive grandparental childcare, 14% of the total unexplained variance was accounted for by countries. When individual characteristics of all three generations were controlled, this variance did not change, showing that country-level factors remained important. When the grandparent policy regime variable for each country was introduced, together with country-level indicators representing the different structural and cultural contexts, the country-level variance reduced to less than 2% of the total residual variance. This revealed that it is a country's policies, labour-market structures, formal childcare provision and cultural norms, rather than compositional demographic and socioeconomic differences, which capture most of the cross-country variation in intensive grandparental childcare. Our results therefore support the hypothesis that policies, structure and culture strongly influence the provision of childcare in European countries.

Conclusions

We have argued in this chapter that to understand the ways that policy, structure and culture all shape the extent to which non-co-resident grandmothers care for children, we need to rethink our approach to these issues. We need in particular to think about policies in terms of how they impact on mothers and grandmothers simultaneously, providing different and complex incentives and opportunities in each generation. This leads us to conceptualise childcare as something that is organised in the wider family, and to think of family care versus formal care when considering the wider impacts on individuals and society, rather than focusing solely on mothers. It also necessitates thinking about how cultures of gender, family and paid work might be influencing family-level discussions and negotiations.

Some important messages emerge from this analysis. Particularly important is the extent to which mothers in a country are not in the paid labour force, which we hypothesise influences the degree of policy attention paid to providing formal, affordable childcare, particularly for very young children. In countries where the norm is that mothers are at home, mothers who work full time, and especially those who work long full-time hours, *need* the cooperation of grandmothers. The availability of grandmothers – which we have examined here through looking at the working patterns of women aged 50–64 – and the cultural expectations these patterns reflect and create also influence grandparental childcare. Alongside this, normative cultural factors help to shape whether children of working mothers are cared for in the family (including grandmothers) or in formal care, which in turn has the potential to influence policy and societal demands. If grandmothers are providing childcare in the absence of formal provision, this may lead to certain complacency about whether such provision is needed.

This is becoming an ever-more critical discussion, as the ageing of populations around the world leads to greater expectations that grandmothers should be in the paid workforce themselves to ever-later ages. Extensions of state pension ages and both paradigmatic and parametric changes to pension systems suggest greater reliance on paid work in the future to have a reasonable expectation of a decent level of income in later life. This suggests a growing conflict between retirement and childcare policies, which has the potential to severely disadvantage middle-aged grandparents and younger mothers in the absence of policy reforms. Extended families clearly play a very important role in caring for children across welfare states. These issues need our attention.

Notes

[1]   The detailed tables for each country are available from Karen Glaser, King's College London.

[2]   For further tables and variables and further discussion of this analysis, see Chapter Six in Glaser et al. (2013).

References

Aassve, A., Arpino, B. and Goisis, A. (2012) 'Grandparenting and mothers' labour force participation: A comparative analysis using the generations and gender survey', *Demographic Research*, 27(3): 53–84.

Albert, I. and Ferring, D. (2013) *Intergenerational relations: European perspectives in family and society*. Bristol: Policy Press.

Arber, S., and Timonen, V. (eds) (2012) *Contemporary grandparenting: Changing family relationships in global contexts*. Bristol: The Policy Press.

Arpino, B., Pronzato, C. and Tavares, L. (2010) *All in the family: Informal childcare and mothers' labour market participation*. Essex: Institute for Social and Economic Research working paper series. Available at: https://www.iser.essex.ac.uk/files/iser_working_papers/2010-24.pdf.

Bordone, V., Arpine, B. and Aassve, A. (2017) 'Patterns of grandparental child care across Europe: The role of the policy context and working mothers' need', *Ageing and Society*, 37(4): 845–873.

Daly, M., and Lewis, J. (2000) 'The concept of social care and the analysis of contemporary welfare states', *British Journal of Sociology*, 51(2): 281–298.

Di Gessa, G., Glaser, K., Price, D., Ribe, E. and Tinker, A. (2016a) 'What drives national differences in intensive grandparental childcare in Europe?', *Journals of Gerontology – Series B Psychological Sciences and Social Sciences*, 71(1): 141–153.

Di Gessa, G., Glaser, K. and Tinker, A. (2016b) 'The health impact of intensive and nonintensive grandchild care in europe: New evidence from SHARE', *The Journals of Gerontology Series B: Psychological Sciences and Social Sciences*, 71(5): 867–879.

Frericks, P., Jensen, P. H. and Pfau-Effinger, B. (2014) 'Social rights and employment rights related to family care: Family care regimes in Europe', *Journal of Aging Studies*, 29: 66–77.

Fuller-Thomson, E. and Minkler, M. (2001) 'American grandparents providing extensive child care to their grandchildren', *The Gerontologist*, 41(2): 201–209.

Geurts, T., Van Tilburg, T., Poortman, A.-R. and Dykstra, P. (2015) 'Child care by grandparents: changes between 1992 and 2006', *Ageing and Society*, 35(6): 1318–1334.

Glaser, K., Montserrat, E., Ribe, E., Montserrat, U. W., Price, D., Stuchbury, R. and Tinker, A. (2010) *Grandparenting in Europe*. London: Grandparents Plus.

Glaser, K., Price, D., Di Gessa, G., Ribe Montserrat, E., Stutchbury, R. and Tinker, A. (2013) *Grandparenting in Europe: Family policy and grandparents' role in providing childcare*. London: Grandparents Plus.

Gray, A. (2005) 'The changing availability of grandparents as carers and its implications for childcare policy in the UK', *Journal of Social Policy*, 34(4): 557.

Hank, K., and Buber, I. (2009) 'Grandparents caring for their grandchildren', *Journal of Family Issues*, 30(1): 53–73.

Hantrais, L. (2000) *Gendered policies in Europe: Reconciling employment and family life*. New York: St. Martin's Press.

Harrington Meyer, M. (2014) *Grandmothers at work: Juggling families and jobs*, New York and London: New York University Press.

Herlofson, K. and Hagestad, G. (2012) 'Transformations in the role of grandparents across welfare states', in S. Arber and V. Timonen (eds), *Contemporary grandparenting: Changing family relationships in global contexts*, Bristol: Policy Press, pp 27–50.

Igel, C. and Szydlik, M. (2011) 'Grandchild care and welfare state arrangements in Europe', *Journal of European Social Policy*, 21(3): 210–224.

Jappens, M. and Van Bavel, J. (2012) 'Regional family norms and child care by grandparents in Europe', *Demographic Research*, 27(4): 85–120.

Koslowski, A. (2009) 'Grandparents and the care of their grandchildren', in J. Stillwell, E. Coast, and D. Kneale (eds) *Fertility, living arrangements, care and mobility*, Dordrecht: Springer Netherlands, pp 171–190.

Lakomý, M. and Kreidl, M. (2015) 'Full-time versus part-time employment: Does it influence frequency of grandparental childcare?', *European Journal of Ageing*, 12(4): 321–331.

Leitner, S. (2003) 'Varieties of familialism: The caring function of the family in comparative perspective', *European Societies*, 5(4): 353–375.

Lewis, J. (1992) 'Gender and the development of welfare regimes', *Journal of European Social Policy*, 2(3): 159–173.

Lewis, J. (2009) *Work–family balance, gender and policy*. Cheltenham: Edward Elgar.

Mätzke, M. and Ostner, I. (2010) 'Introduction: Change and continuity in recent family policies', *Journal of European Social Policy*, 20(5): 387–398.

Neuberger, F. and Haberkern, K. (2014) 'Structured ambivalence in grandchild care and the quality of life among European grandparents', *European Journal of Ageing*, 11(2): 171–181.

O'Connor, J., Orloff, A. and Shaver, S. (1999) *States, markets, families: Gender, liberalism, and social policy in Australia, Canada, Great Britain, and the United States*, Cambridge: Cambridge University Press.

Parsons, T. and Bales, R. (1955) *Family, socialization, and interaction processes*, New York: Free Press.

Pfau-Effinger, B. (2005) 'Culture and welfare state policies: Reflections on a complex interrelation', *Journal of Social Policy*, 34(1): 3–20.

Sainsbury, D. (1999) *Gender and welfare state regimes*, Oxford: Oxford University Press.

Saraceno, C. (2010) 'Social inequalities in facing old-age dependency: a bi-generational perspective', *Journal of European Social Policy*, 20(1): 32–44.

Saraceno, C. and Keck, W. (2010) 'Can we identify intergenerational policy regimes in Europe?', *European Societies*, 12: 675–696.

Saraceno, C. and Keck, W. (2011) 'Towards an integrated approach for the analysis of gender equity in policies supporting paid work and care responsibilities', *Demographic Research*, 25(11): 371–406.

Van Bavel, J. and De Winter, T. (2013) 'Becoming a grandparent and early retirement in Europe', *European Sociological Review*, 29(6): 1295–1308.

Wheelock, J. and Jones, K. (2002) '"Grandparents are the next best thing": Informal childcare for working parents in urban Britain', *Journal of Social Policy*, 31(3): 441–463.

PART 2
Grandparenting in contexts of economic and societal development

Grandparenting in developing South East Asia: comparative perspectives from Myanmar, Thailand and Vietnam

John Knodel and Bussarawan Teerawichitchainan

Introduction

The extent, nature and consequences of grandparenting are profoundly shaped by social contexts and how these contexts change over time (Arber and Timonen, 2012; Hermalin et al., 1998). For instance, grandparental care in the United States is often prompted by problematic situations (for instance, death or incarceration of the grandchild's parent) that require grandparents to step in and provide care for grandchildren. By contrast, grandparenting in China is considered a normative part of reciprocal intergenerational exchanges. Thus, analyses of grandparental care across different settings can broaden our understanding of how social contexts affect grandparenting. A few exceptions notwithstanding (such as Baker and Silverstein, 2012), comparative studies of grandparental care remain relatively sparse. Among the few existing studies, there is a tendency to focus on cultural factors, thus often dismissing the roles of economic development and demographic trends in explaining cross-country differences in grandparental care.

To address these pertinent research gaps, this study examines the prevalence, correlates and older persons' perceptions about grandparental care in Myanmar, Vietnam and Thailand. A combination of similarities and differences, especially in recent demographic histories and economic development levels that characterise these three South East Asian countries, make them suitable for comparative analyses of grandparenting. Importantly, ongoing debates concerning how development impacts on intergenerational relations add further interest to the cross-country comparisons (Aboderin, 2004; Hermalin,

2002; Knodel, 2014); for example, whether it will increase or decrease solidarity between generations.

Based on recent nationally representative surveys of older persons in the three countries, our analyses begin by describing trends in living arrangements among older persons. We specifically focus on the prevalence of older persons living with co-resident grandchildren. Additionally, we explore the extent to which skip-generation households (that is, households with only grandparents and grandchildren) prevail in the three countries. Furthermore, we address the extent and patterns of grandparental care. In particular, we consider variations of care provision by age of grandchildren and by presence of their parents. Using multivariate analyses, we examine the correlates of older persons providing care for grandchildren with and without the presence of the grandchild's parents in the household. Finally, to understand older persons' perceptions of grandparental care, we examine the extent to which grandparents caring for grandchildren in these countries perceive care provision as burdensome.

Country settings

Myanmar, Vietnam and Thailand are characterised by both commonalities and differences in cultural underpinnings, societal structure, demographic trends, economic development and political systems. One of the most distinct features common across all three countries is the old–age support system. Adult children in these settings have traditionally played a predominant role in supporting ageing parents. Intergenerational co-residence serves as a crucial linchpin for this system. The family support system is nevertheless reciprocal (Croll, 2006). Older persons commonly make important contributions to their adult children; for example, doing household chores and providing grandchild care. The latter includes custodial care for grandchildren whose parents have migrated elsewhere for employment (Prachuabmoh et al., 2017).

In addition to cultural features related to intergenerational exchanges, the three countries are similar in several key demographic aspects. These include fertility transition and population ageing. They experienced significant fertility decline during the last half-century. According to Table 4.1, fertility levels in the 1960s were high for all countries, with a woman having on average six children in her lifetime. In Thailand, fertility started to fall first, declined the fastest and is currently well below the replacement level. Trends in Myanmar and Vietnam do not differ much from each other. However, the decline

Table 4.1: Demographic trends and economic development indicators, Myanmar, Vietnam and Thailand

	Myanmar	Vietnam	Thailand
Demographic trends			
Total population, 2015 (in millions)[a]	53.9	93.4	68.0
Total fertility rate, 1960–65[a]	6.10	6.42	6.13
Total fertility rate, 2010–15[a]	2.25	1.96	1.53
% aged 60+, 2015[a]	9	10	16
% aged 60+, 2050 (medium projection)[a]	19	28	37
Economic development indicators			
GDP per capita, current US dollars, 2015[b]	1,162	2,111	5,815
% population in urban areas, 2015[c]	34	34	50
% main roads paved[b]	11 (2005)	48 (2007)	99 (2000)
% population with access to electricity, 2014[b]	52	99	100
Human Development Index rank (out of 188 countries), 2016[d]	145th	115th	87th

Sources:
[a] UN (2015); [b] World Bank (2017); [c] UN (2014); [d] UNDP (2016)

in Vietnam is steeper. Besides dramatic fertility decline, substantial population ageing is expected to take place in all three settings in the coming decades. The Thai population aged 60 and older is projected to increase most rapidly, approaching two fifths by mid-century. Even in Myanmar, where population ageing will be the slowest, the population aged 60 and above is projected to double – from 9% in 2015 to 19% in 2050.

Various indicators of economic development show significant differences among the three countries. They clearly suggest that Myanmar is by far the least developed and Thailand the most developed, with Vietnam falling in between. This is apparent in comparisons of per-capita GDP, which in Myanmar is slightly over half of that in Vietnam and only one fifth of that in Thailand. Furthermore, a substantial proportion of the population in all three countries still lives in rural areas. Nevertheless, the percentage living in urban areas is distinctively highest in Thailand at 50%, compared to about one third in Myanmar and Vietnam.

Other indicators shown in Table 4.1 also confirm the sharp contrast in the ranking of the three countries regarding economic development. Almost all major roads in Thailand are paved, compared to almost half of those in Vietnam and only 11% in Myanmar. Access to electricity is virtually universal in Vietnam and Thailand, but this is true for only about half the population in Myanmar. Perhaps the United Nations Development Programme human development index (UNDP, 2016) best sums up the cross-national differences in levels of development. It reveals that Myanmar is considerably further down the list than Vietnam, which in turn has a lower ranking than Thailand.

Furthermore, the political systems in the three countries are vastly different. Thailand has a constitutional monarchy with a military-led government, Vietnam has a one-party system led by the Communist Party and Myanmar recently transitioned from five decades of military rule to a free democratic system. These different and evolving political systems may affect social protection measures that have implications for state assistance for older persons. At present, government policies in these countries presuppose the primacy of family care for older persons (World Bank, 2016a). Government policies to facilitate and supplement the role of family support and care are most advanced in Thailand and least developed in Myanmar. Thailand not only has effective universal healthcare coverage but is also the only country of the three that provides an old-age allowance programme with universal coverage for persons 60 and older (Suwanrada, 2012).

In sum, the three countries provide an appropriate combination of settings to explore the influence of demography and economic development on grandparental care. Emphasis in the interpretation of results is on the critical role that differences in demographic trends and economic development trends play, in interaction with each other, in accounting for observed differences. It thus fills what has been a gap in previous comparative research. In so doing, it serves to make a case that these aspects of social context deserve a prominent place within conceptual frameworks that guide comparative studies on grandparenting.

Data and methods

We analyse three nationally representative samples of persons 60 and older in South East Asia. Data are from the 2012 Myanmar Ageing Survey (MAS), the 2011 Vietnam Ageing Survey (VNAS) and the 2011 Survey of Older Persons in Thailand (SOPT). Both MAS and VNAS were the first national-level surveys of older people in their respective countries. The MAS sample consisted of 4,080 adults aged 60 and older throughout Myanmar, except Kachin State. The VNAS sample consisted of adults aged at least 50, including 2,789 persons aged 60 and older. The SOPT sample consisted of persons aged 50 and over, among whom 34,173 were aged 60 and older.

The designs of all three surveys require that results be weighted to be nationally representative. Results are thus based on weighted data. Further details about each survey's methodology, including sampling strategy, are available elsewhere (see Myanmar Survey Research, 2012; National Statistical Office, 2012; Vietnam Women's Union, 2012). In interpreting the Thai data, we are mindful that given its relatively large sample size, the same substantive difference observed in all three countries is more likely to be statistically significant for Thailand, all else being equal.

Variable measurements

There are two important issues to note for variable measurements. First, while information on grandchild care is rather limited in the three ageing surveys, sufficient information is available to explore important issues. Second, the numerous challenges in harmonisation of variables faced by this study are a typical issue in comparative research, especially when based on surveys conducted by different organisations. This section describes how key variables are operationalised to address these challenges.

Living arrangements: We examine two aspects of old-age living arrangements, including co-residence with grandchildren and skip-generation living arrangements. First, we incorporate a dichotomous variable indicating whether the respondent co-resides with at least one grandchild. Since the age of grandchildren is suggestive of whether they need care from older persons or may instead be able to provide support for older kin, we further include two additional variables indicating whether the respondent lives with at least one grandchild under age 10 and whether they co-reside with a grandchild aged 18 and over. The second aspect of old-age living arrangements examines whether the respondent (with or without spouse) lives with one or more grandchildren but not with other family members. Given that young children are more dependent than older ones, we pay particular attention to skip-generation living arrangements with at least one grandchild under age 10.

Provision of grandchild care: Unlike co-residence with grandchildren, measures of grandparental care for grandchildren cannot be harmonised completely because information relevant to grandparenting in the three surveys is not identical. Nevertheless, since information across the surveys addresses similar aspects of care provision, comparisons can still be very informative. Based on our data, we incorporate key measures of grandchild care provision, including whether the respondent provides care for grandchildren under age 10 and whether the respondent cares for grandchildren with absent parents.

We are mindful of the differences across the surveys, particularly related to the timing of care provision and the age of grandchildren under care. The Myanmar survey, for example, allows us to examine not only whether the respondent has ever cared for grandchildren (with or without absent parents) but also whether they are currently providing such care. However, the survey does not specify the age of grandchildren under the care of older persons. The Vietnam survey enquires about care provision for grandchildren under age 10. For care provision for grandchildren with absent parents specifically, the survey probes whether such caregiving took place both in the past and more recently (during the last year). It is important to note that the Vietnam survey refers to grandchild care provided by either the respondent or spouse. Compared to Myanmar and Vietnam, information about provision of grandchild care is more limited in the Thai survey. It nevertheless contains information about whether the respondent cared for a young grandchild in the past year and whether they are currently the main carer for co-resident grandchild(ren) whose parents are absent.

Perception of grandchild care: Information about older persons' perceptions of grandchild care is available only in the Myanmar and Vietnam surveys. Both surveys probe the extent to which the respondent views caring for grandchildren under their current or recent care as burdensome. Additionally, the data allows us to examine the perception of care for grandchildren whose parents are present or absent in the household. Possible responses differ slightly across the two surveys. Myanmar respondents were asked if they mostly enjoyed caring for the grandchildren or if it was mostly a burden. Vietnamese respondents were asked about the extent to which caring for grandchildren was a physical burden. It is important to note that the differences in the questions and responses limit precise comparisons between the two countries.

Sociodemographic characteristics: Background characteristics incorporated into the analyses include gender; age; current marital status; location of residence; health status; household wealth, work status and presence of co-resident children aged 18 and older. These variables are treated as independent variables in the multivariate analyses of correlates of grandparental care, since previous studies suggest that they often correlate with care provision.

Age is incorporated as a categorical variable divided into 10-year age groups up to ages 80 and over. Current marital status is measured as a dichotomous variable indicating whether the respondent is married at the time of survey. Health status is generally measured as a categorical variable indicating whether the respondent assesses their health to be good, fair or poor. For Vietnam, because of the small number of respondents who assessed their health status as good, the reference category is average and good and the other categories are poor and very poor.

Household wealth is constructed based on the respondent's housing quality and ownership of household assets such as a TV, refrigerator, phone, motor vehicle, floor constructed using modern materials and access to safe water sources. Based on the household wealth index scores, we divide the respondents into three terciles of low, middle and high household wealth. Furthermore, work status is measured slightly differently for each country based on available information in each survey. For Myanmar, 'work' refers to work status last year; for Vietnam, 'work' refers to whether either respondent or spouse is currently working; and for Thailand, 'work' refers to whether the respondent was working at the time of the survey.

Results

Sample descriptions

Table 4.2 compares sociodemographic characteristics of the survey samples of persons aged 60 and older. The three country samples are quite similar on some measures. The mean ages are around 70. Women constitute modest majorities of older persons in each sample, ranging from 54% to 57%. Approximately two thirds reside in rural areas and around 90% have at least some education. In terms of work status, however, Myanmar respondents are less likely to report having worked in the past year compared to those in Vietnam and Thailand, possibly reflecting their relatively poorer levels of health.

Information on several key household possessions indicates that cross–country differences are substantial. Older persons in Myanmar live in households with the fewest possessions, whereas those in Thailand live in households with the most. Overall, the differences are quite stark and consistent with statistics on country-level indicators of economic development reported in Table 4.1. Only 10% of the Myanmar sample have a phone in the household, compared to the vast majority in Vietnam and Thailand. This is particularly striking, since the lack of ready access to a phone in the household has important implications for grandparents' ability to communicate with parents of grandchildren under their care who live elsewhere.

Table 4.2: Descriptive statistics: sociodemographic characteristics of survey samples of adults aged 60 and older, Myanmar, Vietnam and Thailand

	Myanmar	Vietnam	Thailand
Unweighted N	4,080	2,789	34,173
Mean age	70.5	70.7	69.2
% female	54	57	56
% rural	69	67	67
% with some education	89	92	88
% worked last year	30	40	43
% in households with:			
television	40	93	99
motor vehicle (motorcycle, car, truck)	27	68	81
phone	10	85	89
refrigerator	7	48	93
Mean number of living children	4.6	4.7	3.5
% co-resident with adult children	77	66	57
% with 1+ children outside province/township	43	50	59

Sources: The 2012 Myanmar Ageing Survey; 2011 Vietnam Ageing Survey; 2011 Survey of Older Persons in Thailand

Furthermore, older Thais have on average fewer living children than their counterparts in Myanmar or Vietnam, reflecting Thailand's earlier and more advanced fertility decline. The living arrangements of older persons also differ. Co-residence with at least one adult child (aged 18 and over) is highest for Myanmar and lowest for Thailand. The percentage of older persons with at least one child living at some considerable distance also differs; it is highest in Thailand and lowest in Myanmar. Only 43% of older people in Myanmar have at least one child living outside their township, compared to 50% in Vietnam and nearly 60% in Thailand who have at least one child residing outside the province. These differences likely reflect the differing levels of economic development, and consequent job creation, which spurs migration in the three countries.

Prevalence of co-resident grandchildren and skip-generation households

According to the surveys, 87% of older persons in Myanmar and 93% of their Vietnamese counterparts have at least one grandchild. While the equivalent information is unavailable for Thailand, the proportion is likely lower, given the lower mean number of offspring of Thai elders combined with the lower fertility levels of their adult children. Of greater relevance to our study is the share of older persons who have co-resident grandchildren, particularly those of very young ages, since such living arrangements increase the probability of more intensive grandparental care (Timonen and Arber, 2012).

Table 4.3 compares trends in living with co-resident grandchildren and prevalence of skip-generation living arrangements among older persons in the three countries. Results indicate that about half of elders in Myanmar and Vietnam reside with at least one co-resident grandchild of any age, while the percentage is lower for Thais (44%). Moreover, older persons tend to have multiple grandchildren living with them. The mean number among older adults with co-resident grandchildren is 2.3 in Myanmar, 1.9 in Vietnam and 1.7 in Thailand (not shown in Table 4.3). Close to one third of older persons in Myanmar and Vietnam but only about a quarter in Thailand live with a grandchild under age 10. This likely reflects the more advanced stage of fertility decline in Thailand. Although information is lacking for Thailand, approximately 15% of older persons in Myanmar and Vietnam co-reside with at least one grandchild aged 18 and above.

The phenomenon of skip-generation households consisting only of grandparents and grandchildren is a topic of considerable interest to both researchers and organisations working for the welfare of older persons and children (HelpAge International, 2012; Timonen and Arber, 2012; UNICEF Thailand, 2009). Table 4.3 suggests that relatively few older persons in all three countries live in skip-generation households. Nevertheless, older Thais are clearly the most likely to live in skip-generation households; about one in 10 do so. This is also true for the prevalence of skip-generation households where at

Table 4.3: Descriptive statistics: trends in co-residence with grandchildren and skip-generation households among persons aged 60 and older, Myanmar, Vietnam and Thailand

	Myanmar	Vietnam	Thailand
Co-residential arrangements			
% with co-resident grandchild of any age	49	50	44
% with co-resident grandchild under age 10	32	31	23
% with co-resident grandchild aged 18+	16	15	—
Skip-generation households			
% living with only grandchildren of any age	4	5	10
% living with only grandchildren and at least one is under age 10	2	2	5

Sources: The 2012 Myanmar Ageing Survey; 2011 Vietnam Ageing Survey; 2011 Survey of Older Persons in Thailand

least one grandchild is under the age of 10. While only about 5% of Thai elders live only with young grandchildren, this figure is twice as high as in Vietnam and Myanmar. Overall, the considerably greater prevalence of skip-generation living arrangements in Thailand is all the more striking because older people in Thailand are likely to have fewer grandchildren than those in the other two countries.

The difference in the prevalence of skip-generation households corresponds to differences in the levels of economic development in the three countries. The more advanced development in Thailand compared to the other two countries has generated greater employment opportunities for young adults outside their parents' locality, thus stimulating migration from their place of origin. Results (not shown) reveal that older Thais living in rural areas are considerably more likely than their urban counterparts to be in skip-generation households, whereas rural–urban differences are not pronounced in Myanmar or Vietnam. The more pronounced urban–rural differences in Thailand reflect substantially higher out-migration of adult children from rural areas, stimulated by urban employment opportunities generated by the more advanced Thai economy.

Prevalence and patterns of care provision for grandchildren

Table 4.4 shows proportions of older persons across the three countries who provide care for grandchildren, both regarding any grandchild and those whose parents are absent. Note that absent-parent cases include situations in which other persons besides grandparents and grandchildren may be present in the household, and thus are not limited to skip-generation households as defined in Table 4.3. In this and subsequent analyses, the small number of cases in which both parents are deceased are not included with grandchildren with absent parents, since such cases are not treated consistently across the three surveys.

Overall, substantial proportions of older persons in all three countries are involved in providing care and support for grandchildren. In Myanmar, almost half of respondents had ever cared for grandchildren and almost one third were currently doing so. The proportions of those who ever cared for a grandchild whose parents were absent (13%) or who were currently doing so (4%) are far lower. In Thailand, slightly over a quarter (28%) provided care to a grandchild younger than age 10 during the past year and 10% reported they were currently the main carer for co-resident grandchild(ren) of any age whose parents were absent. In Vietnam, one third of older persons reported they had

Table 4.4: Descriptive statistics: prevalence of care provision for grandchildren among persons aged 60 and older, Myanmar, Vietnam and Thailand

	Percentage
Myanmar	
% ever cared for:	
any grandchild	47
one with absent parents	13
% currently caring for:	
any grandchild	33
one with absent parents	4
Vietnam	
% cared for grandchild < 10 in past year	34
% cared for grandchild < 10 with absent parent in past year	4
% ever cared for grandchild < 10 with absent parent	8
Thailand	
% cared for grandchild < 10 in past year	28
% currently main carer for co-resident grandchild with absent parent	10

Sources: The 2012 Myanmar Ageing Survey; 2011 Vietnam Ageing Survey; 2011 Survey of Older Persons in Thailand

cared for a grandchild under age 10 during the previous year but only 4% had cared for one with absent parents.

Given that the measures of grandchild care are not identical across the three surveys, the ability to make definitive statements about cross-national differences in prevalence is limited. Still, it is clear that older persons in Thailand are more than twice as likely as those in Myanmar to currently be providing care to grandchildren with absent parents. Again, this very likely reflects the higher levels of migration of adult children associated with Thailand's more advanced economic development. Comparison with Vietnam is more complicated. While the Thai questionnaire refers to current main care without a limitation on the age of the grandchild, the Vietnamese questionnaire refers to children under age 10 during the past year and does not specify main care. Nevertheless, since results indicate that current main care for grandchildren with absent parents is much higher in Thailand than is recent care of grandchildren under 10 with absent parents in Vietnam, this strongly implies that such care is considerably more frequent for older Thais than their Vietnamese counterparts.

Correlates of care provision for grandchildren

The prevalence of grandchild care varies with the characteristics and situation of older persons. Based on multivariate frameworks, Table 4.5 examines the correlates of current or recent care of grandchildren in general. Although not shown in a table, we also examined care of grandchildren whose parents are absent. We use binary logistic regressions to examine the correlates of care provision. For each country, we incorporate two models: an unadjusted model treating each variable as a sole correlate of care provision (that is, zero-order effect) and an adjusted model considering all covariates simultaneously. For each variable, coefficients are expressed as the ratio of the odds of providing care versus not doing so for each category relative to the comparable odds of the reference category. Odds ratios above one indicate that the particular category is associated with higher likelihood of care provision than the reference category, whereas values below one indicate the opposite. For statistical significance levels, we consider the joint statistical significance level of the subset categories within each variable based on the Wald test. Odds ratios significant at the $p<0.05$ level are shown in bold. For the Myanmar and Vietnam analyses, consideration is limited to older people who have at least one grandchild.

In all three countries, persons in their 70s – and even more so those in their 80s – are substantially less likely to provide grandchild care relative to those in their 60s, whether in general or for grandchildren with absent parents. Adjusting for other covariates makes little difference. This inverse association between care provision and the respondent's age likely reflects greater frailty of persons of more advanced ages, as well as the ageing of the grandchildren reducing the need for grandparental care (Lee and Bauer, 2010). Contrary to the general assumption that grandchild care is far more a grandmother's than a grandfather's responsibility, results indicate that differences with respect to gender are relatively modest. Nevertheless, in Thailand, after taking other covariates into account, the odds of caring for a grandchild are significantly higher for women than for men. In results not shown, older Thai women experience considerably greater likelihood of caring for a grandchild with absent parents compared to their male counterparts. Results for Vietnam are unavailable because the question asked about care by the respondent or their spouse, making interpretation ambiguous for married respondents. Moreover, unadjusted results indicate that currently married older persons are more likely to provide grandchild care than those not

Table 4.5: Odds ratios of care provision for grandchild, unadjusted and adjusted for sociodemographic covariates, persons aged 60 and older, Myanmar, Vietnam and Thailand

	Myanmar (if has a grandchild)		Vietnam (if has a grandchild)		Thailand (all persons 60+)	
	Current care of grandchild, any age		Recent/current care for grandchild under 10[a]		Recent/current care for grandchild under 10[a]	
	Unadjusted	Adjusted	Unadjusted	Adjusted	Unadjusted	Adjusted
Age (60–69=Ref)						
70–79	0.77	0.79	0.53	0.56	0.67	0.65
80+	0.39	0.41	0.15	0.15	0.32	0.30
Gender (Male=Ref)						
Female	0.96	1.06	—[b]	—[b]	1.01	1.12
Current marital status (Not married=Ref)						
Married	1.33	1.13	2.03	1.35	1.48	1.32
Location of residence (Urban=Ref)						
Rural	0.96	1.02	0.89	0.82	1.54	1.61
Health status (Good=Ref)						
Fair	0.89	0.95	0.74	0.82	0.85	0.87
Poor	0.72	0.83	0.27	0.37	0.67	0.75
Household wealth (Low=Ref)						
Middle	1.50	1.42	1.31	1.04	1.61	1.35
High	1.48	1.42	1.34	0.88	1.21	1.07

(continued)

Table 4.5. Odds ratios of care provision for grandchild, unadjusted and adjusted for sociodemographic covariates, persons aged 60 and older, Myanmar, Vietnam and Thailand (continued)

	Myanmar (if has a grandchild)		Vietnam (if has a grandchild)		Thailand (all persons 60+)	
	Current care of grandchild, any age		Recent/current care for grandchild under 10[a]		Recent/current care for grandchild under 10[a]	
	Unadjusted	Adjusted	Unadjusted	Adjusted	Unadjusted	Adjusted
Work status (Not working=Ref)						
Worked	1.20	1.04	1.78	0.95	1.20	0.91
Co-resident children aged 18+ (None=Ref)						
One	1.61	1.63	1.40	1.72	2.04	2.23
Two or more	1.69	1.49	1.05	0.96	1.99	2.18

Notes:
[a] Question referred to care during past year.
[b] Question referred to care by respondent or spouse. Therefore, gender of carer was unknown.

Significance levels: Odds ratios significant at the p<0.05 level are shown in bold face. The p-values refer to the joint statistical significance level of the subset of categories within each predictor variable based on the Wald test.

Sources: The 2012 Myanmar Ageing Survey, 2011 Vietnam Ageing Survey, and 2011 Survey of Older Persons in Thailand

currently married. This association is, however, reduced remarkably when other covariates are considered.

Results further indicate that the odds of grandchild care are considerably higher for rural than urban dwellers in Thailand, especially in terms of care of grandchildren whose parents are absent. This is consistent for both unadjusted and adjusted models. In Myanmar and Vietnam, however, differences by place of residence are mostly statistically insignificant and inconsistent in direction. Findings further suggest that in Vietnam and Thailand (but not Myanmar) the odds of grandchild care provision in general significantly decrease with poor health of the respondent. This is also true with respect to care of grandchildren with absent parents in Thailand, although not in Myanmar and Vietnam.

Unadjusted results indicate that in all three countries, older persons in households with lowest levels of wealth are less likely to care for grandchildren. However, when statistically adjusted for other covariates, the differences by household wealth are noticeably reduced in Myanmar and Thailand and become statistically insignificant in Vietnam. The association of household wealth and care for a grandchild with absent parents is less consistent across countries. In Myanmar, the odds significantly increase with wealth levels; in Thailand, those in the highest wealth category have the lowest odds of caring for such a grandchild; and in Vietnam, there is no significant difference by household wealth in care of grandchildren whose parents are absent. Unadjusted results show that current or recent work is positively associated with care of grandchildren in general as well as those with absent parents. However, controlling for other covariates either considerably reduces or reverses this association.

Finally, the presence of co-resident adult children increases the odds of taking care of a grandchild in general (with the exception of having two co-resident adult children in Vietnam) but decreases them sharply for taking care of a grandchild with absent parents. The general patterns with regard to co-resident adult children are not surprising. Co-resident adult children may have children of their own whom the older person can help care for; but in cases where no adult child is present, unless a child-in-law is in the household the parents of any grandchild in the household would be absent.

In brief, while interpretations of the similarities and some of the differences in the relationships between grandchild care provision and the covariates examined appear to be fairly straightforward, interpretation for some differences remains elusive. Putting aside possible measurement error, this may simply reflect that the interplay of influences on grandchild care can be quite complex, and to some degree specific, to the particular society under consideration.

Perceived burden of grandparental care

Relatively little attention has been paid to grandparents' own perceptions of providing grandchild care (Arber and Timonen, 2012). While the media often portrays grandparental care as primarily a burden for older persons, existing studies in Asia found positive reactions among grandparents (Baker and Silverstein, 2012; Chyi and Mao, 2012; Sun, 2013; Tsai et al., 2013). The analysis presented in Table 4.6 adds to this emerging literature by examining the extent to which older persons providing recent or current care to a grandchild in Myanmar and Vietnam perceived caregiving as burdensome. The

Table 4.6: Perception of grandchild care as burden among persons aged 60 and older, by presence or absence of grandchild's parents, Myanmar and Vietnam

| | Grandchildren under recent/current care[a] | | |
	All	With parent present in household or locality[b]	With parent outside household or locality[b]
Myanmar			
Total	100%	100%	100%
Mostly enjoyed	73	75	60
Mostly a burden	5	6	5
Both enjoyed and a burden	22	20	35
N (unweighted)	1,290	1,055	145
Vietnam			
Total	100%	100%	100%
Not a physical burden	26	26	26
Only a little burden	27	27	30
Somewhat of a burden	35	34	37
Considerable burden	12	13	7
N (unweighted)	968	784	108

Notes:

[a] Results for Vietnam refer only to grandchildren under age 10. Parents present include only those co-resident in the household for Myanmar but for Vietnam include those living nearby. Information for Thailand is not available. Vietnam's results for current care refer to grandchildren cared for by respondent or spouse during the past 12 months, some of whom may no longer be under their care.

[b] Excludes cases in which care is provided to both grandchildren with present and with absent parents and those with deceased parents.

Sources: The 2012 Myanmar Ageing Survey; 2011 Vietnam Ageing Survey

analysis distinguishes between situations in which a grandchild's parent was present or absent in the household.

Findings indicate a similar picture from both countries: overall, relatively positive perceptions predominate over negative ones. In Myanmar, almost three quarters of grandparents currently providing care to a grandchild replied that they mostly enjoyed it and only 5% said it was mostly a burden. In Vietnam, slightly over half of respondents who recently provided care for a grandchild under age 10 indicated that it was either not at all a physical burden or only a little burdensome, while only 12% viewed it as a considerable physical burden. In Vietnam, there is little difference in the replies of grandparents who cared for a grandchild with a parent present and those whose parents were absent. In Myanmar, however, noticeably lower percentages of respondents currently caring for a grandchild with absent parents expressed positive perception (mostly enjoyed), compared to those currently caring for a grandchild whose parent was present in the household.

In sum, the findings for both Myanmar and Vietnam are reasonably consistent with the studies in other Asian settings. It is plausible that Asian grandparents often gain satisfaction from carrying out a culturally valued family role or find it gives meaning to their lives. Our finding that grandparenting tends not to be viewed as a burden gains additional credibility from the fact that older persons across all three countries who currently care for grandchildren are more likely than those who do not to say they are not lonely, as well as to say that they are happy (results not shown). Even though causality between grandchild care and these measures cannot be implied from these associations, it is at least interesting that they are in contrast to evidence from the US context, which indicates that older persons who care for grandchildren are more likely to experience depression than other older persons (Musil et al., 2011, 2013).

Study limitations

This study has a number of limitations. First, grandparental care was only one of many topics covered by the surveys, thus limiting the amount of information collected. Moreover, responses were recorded in precoded categories and may not capture nuances or complexities of particular answers. Additionally, as mentioned earlier, differences across the three surveys pose numerous challenges for harmonisation of variables. While several efforts have been made to minimise comparability problems, they cannot be entirely discounted. Where possible, we have provided appropriate caveats accompanying the interpretation of results.

Importantly, our data are cross-sectional and not longitudinal. Thus, analyses are primarily descriptive and correlational. Relationships found between grandparenting issues and other variables (such as health status) are simply associations. Their causality cannot be inferred. Moreover, it is not possible to determine the extent to which differences found between groups reflect prior selection or derive from impacts of the caregiving experience. Furthermore, while we interpret the impact of past demographic trends based on direct empirical analysis, our efforts to relate macro-level societal differences in the survey findings (for example, levels of economic development) represent interpretations based on logical arguments rather than direct empirical tests.

Conclusions

Analysing data from recent national-level surveys of older persons in Myanmar, Vietnam and Thailand, this study shows that substantial proportions of persons aged 60 and older in these South East Asian settings live in households with co-resident grandchildren and commonly provide grandparental childcare. By providing such services, the grandchild's parents have more time to pursue economic activities outside the household, including both those who co-reside and those who migrated to work elsewhere. Our analysis thus documents one of the most important services older persons contribute to the household and underscores an important aspect of productive ageing.

The fact that grandparental care is common in the three countries reflects the widespread acceptance across Asia of reciprocal intergenerational obligations between parents and adult children. This includes co-residence of older persons with their adult children as part of the arrangement. Although declining, co-residence is still common in all three countries, and intergenerational obligations remain strong even as they are adapted to changing circumstances (Knodel, 2014; Teerawichitchainan et al., 2015).

In addition to recognising the influence of cultural context on the prevalence and nature of grandparenting, our results illustrate that recent demographic trends and levels of development in interaction with each other serve as major conditioners of grandparental care, and account for a substantial share of the observed cross-country differences. Together, they operate by affecting the numbers of grandchildren available, the extent of migration of adult children and the living arrangements of older persons.

All three countries have experienced substantial declines in fertility, brought about in part through socioeconomic development, which also influenced their timing and pace. Adult children of the older generation are having small families, thereby reducing the number of grandchildren available for older persons to care for. The timing and extent of fertility decline in the three countries differed, with fertility falling earliest, fastest and furthest in Thailand. Thus, the reduction in family sizes among Thais entering later life during recent years is far more pronounced than in the other two countries. These cross-national differences in past fertility trends help account for why proportions of older Thais who have co-resident grandchildren, and particularly young (under age 10) grandchildren, are the lowest.

While differences in economic development likely contribute indirectly to differences in fertility trends, they are much closer linked to differences in levels of migration of adult children. Throughout the developing world, economic development generates modern-sector jobs that stimulate migration of young adults, especially from rural areas seeking employment opportunities elsewhere. This in turn affects the living arrangements of older persons, who generally remain in the place of origin, by contributing to a reduced presence of adult children in their households or those living nearby. At the same time, migration generates a need for custodial care for the grandchildren whose parents leave but are unable to bring them along. As already noted, the percentage of adult children that migrated is by far highest among older persons in Thailand and by far lowest in Myanmar, in accordance with the sharp differences in their levels of economic development. Thus, although skip-generation households remain rather uncommon in all three countries, in accordance with levels of development they are by far most common in Thailand and least in Myanmar.

Looking ahead, the situation is very likely to change. Myanmar's ongoing transformation of its political system and the country's opening up to the world economy and foreign investment have already propelled rapid economic growth and other social changes (Knodel and Teerawichitchainan, 2017; Park et al., 2012). This has resulted in increased internal migration in response to expanding employment opportunities and improved standards of living (World Bank, 2016b). Likewise, there is little reason to doubt that socioeconomic development will continue in both Vietnam and Thailand and contribute to increased internal migration of adult children of older persons, although the disjuncture with the past is unlikely to be as prominent as in Myanmar.

Concerning future demographic trends, it is anticipated that the average number of children of older persons will decline over the next few decades as cohorts with fewer children enter older ages and those characterised by larger families die out. Moreover, the decreased number of adult children of the future cohorts of older people will themselves likely be characterised by smaller families. Together, these trends will result in substantially decreased availability of grandchildren, thus lowering the prevalence of grandparental care among the older population. The combined impact on the extent of custodial care of grandchildren with absent parents is less certain. On the one hand, increased migration promotes leaving children behind; on the other, lower fertility reduces the numbers of grandchildren. In Thailand, where these trends have progressed furthest, skip-generation families increased noticeably between 1994 and 2007 but declined modestly in 2011. Apparently, in the last few years, the impact of fertility decline more than counteracted the increased migration of adult children (Knodel et al., 2013). This decline may well continue in the future, and possibly portends eventual decline in skip-generation households in Vietnam and Myanmar as well.

Despite substantial economic development and social change, the intergenerational contract through which adult children fulfill filial obligations to their ageing parents remains strong (Croll, 2006). However, it is maintained through a process of renegotiation in which the exchange of services (including grandchild care) between the two generations plays an increasingly essential role. Rising employment in the modern sector has heightened the need for assistance with the care of young children among working-age adults. By providing such care, older persons reinforce the sense of obligation on the part of their adult children to provide care and support in old age. Given that demographic trends are almost certain to decrease the availability of grandchildren and possibly the need for grandparental childcare, how this may affect the ongoing renegotiation and reinterpretation of the intergenerational contract in the coming decades remains an open question.

In conclusion, in the case of the three South East Asian countries, differences in recent demographic trends and levels of development help account for differences in various aspects of grandparenting. Comparative studies of grandparenting will likely benefit by including these important aspects of the societal context in the conceptual frameworks guiding their research and paying explicit attention to them in their analyses.

References

Aboderin, I. (2004) 'Modernisation and ageing theory revisited: Current explanations of recent developing world and historical western shifts in material family support for older people', *Ageing & Society*, 24(1): 29–50.

Arber, S. and Timonen, V. (2012) 'Grandparenting in the 21st century: New directions', in S. Arber and V. Timonen (eds) *Grandparenting: Changing family relationships and global contexts*, Bristol: Policy Press, pp 247–264.

Baker, L. and Silverstein, M. (2012) 'The well-being of grandparents caring for grandchildren in China and the United States', In S. Arber and V. Timonen (eds) *Grandparenting: Changing family relationships and global contexts*, Bristol: Policy Press, pp 51–70.

Chyi, H. and Mao, S. (2012) 'The determinants of happiness of Chinese elderly population', *Journal of Happiness Studies*, 13: 167–185.

Croll, E. (2006) 'The intergenerational contract in the changing Asian family', *Oxford Development Studies*, 34(4): 473–491.

HelpAge International. (2012) *The neglected generation: The impact of displacement on older people*, London: HelpAge International and the Internal Displacement Monitoring Centre.

Hermalin, A.I. (2002) 'Theoretical perspectives, measurement issues, and related research', In A.I. Hermalin (ed) *The well-being of the elderly in Asia: A four country comparative study*, Ann Arbor, MI: University of Michigan Press, pp 101–142.

Hermalin, A.I., Roan, C. and Perez, A. (1998) 'The emerging role of grandparents in Asia', *Elderly in Asia research report series*, No. 98-52, Ann Arbor, MI: Population Studies Center, University of Michigan,

Knodel, J. (2014) 'Is intergenerational solidarity really on the decline? Cautionary evidence from Thailand', *Asian Population Studies*, 10(2): 176–194.

Knodel, J. and Teerawichitchainan, B. (2017) 'Ageing in Myanmar', *The Gerontologist*, 57(4): 599–605.

Knodel, J., Prachuabmoh, V. and Chayovan, N. (2013) *The changing well-being of Thai elderly: An update from the 2011 Survey of Older Persons in Thailand*, Chiang Mai: HelpAge International.

Lee, J. and Bauer, J. (2010) 'Profiles of grandmothers providing child care to their grandchildren in South Korea', *Journal of Comparative Family Studies*, 41(3): 455–475.

Musil, C.M., Gordon, N.L., Warner, C.B., Zauszniewski, J.A., Standing, T. and Wykle, M. (2011) 'Grandmothers and caregiving to grandchildren: Continuity, change, and outcomes', *The Gerontologist*, 51(1): 86–100.

Musil, C.M., Jeanblanc, A.B., Burant, C.J., Zauszniewski, J.A. and Warner, C.B. (2013) 'Longitudinal analysis of resourcefulness, family strain, and depressive symptoms in grandmother caregivers', *Nursing Outlook*, 61(4): 225–234.

Myanmar Survey Research (2012) *Survey on Ageing in Multiple Regions 2012: Technical Report.* Available at: https://umich.box.com/s/g5vwniltsrszfic18jth.

National Statistical Office (NSO) (2012) *Survey of Older Persons in Thailand 2011,* Bangkok: NSO (in Thai).

Park, C-Y., Khan, M.E. and Vandenberg, P. (2012) *Myanmar in transition: Opportunities and challenges,* Manila: Asian Development Bank.

Prachuabmoh, V., Knodel, J. and Teerawichitchainan, B. (2017) *Productive ageing: Comparative analysis between Myanmar, Thailand, and Vietnam.* Paper presented at Contextualising Productive Ageing in Asia conference, National University of Singapore, 13–14 March.

Sun, J. (2013) 'Chinese older adults taking care of grandchildren: Practices and policies for productive ageing', *Aging International*, 38: 58–70.

Suwanrada, W. (2012) 'Old-age allowance system in Thailand', *Poverty in Focus,* 25: 14–16.

Teerawichitchainan, B., Pothisiri, W. and Giang, T.L. (2015) 'How do living arrangements and intergenerational support matter for psychological health of elderly parents? Evidence from Myanmar, Vietnam, and Thailand', *Social Science & Medicine*, 136–137: 106–116.

Timonen, V. and Arber, S. (2012) 'A new look at grandparenting', In S. Arber and V. Timonen (eds) *Grandparenting: Changing family relationships and global contexts*, Bristol: Policy Press, pp 1–24.

Tsai, F.J., Motamed, S. and Rougemont, A. (2013) 'The protective effect of taking care of grandchildren on elders' mental health?', *BMC Public Health*, 13(1): 1–9.

UN (2014) *World urbanisation prospects: The 2014 revision.* New York: UN.

UN (2015) *World population prospects: The 2015 revision.* New York: UN.

UNDP (2016) *Human development report 2016.* New York: UNDP.

UNICEF Thailand (2009) *Global study on child poverty and disparities: National report, Thailand*, Bangkok: UNICEF Thailand.

Vietnam Women's Union (2012) *Vietnam Ageing Survey (VNAS): Key findings*, Hanoi: Vietnam Women's Union.

World Bank (2016a) *Live long and prosper: Ageing in East Asia and Pacific,* Washington, DC: World Bank East Asia and Pacific Regional Report.

World Bank (2016b) *A country on the move: Domestic migration in two regions of Myanmar*, Yangon: World Bank Myanmar.

World Bank (2017). *World development indicators data bank*, June. http://databank.worldbank.org/data/reports.aspx?source=world-development-indicators

FIVE

Second-parenthood realities, third-age ideals: (grand)parenthood in the context of poverty and HIV/AIDS

Jaco Hoffman

Introduction

Within contexts of poverty and the AIDS-related epidemics in (South) Africa, this chapter positions itself at the interface of the historical–moral engagement of grandparents in the care and nurturing of grandchildren with contemporary social realities and aspirations. Grandparents, specifically grandmothers,[1] in (South) Africa have always found themselves in a situation of reciprocal exchanges: grandmothers raised and/or nurtured children, young children assisted with house and agricultural work, and absent adult children (the migratory parents of the children being raised by these grandmothers) provided income. The phenomenon of the oldest generation in (South) Africa caring for younger generations thus builds on a long-established continuum of social structures and norms related to intergenerational support, including childcare. What distinguishes the current role of grandparents in the HIV/AIDS context is that, rather than forming part of a web of complementary socialising agents within communities, they are increasingly being forced – as their children become incapacitated and even die – to take sole responsibility for their grandchildren, including legal guardianship. The responsibility for focused childcare in the HIV/AIDS context is further – at least for part of the time – compounded by dedicated care of sick and dying children and/or grandchildren, chronic poverty and the unemployment of younger generations.

Background

The uncertain situation of grandparents (specifically grandmothers) in relation to their own care futures should be understood against the backdrop of poverty exacerbated by the HIV/AIDS pandemic.

Poverty

Most singularly, entrenched poverty characterises Sub-Saharan Africa (SSA), with its otherwise huge diversity of populations. Of the 41 countries with the lowest human development ranking listed in the 2016 *Human Development Report* of the UN Human Development Index (UNDP, 2016), 35 are situated in SSA. Although South Africa ranks 119th out of 188 positions and is categorised as a medium development country, it has one of the highest levels of economic inequality in the world, with a Gini coefficient of 0.68 in 2015 (Stats SA, 2017). A legacy of previous policies related to colonialism and apartheid, the group most affected by this entrenched inequality is Black Africans (categorised as such by Statistics South Africa). South Africa's unemployment rate hit a 12-year high in 2016 at 27.3% in the third quarter, while the youth unemployment rate is close to 50% (Stats SA, 2017).

With 17,443,994 beneficiaries of social security grants in 2017 (South Africa Social Security Agency, 2017), the South African government currently oversees, along with Brazil, one of the most rapidly expanding social welfare systems in the developing world. The four social assistance programmes in post-apartheid South Africa that provide the largest benefits and have the widest spread are the Old Age Pension (OAP) at R1,690 (£143) per month, the Disability Grant at R1690 (£143) per month, the Foster Care Grant at R962 (£81) per month and the Child Support Grant at R400 (£34) per month (see Lund, 2008 for more detail on the respective programmes). Over 3.1 million persons aged 60 years and older were recipients of OAP in 2015 compared to 2.7 million in 2011. Since the start of the implementation of a social security plan in 1928, African pensioners have been under considerable moral and normative pressure to share their grants downwards as an acknowledgement of kin relationships (Sagner and Mtati, 1999). Given the gap in the safety net for unemployed persons between 18 and 60 years, coupled with the high unemployment rate, there is a high asymmetrical dependency on and expectancy of support among younger generations from their older relatives (especially grandmothers). This dependency of the younger on older generations is exacerbated by the impact of HIV/ AIDS (Chepng'eno-Langat, 2014; Schatz and Seeley, 2015).

HIV/AIDS

It is estimated that around 7 million people in South Africa are HIV-positive (Stats SA, 2016), with a concentrated toll on young adults. However, the pandemic's long-term generational momentum affects both ascending and descending generations, as illustrated by the high proportion of affected grandchildren that live in households headed by older persons (mostly grandmothers) – estimated to be up to 60% (Makiwane et al., 2004; UNICEF, 2007). With virtually no institutional care options for AIDS patients or orphans, grandmother-headed networks must provide the necessary shelter and care in-house.

Older carers' contribution to HIV/AIDS care management and recognition of their own vulnerability and need for support have been acknowledged in several global policy instruments (United Nations, 2002), the African Union's *Policy framework and plan of action on ageing* (AU/HAI, 2003) and the *Valletta declaration on HIV/AIDS and older persons* (Help the Aged/International Institute on Ageing (UN–Malta), 2005). These policy instruments all call for mainstreaming older persons into the design and implementation of response programmes as both care providers and care recipients (Ferreira, 2006).

A fairly substantial body of research already exists on the effects of the AIDS epidemics on older persons in SSA countries. Studies on the impact of the disease on older persons in African countries have mainly focused on associated morbidity and mortality rates (Ferreira et al., 2001; Lawn et al., 2008; WHO, 2006) and resultant dysfunction in affected households (Hosegood et al., 2007; Hosegood, 2009; Nankwanga et al., 2013; Oramasionwu et al., 2011). Localised qualitative studies in South Africa, although not exclusively focused on AIDS, have assessed the perceived needs of older carers in poor settings (Ferreira et al., 2001; Ferreira and Van Dongen, 2004; Singo et al., 2015). Ferreira and co-authors (2001), Ogunmenfun (2007) and Petros (2010) have prioritised the needs of older caregivers affected by HIV and AIDS for government intervention. Kuo's (2010) study is one of the few employing quantitative research methods and focuses on assessing the wellbeing of adults, including older carers, providing noninstitutional care to children orphaned by HIV/AIDS in South Africa and identifying factors that mediate wellbeing. Other studies with implications for older carers have been conducted specifically on the effects of AIDS orphanhood and parental AIDS illness on children, particularly mental health, physical health and educational outcomes (Cluver et al., 2006, 2007; Lang, 2005).This research explores the types of challenges faced by people caring for children orphaned and made vulnerable by HIV/AIDS in communities with high levels of poverty, unemployment, and HIV/AIDS.

Overall, these studies highlight the burden of care (financial, emotional and physical) and the multiple responsibilities of older carers, particularly women. General findings furthermore include inadequate knowledge and lack of support for older carers. These range from a loss of economic support in affected households through the illness or death of a breadwinner, a lack of material resources (money, food and clothing) experienced by older carers and challenges in accessing medical treatment for sick household members due to inability to pay for the treatment and/or to travel to a healthcare facility. Apart from the financial and practical effects of caregiving and loss of kin, older persons experience grief, pain and anxiety regarding the future. Many neglect their own healthcare needs because of the time and resources they devote to caregiving (Ferreira et al., 2001; Kuo, 2010; Small et al., 2017).

Over the last decade, evidence on the position of older persons largely evolved into two main streams, namely older individuals' vulnerability to poverty and ill health (HAI, 2008; Lloyd-Sherlock et al., 2014; WHO, 2017) and evidence of the significant contributions that older persons, in particular older women, make to the welfare and capacity development of younger family generations and their communities more generally (Cohen and Menken, 2006; HAI, 2015). Older people's care roles in the context of HIV/AIDS and their use of pension income to support the education and healthcare of children and grandchildren are particularly emphasised (see HAI, 2004, 2006; IDPM/HAI, 2003; Murphy et al., 2017; Ralston, et al., 2016).

Evident against this background are two interrelated trends (Aboderin and Hoffman, 2015). This chapter will focus on the second with reference to the first:

- continuous ascending family support patterns with indications of growing inadequacies in support for older persons; and
- descending pattern of care where older persons are increasingly looked upon as continuous providers of family support – especially evident against the backdrop of poverty/social protection and HIV/AIDS.

Drawing on qualitative research (in-depth interviews and focus groups in urban settings in South Africa) over the past decade (2007–17), this chapter aims to explore how grandmothers experience their positions where they have to continue to provide support to younger generations despite a skewed cycle of reciprocity. I argue that the point of departure for these grandmothers is an obligatory contribution perspective, which often overrides their own needs and aspirations. However, during the past decade there has been increasing evidence of a more rights-based discourse, through which expectations and demands of younger generations are questioned and the obligatory contribution discourse is contested, or at least relativised, through negotiation (also see Hoffman, 2016).

Dichotomous discourses

Contribution discourse

A prominent discourse underpinning downward support and care relates to older persons as contributors, with a focus on issues such as intergenerational solidarity, collectivism, home-based care, surrogate parenting of orphans, resilience, coping and poverty alleviation. By emphasising home- and community-based care, the discourse aims to draw on and enhance communal solidarity and mutual assistance. As such, home-based care is seen as a more African way of care, as opposed to so-called western ways. Here, dominant policy discourses support the relative strength of Africa's families and 'traditional' family values as a major, even moral, asset upon which development can and must build (Aboderin and Hoffman, 2015).

Within the post-1994 South African context, the search for an authentic African culture led to an essentialist and unproblematised notion of *ubuntu*.[2] The renewed interest in doing things the African way in the post-apartheid period and the pan-African vision of an African Renaissance lend a positive, if not utopian, connotation to traditional African values and philosophies (Blomkamp, 1995; Broodryk, 1995; Mbiti, 1985; Ntuli, 2002). However, the interpretation of so-called traditional social relations may not always be an accurate reflection of the past, and often represents mythical reconstructions of a golden age of intergenerational support (Sagner, 1999a, 1999b; Soyinka, 1976;).

Although home- and community-based care might reduce the cost of social and health care for the health system (the state), it does so in the main by displacing costs onto caregivers, with older women bearing the brunt (Marais, 2005). Generally, this means that care as a household and community responsibility is consigned to the intimate spheres of homes headed by grandmothers. One school of thought argues that this thinking is in line with the neoliberal ideal that the responsibility for care should be entrusted to ever-smaller units of society to ultimately be ceded to the individual as an empowered agent; another, as Aboderin and Ferreira (2009) argue, that this normative emphasis on the centrality of family obligations and contributions is only an extension of neoconservative macro-economic policy arguments that seek to limit formal welfare provision and thus public spending. Whichever angle is taken, it involves the assumption that the extended family (and in this context, older women) functions as a substitute for the state to ensure arrangements such as primary healthcare and social security provision, with consequent pressures on grandparent–headed households.

The vulnerability discourse

The concept of vulnerability in relation to mutual intergenerational support and whether these bonds could be sustained features prominently in the literature on AIDS. These vulnerability arguments tend to focus on strong assumptions of the exceptionality of HIV/ AIDS (Altman, 2006), whereby the issues of poverty, migration, food insecurity and past family and intergenerational relationships are largely neglected (Chazan, 2008; Marais, 2005). These discourses tend to portray the AIDS epidemics as a unique phenomenon, characterised by frailty, disempowerment, insecurity and rupture, which inevitably translates into an expected inability to manage. Much of the AIDS-impact literature forecasts eventual disintegration of family support in vulnerable countries that are unable to cope with the epidemic's effects (Hoffman, 2014).

According to this discourse, if it were not for AIDS, grandmothers in high-prevalence African countries would be 'enjoying a restful retirement' (Chazan, 2008). Yet sight is often lost that the phenomenon of the oldest generation in South Africa caring for the younger generations (grandchildren) builds on a long-established continuum of social structures and norms related to intergenerational support, specifically childcare. South Africa has a history of labour migration that dates to the early 20th century. For many decades, young adults (especially men) have worked away from their homes in urban centres and mines. Grandmothers customarily – and throughout the apartheid era – stayed behind to care for their grandchildren and were dependent on remittances from their adult children (Beinart, 1980; Kalule-Sabiti et al., 2012; Marais, 2005; Posel et al., 2006).

It is nonetheless undeniable (as Marais already pointed out in 2005) that, in the context of the extremely high rate of unemployment, HIV/AIDS further and significantly undermines potential traditional reciprocal care arrangements. Children who become ill and die can no longer provide remittances to the grandparents caring for their children, and they may even return home to be nursed. What has changed in the context of HIV/AIDS is the intensity, duration and range of the support responsibilities on older people. For most of the time, grandparents are now solely responsible for the economic and psychosocial wellbeing of younger dependants, with resultant financial and socioemotional stresses and impact on their health (Small et al., 2017).

The tendency to 'dichotomize human experiences is persistent, powerful, and pernicious' (Belenky et al., 1997, p 119). However tempting it may be to reduce complex situations to a simple classification, such as the vulnerability and contribution dichotomy, these polarised views consistently fail to adequately explain the patterns of grandmothers' contemporary lived experiences.

Contemporary lived experiences of grandmothers

Drawing on two rounds of data collection (2008–09 and 2016–17), the overall sense is that most of the grandmothers' accounts range between total, almost fatalistic acceptance of the situation that grandmothers have to support younger generations to a frustrated acceptance of an **entrapped responsibility** (Aboderin and Ferreira, 2009; Hoffman, 2014, 2016) related to a moral **duty-boundness** (Schatz, 2005; Schatz and Ogunmefun, 2007). However, data from the latter period do indicate some transitioning towards a more critical and rights-based perspective from the next cohort of grandmothers.

Entrenched vulnerability, reluctant obligation and expected reciprocity

Grandmothers' earlier accounts (2008–09) are underpinned by an overwhelming sense of duty to contribute to younger generations through their pensions and care management – a so-called **cash and care** response. The cross-cutting, overarching theme in all these HIV-affected and -nonaffected grandmother-headed networks is one of pervasive and desperate poverty – in the widest sense of the word

– revolving around continuous material and instrumental provision for younger generations. This reality is verbalised in two interrelated themes in which the economics of these intergenerational relationships are related to the moral politics of care, namely the reliance of younger generations on the pension (cash) of the grandmother and provision of care by older generations. The first – the pension (also called the grant) – serves as not only a metaphor for hope and an important (if not the only) material resource for survival but also an indication of vulnerability. The lack of such a grant symbolises even more desperation and vulnerability, as the younger grandmothers not eligible for the OAP experience. Encompassing the first, the second issue (care) deals with the consequences of this struggle for survival in the context of poverty and HIV/AIDS, offering a point of overlap between the material, the physical, the emotional, the symbolic and the sociological.

At present, older generations (grandmothers specifically) are alleviating many of the cumulative effects of poverty; high rates of unemployment, migration, consumerism and increasing individualism and HIV/AIDS at a high cost to themselves (Hoffman, 2014). The irony, of course, is that this is the case precisely because grandparents (especially grandmothers) are mainly doing what they have always done: caring and sacrificing. Data from the 2008–09 research participants suggest that these grandmothers have mitigated many of poverty's and the epidemic's most immediate negative consequences by caring for growing networks of younger dependants, and are doing so on shrinking incomes. However, for most of these participants in survivalist positions – physically unwell, emotionally distraught and struggling to make ends meet – these impacts come at a high personal cost:

> LENA: 'I just have to look at them no matter what. It is my responsibility and through this I am honouring my child. I just have to do it.'
>
> SOPH: 'There is nothing good in my life at the moment. If I sleep, I still think in the morning about the difficulties … my grandchild is sick and his mother is dead. I cope because I just have to … Sometimes it is hard but there is nothing else I can do … I go to church and I pray. But it is because I must do it that I just have to continue.'

Overall, the support responsibilities of older generations have considerable financial, practical and emotional impacts on both older and younger generations, which are compounded by a myriad of other stresses in their lives, including those particularly related to HIV/AIDS. As strains build up, the older generations try to adapt and assume ever-greater responsibilities for the growing and changing needs of their families.

With regard to the continuous and perceived asymmetrical need and dependency of younger generations on them, these grandmothers paint a scenario that can broadly be described in the following key phrase:

> 'This is how it is: I have to, even if I don't necessarily want to.'

The older participants tend to explain their relationship with younger generations as a duty that transcends exchange and even the principle of reciprocity; a dutiful obligation that entails sacrifice as an ultimate contribution. This corresponds to the notion that younger generations should take precedence over older generations.

In this sense, obligation is seen as a natural part of the order of life – the contract. As Gouldner (1960; 1973) argues in connection with status duties: 'by virtue of the socially standardised roles (people) play' (1960, p 171), these are 'binding in their own right' because they 'possess a kind of *prima facie* legitimacy for properly socialised group members' (1960, p 175). Support in this sense is not primarily driven by discretionary motives arising from the relationship but rather by structural norms of obligation (Nydegger, 1983). This draws on the premise that neither affection nor reciprocity is necessarily a precondition for the provision of support. Acknowledging the dangers of essentialist approaches, the roots of this perspective of filial obligation are typically seen as lying in African collectivism, African metaphysics and Judaeo-Christian values. The public ideology of caregiving and familialism furthermore portrays family caregiving as a natural responsibility of women, which is even more internalised through patriarchy.

Some of the accounts in this research would suggest that affection is not necessarily involved; rather, duty. It can, then, be argued that the extended family in this sense is not essentially a caring institution for its members; instead, individuals must maintain and cultivate their relations of kinship and shape them as relations of social security.

Data from the 2008–09 research suggest that a dichotomous view of affection and obligation at opposite ends should give way to the recognition of filial support as the result of both personal motives and structural norms, and that the role of each is variable and complex; it will vary by gender, age, personality, the type of support provided and the context. These relationships and sentiments are not necessarily symmetrical in nature (see, for example, the **intergenerational stake** hypothesis; Giarrusso et al., 1995).

However, considering the uncertain, resource-constrained and survivalist context in which this research is set, a more realistic explanation might tend towards the moral, obligatory nature of material support. This relates to the pensioner identity of most members of the older generations. Those with state pensions are often, in the context of unemployment and HIV/AIDS, the ones with the only reliable income. While these pensioners are perceived as more self-sufficient financially, the money might ironically reinforce their dependency status, as it heightens moral pressure on them to provide services and care to vulnerable family members (Sagner, 2000).

The grandmothers argue that if they continue to fulfil their obligations to the younger generations, some of these younger relations will at least feel obliged to respond when they as older generations need support – out of gratitude and based on the example set. This is, in essence, the very basis of the intergenerational contract – the **logic of debt** – and, in its most reductionist sense, the idea that by raising (grand)children as their debtors these younger generations will later repay the debt of gratitude of their own accord by caring for their (grand)parents.

Although reciprocal action is an important component of solidarity between generations, it is sometimes found to be weak or nonexistent in practice. This corpus of research (2008–09 and 2016–17) builds on earlier (2004) work in Mpumalanga, which found that strong acts of solidarity expressed by older persons, in supporting younger generations with their pensions, elicited little practical or material reciprocal action (Makiwane et al., 2004). Older generations perceive that they generally and persistently invest much more than their children and grandchildren in the relationships. This does not necessarily lead to reciprocity of care; some older persons in fact feel disrespected and abused, not only financially but also emotionally. The majority of these older generations had already realised they might never get back what they invested, as a consequence of HIV/AIDS (incapacitated children; children who died; being responsible for too many affected grandchildren), unemployment of adult children or the inadequacy or infrequency of any reciprocal arrangements from the younger generations. That very investment in the younger generation now becomes their biggest vulnerability.

It could consequently be hypothesised that continuous downward support of younger generations by older generations in resource-constrained contexts is a precursor for entrenched vulnerability – more so if it is exacerbated by HIV/AIDS. The epidemics do not make kinship irrelevant but instead alter the dynamics and quality of certain relationships. Whereas the older carers in the 2008–09 research contribute in spite of the impact of the context (personal or structural), because they believe younger generations should enjoy precedence, both generations argue that providing support to older generations will be mediated by context according to certain limitations. The overarching limitation is that younger generations are only expected to support older generations to the extent that they are in a position to provide it, and that it fits into their hierarchy of priorities. This ultimately elucidates the aspect of the intrinsic vulnerability of older carers. In practice, this vulnerability equates a compulsory contribution, turning the contributing carer into the sacrificing grandmother.

The normative entrenched intergenerational vulnerability of these older carers in resource-constrained and uncertain contexts has implications for them at the nexus of two interrelated levels; namely, the issue of their rights and their future care outcomes. These implications relate to not only the individual older carer but also a national policy level in view of global ageing trends. Caregivers in general are a growing population at risk, with these older caregivers at the extreme end of vulnerability. An almost exclusive continuous reliance of older persons on informal (family) care is not sustainable.

Agency and rights

In the 2016–17 round of data collection, the grandmothers demonstrated their increasing sense of agency (bordering on activism) and voiced their needs and rights in a 'corrective' and rights-based discourse. Participants not only complained that caregiving for their children and grandchildren was hard but also pushed against the normative assumption that such care should systemically be part of their role now they had aged. A strong narrative developed of older adults in search for a life of their own. They presented themselves as trapped by the traditional organisation of family and care but nevertheless with some agency and aspirations:

> MARY: 'Because really women, women have become slaves of their grandchildren! That's what I don't like about it. … So, if you talk to them, they are not happy but

they don't know how to get out of this because when you tell them about old-age home they will say, "haai, I don't know, what about my grandchildren? My son or my daughter is not working, so, what will happen to them?" I said but there are grants. They can get grants. "No, no, just to be around them!" But now you are sick, you say they can hardly give you a cup of tea, but you still want to stay with them? Why don't we just let go at some time? You have looked after these people from birth up to now. You have done everything for them and now you are running the role again. You are becoming a mother to their children. When are you going to rest? Perhaps in the graveyard.'

LILLY: 'I wouldn't mind going to a [retirement] home. As much as I would love to stay in my house with my grandchildren, but I don't want to look after the children because, when I'm with my grandchildren, and their parents, they're gonna go out and leave me with their children. I don't want responsibility. I think I've been responsible, from day one, "13 children", grandchildren, wharra-wharra, "77 grandchildren" ... Now I want to be free!'

Human beings as social agents are always vulnerable and exposed to contingencies, uncertainties and risks – some more than others. Turner (1993) argues that embodied vulnerability is a universal human condition, compounded by the risky and precarious nature of social institutions. Human vulnerability can, however, be contained or amended by the institution of rights with the potential to protect human beings from uncertainty. It is because of a collective sympathy for the plight of others that moral communities are created that support the institution of rights. From a sociological perspective, rights are thus social claims for institutionalised protection.

The build-up to the democratisation of South Africa as well as the subsequent post-apartheid era are characterised by a discourse of empowerment and a reaction to the inequalities related to a colonial and apartheid past. All these ideas of self-development and equality, economic independence and autonomy are based on the individual's rights. Younger generations are specifically targeted by NGO-initiated programmes, which, with their age-segregated approach, create further dilemmas of power within the intergenerational setup – especially in view of their dependence on older generations. This discourse of empowerment and egalitarian liberalism taken up by younger generations challenges other forms of social power known by the older generations, with consequent tension between the discourse of self-development and ideas of reciprocity in the multigenerational network (Durham, 2007; Stroeken, 2008).

Amid the empowerment discourse greatly dominated by younger generations, there is nevertheless also a growing emphasis on the rights of older persons. This notion has become increasingly prominent in western and international development debates (INPEA, IFA, ILC-US, IAGG, IAHSA and HelpAge International, 2010) and gained particular impetus in South Africa with the ministerial hearings on human rights abuses perpetrated against older persons and the subsequent establishment of the South Africa Older Persons' Forum in 2005. The findings and recommendations of the committee, under the chairmanship of the South African Human Rights Commission, were consolidated into a report titled *Mothers and fathers of the nation: The forgotten people?* (South Africa (Republic), Department of Social Development, 2001). The report represented a serious indictment against the society as a whole and its institutions. Further, the instances of abuse, neglect and marginalisation inflicted on older persons kindled a process that, in the main, has been positive in leading directly to the Older Persons Act (OPA) 13 of 2006 (South Africa (Republic) 2006).

The OPA is, however, silent on (or even oblivious of) addressing older persons suffering ill-treatment or needing care and protection in the family/intergenerational context. It rightly employs broad definitions for situations in which older persons are being abused or are in need of care and protection. The OPA fails to recognise that these are potentially sensitive situations requiring nuanced remedies. Incidents of mistreatment and neglect often originate within the intimate relational space with family members with whom the older person co-resides. That the OPA fails to accord any rights to older persons on matters potentially concerning their family, housing and health, not to mention their privacy and finances, is a prominent gap and intricate to address (see Adkins, 2011).

The dilemma explored in these two rounds of interviews relates to what older carers see as their sacrificial and duty-bound support obligation towards younger generations and how this could possibly interface with their individual human rights. This dilemma directly challenges idealised versions of intergenerational relations and foregrounds the notion of sacrifice (Land and Rose, 1985). Where does sacrifice (**generativity**) for the sake of the collective ideal end and abuse of individual human rights begin? It is particularly challenging if the sacrificing/contributing grandmother is looked at through the western individualised human rights perspective – when the collective ideal is scrutinised according to individualised human rights principles. To answer the question posed would require a more nuanced understanding of the interactions between personal, interpersonal and systemic factors in the context of a phenomenology of vulnerability.

Conclusion

The space of intergenerational negotiation between the aspirations and the realities of grandparenthood (specifically grandmotherhood, in this case) may offer researchers and policy makers some possibilities for conceptual refinement and policy interventions respectively. It provides an opportunity to transcend the binary opposites currently prevalent in the discourses of older generations, such as contribution–vulnerability, good–bad, past–present, active–passive and victim–perpetrator. Such a binary opposition reduces the possibilities for an empathic understanding of the complexity of relations. The core idea is thus to facilitate a process of reflexivity through which to understand the generational other. Biggs and Lowenstein (2011, p 108) describe this as generational intelligence: 'allowing empathic understanding of oneself and other, and when contesting definitions of generation and ageing coexist, enhancing the possibilities for shared problem-solving'. Such initiatives would take into account cohort expectations, historical and life-course experience and ways to deal with ambivalences. Roos (2011) suggests that the moral space between the generations can be explored through an Intergenerational Group Reflecting Technique, wherein generations voice their needs and expectations in each other's presence to discover the generational other and establish mutual ground. These conceptualisations and programmatic initiatives are initial attempts; hardly any research has been done into the dynamics of vulnerability and abusive intergenerational relationships beyond the binary of opposites.

Some concern has indeed focused on the economic and social costs of care provided by older to younger generations, in particular in contexts of HIV/AIDS. However, little attention is paid to questions of care for older persons. Who will care for the aged carers? In general, participants were not content with the status quo of family care. They wanted a solution to what they regarded as a problem of relying on families for care, at least in some circumstances. However, they had little information about the alternatives to family care, leaving them with much uncertainty and confusion around what forms of care would be possible and accessible.

In the meantime, older carers themselves negotiate and construct pragmatic internal and complementing external solutions to imagine and deal with their own care futures (Hoffman, 2016). Given future care uncertainties, they – within the internal family dynamics – tend to select the 'appropriate' individual according to their needs and/or construct complementary alternative communities within their peer group network or immediate community, such as churches and burial societies, where they generate an extended way of life around the collective ideal (see Klaits, 2001). This involves – given local contexts and personal circumstances – new interpretations and modifications of the meanings and practices of grandparents' own care futures.

Notes

[1] 'Grandmother'/'older woman', in this chapter, is interpreted as a social construct – and, apart from when it is used in the context of the Old Age Grant, not exclusively chronologically defined. 'Older' women in this research implies those with children and grandchildren, who are thus by definition 'grandmothers' – the two terms are used interchangeably. This is also the case with 'older generations' as opposed to 'younger generations' when referring to children and/or (great-)grandchildren.

[2] *Ubuntu* is a Xhosa word referring to a collective human solidarity and a collective morality 'of co-operation, compassion, communalism ... respect ... with emphasis of dignity in social relationships and practices' (Mokgoro, 1998).

References

Aboderin, I., and Ferreira, M. (2009) 'Linking ageing to development agendas in sub-Saharan Africa: Challenges and approaches', *Journal of Population Ageing*, 1(1): 51–73.

Aboderin, I., and Hoffman, J. (2015) 'Families, intergenerational bonds, and ageing in Sub-Saharan Africa', *Canadian Journal on Aging/ La Revue canadienne du vieillissement*, 34(3): 282–289.

Adkins, J. (2011) 'Advancing the socio-economic rights of older persons in South Africa: Leaping the implementation barriers of the Older Persons Act', *Economic and Social Rights in South Africa*, 12(1): 16–19.

Altman, L.K. (2006) Grandmothers rally to raise AIDS orphans, *The New York* Times, 12 August. Available at: http://www.nytimes.com/2006/08/13/world/africa/13aids.html?_r=1.

AU (African Union)/HAI (HelpAge International) (2003) *The African policy framework and plan of action on ageing*, Nairobi: HelpAge International Africa Regional Development Centre.

Beinart, W. (1980) 'Labour migrancy and rural production: Pondoland, 1900–1950', in M. Mayer (ed) *Black villagers in an industrial society*. Cape Town: Oxford University Press, pp 81–108.

Belenky, M., Bond, L., and Weinstock, J. (1997) *A tradition that has no name*. New York: Basic Books.

Biggs, S. and Lowenstein, A. (2011) *Generational intelligence: A critical approach to age relations*. Abingdon: Routledge.

Blomkamp, P.J. (1995) S v Makwanyane and Another. *Butterworths Law Reports: Constitutional Law*, June(6), 665–792.

Broodryk, J. (1995) *Ubuntuism as a worldview to order society*. University of South Africa. D. Litt et Phil thesis.

Chazan, M. (2008) 'Seven "deadly" assumptions: Unraveling the implications of HIV/AIDS among grandmothers in South Africa and beyond', *Ageing and Society*, 28(7): 935. DOI: 10.1017/S0144686X08007265.

Chepng'eno-Langat, G. (2014) 'Entry and re-entry into informal caregiving over a 3-year prospective study among older people in Nairobi slums, Kenya', *Health & Social Care in the Community*, 22(5): 533–544.

Cluver, L., Gardner, F. and Operario, D. (2007) 'Psychological distress amongst AIDS-orphaned children in urban South Africa', *Journal of Child Psychology and Psychiatry*, 48(8): 755–763.

Cohen, B. and Menken, J. (eds) (2006) *Aging in Sub-Saharan Africa: Recommendation for furthering research*, Washington DC: National Academies Press. Available at: https://www.ncbi.nlm.nih.gov/books/NBK20296/.

Durham, D. (2007). 'Empowering youth: Making youth citizens in Botswana', in: J. Cole and D. Durham (eds), *Generations and globalization: Youth, age, and family in the new world economy*. Bloomington, IN: Indiana University Press, pp 102–131.

Ferreira, M. (2006) 'HIV/AIDS and older people in Sub-Saharan Africa: Towards a policy framework', *Global Ageing: Issues and Action*, 4(2): 56–71.

Ferreira, M., Keikelame, M.J. and Mosaval, Y. (2001) *Older women as carers to children and grandchildren affected by AIDS: A study towards supporting the carers*, Cape Town: Institute of Ageing in Africa, University of Cape Town.

Ferreira, M. and Van Dongen, E. (eds) (2004) *Untold stories: Giving voice to the lives of older persons in new South African society – an anthology*. Cape Town: The Albertina and Walter Sisulu Institute of Ageing, University of Cape Town.

Giarrusso, R., Stallings, M. and Bengtson, V. L. (1995) 'The "intergenerational stake" hypothesis revisited: Parent–child differences in perceptions of relationships 20 years later', in V.L. Bengtson, K.W. Schaie and L. Burton (eds) *Intergenerational issues in aging*. New York: Plenum, pp 227–263.

Gouldner, A.W. (1960) 'The norm of reciprocity: A preliminary statement', *American Sociological Review*, 25: 161–178.

Gouldner, A.W. (1973) *For sociology: Renewal and critique in sociology today*. London: Allen Lane.

HAI (HelpAge International) (2004) *Age and security: How social pensions can deliver effective aid to poor older people and their families*. London: HAI.

HAI (2006) *Why social pensions are needed now*. London: HAI.

HAI (2008) *Annual report*. London: HAI.

HAI (2015) *Global age watch index 2015*. Available at: http://www. helpage.org/global-agewatch.

Help the Aged/International Institute on Ageing (UN–Malta) (2005) *Valletta Declaration on HIV/AIDS and older people*. London: Help the Aged.

Hoffman, J. (2014) 'Families, older persons and care in contexts of poverty: The case of South Africa', in S. Harper and K. Hamblin (eds) *International Handbook of Ageing and Public Policy*, Cheltenham: Edward Elgar.

Hoffman, J. (2016) 'Negotiating care for older people in South Africa: Between the ideal and the pragmatics', in J. Hoffman and K. Pype (eds) *Ageing in Sub-Saharan Africa: Spaces and practices of care*. Bristol: Policy Press, pp 159–182.

Hosegood, V. (2009) 'The demographic impact of HIV and AIDS across the family and household life-cycle: Implications for efforts to strengthen families in Sub-Saharan Africa', *AIDS Care*, 21(Suppl 1): 13–21.

Hosegood, V., Preston-Whyte, E., Busza, J., Moitse, S. and Timæus, I. (2007) 'Revealing the full extent of households' experiences of HIV and AIDS in rural South Africa', *Social Science and Medicine*, 65: 1249–1259.

INPEA, IFA, ILC-US, IAGG, IAHSA and HAI (2010) *Strengthening older people's rights: Towards a UN convention – A resource for promoting dialogue on creating a new UN convention on the rights of older persons*. Available at: globalaging.org/agingwatch/convention/humanrights/.

Institute for Development Policy and Management/HAI (2003) *Non-contributory pensions and poverty prevention: A comparative study of South Africa and Brazil*. London: HelpAge International.

Kalule-Sabiti, I., Mbenga, B., Amoateng, Y. and Hoffman, J. (2012) 'Country monographs: Post-apartheid South Africa', in C. Attias-Donfut, J. Cook, J. Hoffman, and L. Waite (eds), *Citizenship, belonging and intergenerational relations in African migration (migration, diasporas and citizenship)*, Basingstoke: Palgrave Macmillan.

Klaits, F. (2001) *Housing the spirit, hearing the voice: Care and kinship in an apostolic church during Botswana's time of AIDS*. Boston, MA: Johns Hopkins University. Unpublished PhD thesis.

Kuo, C.C. (2010) *Health impacts amongst carers of orphans and other children in a high HIV prevalence community in South Africa*. University of Oxford. DPhil thesis.

Land, H. and Rose, H. (1985) 'Compulsory altruism for some or an altruistic society for all?', in P. Bean, J. Ferris and D. Whynes (eds) *In defence of welfare*, London: Tavistock, pp 74–96.

Lang, S.S. (2005) 'In Africa, children as young as 9 are heading households and turning to other children for help', *Chronicle Online* (University of Cornell). Available at http://www.news.cornell.edu/stories/Nov05/africa.orphan.heads.ssl.html.

Lawn, S.D., Harries, A.D., Anglaret, X., Myer, L. and Wood, R. (2008) 'Early mortality among adults accessing antiretroviral treatment programmes in Sub-Saharan Africa', *AIDS*, 22(15): 1897–1908.

Lloyd-Sherlock, P., Minicuci, N., Beard, J., Ebrahim, S. and Chatterji, S. (2014) 'Hypertension among older adults in low and middle income countries: Prevalence, awareness and control', *International Journal of Epidemiology*, 14(1): 116–128.

Lund, F. (2008) *Changing social policy: The child support grant in South Africa*. Cape Town: HSRC Press.

Makiwane, M., Schneider, M. and Gopane, M. (2004) *Experiences and needs of older persons in Mpumalanga*, Pretoria: Human Sciences Research Council.

Marais, H. (2005) *Buckling: The impact of AIDS in South Africa*, 121, Pretoria: Centre for the Study of AIDS, University of Pretoria.

Mbiti, J.S. (1985) *African religions and philosophy*. London: Heinemann.

Mokgoro, Y. (1998) 'Ubuntu and the law in South Africa', *Buffalo Human Rights Law Review*, 4(17): 15–24.

Murphy, A., Kowal, P., Albertini, M., Rechel, B., Chatterji, S. and Hanson, K. (2017) 'Family transfers and long-term care: An analysis of the WHO study on global AGEing and adult health (SAGE)', *Journal of the Economics of Ageing*. DOI: https://doi.org/10.1016/j.jeoa.2017.08.003.

Nankwanga A., Neema S., Phillips J. (2013) 'The impact of HIV/AIDS on older persons in Uganda', in P. Maharaj (eds) *Aging and Health in Africa: International Perspectives on Aging*, 4. Boston, MA: Springer.

Ntuli, P. P. (2002) 'Indigenous knowledge systems and the African renaissance', in C.A. Odora Hoppers (ed), *Indigenous knowledge and the integration of knowledge systems: Towards a philosophy of articulation*. Claremont: New Africa Books.

Nydegger, C.N. (1983) 'Family ties of the aged in cross-cultural perspective', *The Gerontologist*, 23: 26–32.

Ogunmenfun, C.A. (2007) *The impacts of adult HIV/AIDS mortality on elderly women and their households in rural South Africa*. University of Witwatersrand, South Africa. PhD thesis.

Oramasionwu, C.U., Daniels, K.R., Labreche, M.J. and Frei, C.R. (2011) 'The environmental and social influences of HIV/AIDS in Sub-Saharan Africa: A focus on rural communities', *International Journal of Environmental Research and Public Health*, 8(7): 2967–2979.

Petros, S.G. (2010). *The role of older persons in the management of HIV and AIDS: An assessment of their contribution and support needs in three South African provinces*. University of Cape Town, South Africa. PhD thesis.

Posel, D., Fairburn, J.A. and Lund, F. (2006) 'Labour migration and households: A reconsideration of the effects of the social pension on labour supply in South Africa', *Economic Modelling*, 23: 836–853.

Ralston, M., Schatz, E., Menken, J., Gómez-Olivé, F.X. and Tollman, S. (2016) 'Who benefits – or does not – from South Africa's old age pension? Evidence from characteristics of rural pensioners and non-pensioners', *International Journal of Environmental Research and Public Health*, 13(1): 85.

Roos, V. (2011) '"The generational other": The cultural appropriateness of an intergenerational group reflecting technique', *Journal of Intergenerational Relationships*, 9(1): 90–97.

Sagner, A. (1999a) 'Ageing and old age in pre-industrial Africa: Elderly persons among 19th-century Xhosa-speaking peoples', *Southern African Journal of Gerontology*, 8(2): 7–17.

Sagner, A. (1999b) 'Reflections on the construction and study of elderliness', *Southern African Journal of Gerontology*, 8(2): 1–6.

Sagner, A. (2000) 'Ageing and social policy in South Africa: Historical perspectives with particular reference to the Eastern Cape', *Journal of Southern African Studies*, 26(3): 525–553.

Sagner, A. and Mtati, R.Z. (1999) 'Politics of pension sharing in urban South Africa', *Ageing and Society*, 19(4): 393–416.

Schatz, E. (2005) *'Taking care of my own blood': Older women's relationships to their households in Agincourt*. Research Program on Population Processes working paper. Boulder, CO: Institute of Behavioral Studies, University of Colorado. Available at: http://www.colorado.edu/IBS/POP/pubs/wp.html.

Schatz, E. and Ogunmefun C. (2007) 'Caring and contributing: The role of older women in rural South African multi-generational households in the HIV/AIDS era', *World Development*, 35: 1390–1403.

Schatz, E. and Seeley, J. (2015) 'Gender, ageing and carework in East and Southern Africa: A review', *Global Public Health*, 10: 1185–1200.

Singo, V.J., Lebese, R.T., Maluleke, T.X. and Nemathaga, L.H. (2015) 'The views of the elderly on the impact that HIV and AIDS has on their lives in the Thulamela Municipality, Vhembe District, Limpopo Province', *Curationis*, 38(1): 1–8. Available at: https://dx.doi.org/10.4102/curationis.v38i1.1166.

Small, J., Kowal, P. and Ralston, M. (2017) 'Context and culture: The impact of AIDS on the health of older persons in Sub-Saharan Africa', *Innovation in Aging*, 1(suppl_1). Available at: https://doi.org/10.1093/geroni/igx004.2183.

South Africa (Republic) Department of Social Development (2001) *Ministerial committee on abuse neglect and ill-treatment of older persons: Mothers and fathers of the nation – The forgotten people?* Pretoria: Government Printers.

South Africa Social Security Agency (2017) 'A statistical summary of social grants in South Africa', Fact sheet 10(2017): 31 October 2017. Available at: file:///C:/Users/NWUUser/Downloads/factsheet%20issue%20no%2010%20of%202017.pdf.

Soyinka, W. (1976) *Myth, literature and the African world*. Cambridge: Cambridge University Press.

Stats SA (2016) *Mid Year Estimates 2016: 55,9 million people in South Africa – Planning for a better tomorrow*. Available at: http://www.statssa.gov.za/?p=8176.

Stats SA (2017) *Poverty Trends in South Africa: An examination of absolute poverty between 2006 and 2015*. Pretoria: Stats SA.

Stroeken, K. (2008) 'Tanzania's new generation: The power and tragedy of a concept', in E. Alber, S. Van der Geest and S.R. Whyte (eds), *Generations in Africa: Connections and conflicts*. New Brunswick and London: Transcation Publishers, pp 289–308.

Turner, B. S. (1993) 'Outline of a theory of human rights', *Sociology*, 27(3): 489–512.

UN (2002) *Madrid international plan of action on ageing 2002*. New York: UN.

UNDP (United Nations Development Programme) (2016) *Human development report: Human development for everyone*, New York: UNDP.

UNICEF (2007) *The state of the world's children: The double dividend of gender equality*, Geneva: United Nations Children's Fund.

WHO (World Health Organization) (2006) *The health of the people: The African regional health report*. Brazzaville: WHO Regional Office for Africa.

WHO (2017) *Towards long-term care systems in sub-Saharan Africa: WHO series on long-term care*, Geneva: WHO.

PART 3
Transnational grandparenting

Transnational grandparenting: the intersection of transnationalism and translocality

Yanqiu Rachel Zhou

Introduction

In the past decade the phenomenon of **transnational grandparenting** has received increasing, yet still sporadic, academic attention. The literature shows that the term was coined to describe various forms of new and changing relationships between grandparents and grandchildren in the context of transnationally dispersed families. Despite geographical distance, grandparental relationships can be maintained through, for example, global communications (such as the internet and mobile phones), exchanging gifts, visits and childcare (Chen and Lewis, 2016; Da, 2003; Lie, 2010; Nesteruk and Marks, 2009; Sigad and Eisikovits, 2013; Stephen, 2013; Zhou, 2012).

Transnational grandparenting has been largely examined through a cultural lens. Empirical studies have primarily focused on diaspora families and minority ethnic groups whose cultural values may differ from those of the mainstream society: Chinese immigrants in Australia and the UK (Da, 2003; Lie, 2010); Indian grandparents in Canada (Stephen, 2013); Bangladeshi households in the UK (Lie, 2010); American–Israeli grandparents and their children and grandchildren who live transnational lifestyles (Sigad and Eisikovits, 2013); and Eastern European immigrants in the US (Nesteruk and Marks, 2009). On a conceptual level, furthermore, these groups' cultural norms around, for example, family values, intergenerational relationships and the desired roles of grandparents have been fundamental in explaining those transnational intergenerational families' struggles, negotiations and adaptations in the changing context of grandparenthood.

Ascribing to culture a central role in conceptualising transnational grandparenting, however, neglects the broader structural factors (for example, neoliberal childcare and immigration policies) with which culture intersects. Although the cultures of migrant families have buffered or absorbed the effects of international mobility on 'minority ethnic communities' needs' (Lie, 2010, p 1425), various cultural institutions around grandparenting – not only grandparental roles or relationships but also expectations about ageing – may also evolve or be transformed in the process (Zhou, 2012). Using the case of transnational childcare by Chinese grandparents in Canada, I contend that an exploration of the intersection of transnationalism and **translocality** can contribute to a broader, contextualised perspective from which to understand the dynamics, dissonance and effects of transnational grandparenting.

The intersection of transnationalism and translocality: towards a broader conceptual framework

My analytical approach to transnational grandparenting aims to illustrate the connections between mobility and locality by drawing on theories of transnationalism and translocality. Locality here is not necessarily about geographic location but rather 'simultaneous situatedness across different locales' or 'situatedness during mobility' (Greiner and Sakdapolrak, 2013, pp 375, 376).

From the perspective of transnationalism, international migration is not simply a movement from one country to another or an event that ends with migrants' settlement in the host country; it is a lifelong process that involves complex interactions between migrants and those left behind and evokes a linkage of relationships across nation states and generations (Lunt, 2009; Tsuda, 2012). Challenging 'the container theory of society' or nationally bounded thinking, this approach makes it possible to better contextualise transnational grandparenting by encompassing 'the processes, ties and links between people, places, and institutions that routinely cut across nation states' (Yeates, 2008, p 22). Transnationalism, as 'a social process that is both transborder and simultaneously engages two nation-states', yields a conceptual lens through which to understand how immigrant families' – including grandparents' – double grounding, in both China and Canada, has transformed the conditions and experiences (including the inequalities) of their transnational care arrangements and resultant intergenerational relationships (Tsuda, 2012, p 645; Vertovec, 2009).

Building on 'transnationalism', the concept of translocality expands the analytical focus beyond 'the limit of the nation-state by focusing on various other dimensions of border transgressions', such as local–local negotiations, sociospatial (re)configurations and translocal imaginations (Greiner et al., 2015, pp 7–8). It is also viewed as a more 'grounded' or 'territorialised' notion of transnationalism, given its insistence on locality (Greiner and Sakdapolrak, 2013). In the context of transnational grandparenting, for instance, translocality can help shed light on how the emigration of adult children has turned the intergenerational family and relationship into a multilocal structure through various forms of connectedness across national borders. While emphasising the micro level and local-to-local dynamics of sociospatial phenomena, this theory also distances itself from the dominant frame of the nation state, and may produce a narrative that runs counter to Eurocentric assumptions about indigenous histories, cultures, livelihoods and structures of feeling (Appadurai, 1996; Freitag and Von Oppen, 2009; Ng, 2013). Unlike 'transnational', the word 'translocal' 'carries us from one conceptual realm – that of nations and civilisations – to another – that of places' (Dirlik, 2005, p 397). In addition to producing 'alternate' globalities that challenge Eurocentric and economic-centric activities and narratives, this perspective also suggests practical possibilities – such as a form of transnational care by grandparents – generated from multilocal embedding of actors and livelihood. For grandparents who are mobile or left behind alike, for instance, the use of translocal strategies may broaden their options for viable grandparenthood and livelihoods through accessing resources (both material and immaterial) over distances, and thus overcome some constraints posed by the global forces in the local or micro context (Benz, 2014; McKay and Brady, 2005).

Together, these two theoretical lenses make it possible to better understand transnational grandparenting in the context of multifaceted sociospatial connections, and also to present alternative narratives beyond the culturalised perspectives. This approach shows promise for revealing the complex intersections, including tensions (for example, contradictions, transgressions, disjunctures and even collapses) between mobility and locality, and thus allows a less linear and more open and inclusive conceptualisation of the manifold ways in which transnational grandparenting is constituted.

The study

Since the 1990s, the People's Republic of China (PRC) has become the premier source country of immigrants to Canada (Statistics Canada, 2008). The new wave of emigration of highly educated professionals, entrepreneurial elites and university students from China has changed Chinese immigration to Canada 'beyond recognition' (Pieke, 2006, p 86). Against the background of neoliberal care restructuring, the traditional care burden of women who face work–care conflicts may be transferred onto paid care workers through the global care market, or onto their own family members including ageing kin overseas. A lack of childcare resources within Chinese immigrant families in western countries often leads to two types of transnational caregiving relationship: sending young children back to grandparents in China, and inviting grandparents to the host country for caregiving (Da, 2003; Zhou, 2013a). Although the traditional idea of grandparenting remains crucial for such care arrangements across countries, cultural explanations of transnational grandparenting appear inadequate in that they neglect the broader, structural contexts that have changed the related cultural norms as well as grandparents' later lives.

The larger study, from which the data analysed here were drawn, aims to understand the dynamics, experiences and effects of Chinese grandparents' transnational caregiving experiences in Canada (Zhou, 2012, 2013a, 2013b, 2015, 2017). The data were collected through individual, face-to-face, semistructured interviews with 36 grandparents who had come from the PRC to care for their grandchildren in Canada, and with 34 Chinese skilled immigrant mothers – all college-educated and 14 of whom had master's or higher degrees – in Canada. Of these grandparents, 31 were women and 5 were men; excluding one unknown, they ranged in age from 54 to 77, with an average age of 64 years. Their immigration statuses were divided among 'Canadian visitor visa holder' (27 of 36), 'Canadian permanent resident' (7 of 36) and '(naturalised) Canadian citizen' (2 of 36). Five were living in publicly funded seniors' homes, 12 were in shared rental apartments with their children and grandchildren, and 19 were living in their children's owner-occupied houses or apartments.

Taking into account the role of skilled immigrant families' transnational caregiving practices in structuring intergenerational relationships, I engage in my analysis through three interconnected aspects of transnational grandparenting. First, I explore the dynamic relationship between the notion of intergenerational love and Chinese skilled immigrant families' urgent, pragmatic needs for reliable childcare in the context of post-immigration settlement. Second, I contrast grandparents' unprecedented transnational mobility to provide childcare with the institutional barriers (particularly border control) that have fragmented not only their grandparenthood but also the intergenerational family – and left both unsustainable. Third, I discuss the effects of changing family structures and relationships on the tradition of generational reciprocity (particularly the norm of filial piety), which in turn has shaped the ageing trajectories of these grandparents. It is concluded that a theorisation of transnational grandparenting beyond a narrow cultural lens enables a more contextualised understanding of the intersection of grandparenting and aspects of the immigration process, such as the spatial reconfiguration of the family and cultural change.

It should be noted, however, that the results of this study may not be generalisable for Chinese immigrants to Canada as a whole due to its small sample size and limited number of study sites. Nevertheless, this qualitative exploratory study indicates the importance of situating transnational grandparenting in the broader processes of international migration and attending to the intersection of transnationalism and translocality.

Intergenerational love in the context of the 'care deficit'

In Canada, since the neoliberal welfare restructuring that started in the 1980s, the fairly limited public care provision (including childcare) secured in earlier years has been either downsized or privatised; the consequences have been heavily borne by socioeconomically disadvantaged groups, such as newcomers with constrained access to viable financial and social support (Aronson and Neysmith, 2006; Friendly, 2009; Man, 2002). In the context of the 'care deficit', families with economic resources in wealthy countries like Canada often resort to migrant care labour, obtained through global care markets, to meet their childcare needs (Yeates, 2012). For Chinese immigrants in the west (for example, Australia, Canada, the UK and the US), however, arranging for grandparents to provide transnational childcare reflects both their cultural norms and family-oriented strategies to overcome various socioeconomic challenges in the host country (Da, 2003; Lie, 2010; Zhou, 2013a).

When they were requested to travel overseas to provide childcare, none of the grandparents in this study considered not coming to be an option, because failing to do so often provoked feelings of guilt or conflict. Some even had to leave their own ageing parents or parents-in-law – in their 80s or 90s – behind in China. In addition to the tradition of grandparenting in Chinese culture, they saw themselves as the only viable source of support for their emigrated adult children's families. For them, being a loving parent and grandparent was not only integral to their family obligations but also the way to carry on the cultural notion of family, which is often demonstrated through the practice of intergenerational love:

'My grandmother helped my mother take care of us, and my mother helped me take care of my children. This is passed from generation to generation, and I think this is what a family means.' (Mrs Zhao, 61 years)

'In China we have a term, *ge dai qing* [intergenerational love]: that is, parents pass their love on to their grandchildren as a way to love their own children ... This is a Chinese tradition that I learned from my parents ... I want to contribute to our children's and grandchildren's life, and doing so makes me very happy, very proud and satisfied ... I think this is what family means.' (Mr Qian, 60 years)

Upon arrival, grandparents were immediately integrated into a much faster pace of life. Their typical day started in the early morning, with breakfast preparation, and continued until children and grandchildren went to bed at night. Depending on the children's ages, their childcare workload varied; some completely took over daily baby care so the mothers could go back to work or university while others primarily took care of grandchildren after daycare hours. Despite the wider scope and heavier load of their care work than of those grandparenting back home in China, grandparents viewed their transnational caregiving as necessary to stabilise the lives of their adult children as new parents in Canada. As their daughter – a PhD candidate who was about to graduate – and son-in-law were studying and working in different cities, for example, one couple had become sole caregivers for their three-month-old granddaughter. "If [my daughter was] taking care of the baby on her own," Mrs Wang, the 55-year-old grandmother, said, "I don't think she could even find time to eat". These grandparents also believed that attentive caregiving at home benefits the grandchildren's early development, because "only grandparents have that much time to give holistic attention to the very small details of children's growth" (Mrs Qin, 69 years), and makes them feel "fully cared for and loved" (Mrs Qin, 69 years), especially when the immigrant parents did not have the time to do so.

The grandparents appreciated their adult children's struggles in Canada and sought to accelerate their settlement by relieving those struggles with uncompensated transnational care. Doing those "meaningless" (Mrs Sun, 63 years) household chores, they thought, would allow their immigrant children to use the time for their career development or allow themselves to spend more quality time with their grandchildren – and if they could help their immigrant families save money through unpaid childcare, their children could have more resources for other things, such as further education and house buying. Mrs Sun (63 years old) explained:

> 'Why do we have to work so hard here? … My understanding is that my daughter could work less if I worked more … So if I take good care of these two grandchildren, then my daughter will have peace of mind and can concentrate on her work. And then they will have a better life in the future.'

Coining the term '**family time economy**', Maher, Lindsay and Franzway (2008) argue that women's time for work and activity in the labour market depends on the time required for caregiving and family, given that one's time is limited and time for care (especially for dependants) is less flexible. The need for 'intensive grandparenting', which 'happens on a daily basis, covering a range of different aspects over a prolonged period of time', is also determined by various economic and systematic factors, such as (paid) work commitment required for the mother and barriers to accessing formal childcare (Lie, 2010, p 1436). In this context, it is also important to recognise the multiple values of transnational grandparenting for immigrant women who have to spend time on paid work, and for immigrants' family economy and welfare. Yet the dominant politics and policies of care have devalued and ignored such kin-based care resources as time, emotion and cultural knowledge, which are key to children's development and the overall wellbeing of the family.

Intergenerational families in the context of border control

State borders, through such consequences as geographic separation and border-crossing, have not only separated multigenerational families into different places but also changed the dynamics and meanings of the family as an important sociocultural institution in which both grandparenting and grandparents' transition into old age take place. The fact that "a family is now living in two countries" (Mrs Wang, 69 years) has fundamentally shaken the two interconnected ideals of family and ageing in Asian – including Chinese – cultures, which are closely linked with proximity, intimacy, stability and generational reciprocity and harmony (Desai and Tye, 2009; Kauh, 1997; Lamb, 2002; Mui and Kang, 2006). Moreover, restrictive border control policies mean these grandparents' unprecedented mobility is often accompanied by institutional intrusions and interruptions, reluctant multiple travels and fragmented grandparenthood.

The visa application process was commonly described as unnecessarily complicated, restrictive, discriminatory and expensive. To get a visitor visa, grandparents had to pass a physical checkup and present evidence that they had no intention of staying in Canada illegally. Some grandparents had to travel from their home towns to the cities where Canadian embassies or consulates are located; some, having been rejected the first time, had to go back and wait for months to reapply. The rejection of their visa applications caused some grandparents to miss the birth of a grandchild and created a feeling of being unwanted in Canada: for example, "I felt like Canada does not welcome us as grandparents" (Mrs Chen, 69 years). As 65-year-old Mrs Li commented:

> 'Our children are Canadian citizens now, and our grandchildren are Canadian-born. We are their families, but we may not be allowed to go to see them and to care for them when they need us ... [The Canadian authorities] don't understand our love for our children; what we care about is not living in Canada, but our children.'

The anxiety and uncertainty were also reinforced by the time limit of the visas. To avoid disrupting the childcare arrangements, most grandparents tried to renew their visa after their initial six-month stay. When their visa expired they had to go back to China; in some cases, when no alternative care arrangement could be secured, they brought their grandchildren with them. More than two thirds of the grandparents in this study came to Canada more than once (two to four times) for caregiving primarily because of the time restriction on their visitor's visas. It was not unusual for them to find that the grandchildren they once cared for were, after geographical separation for a couple of years, unable or unwilling to communicate with them in Chinese. While they were in China, Canada – as the home of their children and grandchildren – continued to be present in their daily lives and thoughts. Ultimately, no matter where they were, they had simultaneously lived at a 'home away from home, here and there' (Lamb, 2002, p 304).

The immigration of adult individuals is often followed by the gradual immigration of their extended family members, including their ageing parents (Hwang, 2008; Lai and Leonenko, 2007). To attain greater transnational mobility and proximity to their children, more than half of the grandparents under study had immigrated or applied for immigration to Canada. Permanent resident status also meant grandparents would have access to the universal health care system in Canada, giving them basic, but critical, health security and relief from their fear that an unforeseeable health breakdown could bankrupt their children's families. Some also perceived immigration as their only option for future elder care because their child in Canada was their only child, all their children had emigrated or their living conditions back home were not ideal. Viewing her own immigration to Canada as a dilemma, for example, a widowed, 65-year-old Mrs Zhou commented:

'My life in China is good; all my friends and siblings are there, and I miss them a lot. I would certainly not apply for immigration if any of my children were in China. So I felt like I didn't have a choice.'

The emigration of adult children has interrupted the functioning of the family as an important mechanism of transmitting resources and cultural values across generations in Chinese culture, with the extended family playing an indispensable role in welfare and care provision for its older members (Goh, 2009; Wu and Hart, 2002; Zhan and Montgomery, 2003). Although immigration at older ages means the end of separation from their children and grandchildren, ageing in a foreign country also makes older adults vulnerable to social and health risks, such as poverty and social isolation (Lai, 2004; Lai and Leonenko, 2007; Zhou, 2012). Those who were explicit about not considering immigrating often had better living conditions in China and worried that immigration would further compromise their children's quality of life in Canada. If they decide to stay in China, however, they may end up ageing alone. This issue may become even more salient, given that many recent Chinese immigrants to Canada are members of the one-child-policy generation (those born in the 1980s and later).

In the past decade, Canada's policies on the sponsoring of parents and grandparents for immigration have further tightened. Although the 'parent and grandparent super visa' that grants a longer stay in Canada was introduced, the restrictive eligibility criteria suggest that immigrant families with lower socioeconomic status may not benefit from such policy changes (Chen and Thorpe, 2015).

Generational reciprocity in the context of cultural rupture

Citing the Chinese phrase *shang ci xia xiao* (loving parents and filial children), grandparents often see filial piety as not simply children's responsibility to love and care for their ageing parents but also a continuum of generational reciprocity in everyday family life. Many attributed the cultivation of filial piety to traditional multigenerational households; for example, "three of my four children were brought up by their grandmother, so [they] have learned well to respect them since they were very young" (Mrs Zhu, 73 years), and, "My daughter grew up watching how I cared for my own mother every day" (Mrs Zhen, age unknown). Yet the processes of modernisation, urbanisation and immigration have eroded some aspects of filial piety, such as multigenerational cohabitation and filial care, in China and among overseas Chinese immigrants (Chen and Lewis, 2016; Cheung and Kwan, 2009;Lan, 2002; Lieber et al., 2004).

The arrival of grandparents transformed immigrants' nuclear families into three-generation households. Some grandparents were happy about the new living arrangement; others, however, found they had to cope with challenges such as crowded living conditions, in-law conflicts and communication problems resulting from cultural and age gaps. Some grandparents tried to assume a role of traditional parental authority but often encountered resistance. Many also felt neglected or alienated by insufficient communication with their busy adult children, which, along with the limitations on their interaction with the outside world, exacerbated their sense of isolation. Some joked about their awkward "*san bu* [three nots] identity", a term widely circulated among Chinese grandparents to refer to their situation in their children's homes: not a master (because they cannot make decisions for the families), not a guest (because they have to do care work and housework) and not a servant (because they are not paid).

The fragmented nature of transnational households and the difficult settlement of immigrant families has also made it challenging to carry on the Chinese tradition of filial piety that emphasises generational reciprocal responsibilities. Despite their own devoted filial care for their parents, many grandparents said they would not expect their immigrant children to do the same for them, considering the latter's long-term settlement struggles and the different norms of generational relations and elder care in Canada. Instead, they attended more to the ideational or spiritual aspects of filial piety – such as love, sense of care and happiness – than to its practical and material ones – such as co-residence, day-to-day care and financial support:

'No need for material payback. It's enough if they care about me and think of me.' (Mrs Li, 65 years)

'If their life, career and family are good, and then we are happy. This is them being filial to us.' (Mr Wu, 65 years)

'The best payback for me is that my grandson can grow up well, my daughter and my son-in-law can concentrate on their studies, and our family relationship is good.' (Mrs Zhen, age unknown)

They also tended to rationalise the changing intergenerational relationships with such observations as: "Even if my child's family has this intention, they may not have the material resources to actualise it" (Mr Jiang, 65 years), "Economic survival is now the top priority for them, so having the intention to be filial is good enough" (Mrs Shen, 73 years) and "It is not the children, but the environment that has changed" (Mrs Han, 77 years).

When it came to their grandchildren's generation, most grandparents felt very uncertain about whether the idea of filial piety could be carried on by those "little Canadians" (Mrs Qin, 69 years), who would grow up in a very different environment than their immigrant parents did. They also worried about whether their grandchildren would even understand what the Chinese word *yijiaren* (family) means, because "[if] we are unable to stay together, then family just becomes an abstract term in the end" (Mr Yang, 67 years). Alternatively, some grandparents emphasised their children's filial duty to perpetuate the traditional notions of the family and Chinese identity into their grandchildren's generation.

While the transnational grandparenting under study was driven by the traditional notions of family and generational reciprocity, such notions appear to become increasingly selective for adult children. Although some grandparents were able, to some degree, to adapt the 'modified' tradition, the practical aspects of filial piety as an elder care model are still crucial for those with limited access to resources, whether private or public (Chou, 2011; Sung and Kim, 2002). From the perspective of social welfare, furthermore, such a cultural 'modification' or rupture suggests not only the exploitative, one-way intergenerational redistribution of informal resources (emotion and unpaid care) but also the gap between immigrant families' needs for care in relation to changing family structures and the delayed policy response to such changes.

Discussion and conclusion

Situating grandparenting in the contexts of international migration and transnational care, this study reveals on the one hand that mobility (not limited to physical mobility) of skilled immigrant families has transformed the conditions, dynamics, experiences and effects of grandparenting – as both caregiving practice and generational relation. On the other hand, the family – the geographically resilient kinship imbued with cultural values and resources – has been challenged, transgressed against and reconfigured by the mobility under discussion. Attending to both transnationalism and translocality has enabled us to understand transnational grandparenting as both a culture-informed familial strategy to mobilise resources across national borders, so as to overcome the structural barriers to skilled immigrants' settlement in Canada, and as a sociospatial process through which a new form of intergenerational relationship transcending the geographical territories of nation states emerges.

International migration, as 'a life-long process of complex interaction between individuals and groups who often live far apart' (Lunt, 2009, p 244), has presented extensive impacts on family – not only the nuclear families of Chinese skilled immigrants in Canada but also grandparents living in China or, subsequently, living in transnational and multilocal spaces. State borders – through border control policies – have shaped the effects of mobility on immigrant families (including grandparents); they have also changed the structure and meanings of the family as an indigenous cultural institution. Grandparents' lack of control over the time they spend with their children and grandchildren in Canada has also disrupted their kin bonds, their selfhood (parenthood and grandparenthood) and the ideal of ageing as a time traditionally linked with certainty, relaxation, generational reciprocity and a sense of connection and satisfaction (Sun, 2012). In this light, transforming traditional families 'in place' into a multilocal structure across locales has significantly changed the sociocultural conditions on which both immigrant families' childcare and elder care take place. These grandparents' own transnational mobility, as a byproduct of their children's international migration, also raises questions about the spillover effects of global economic processes – in the form of skilled immigration and neoliberal welfare restructuring – on their later lives.

The fragmented nature of multilocally anchored households and livelihoods has also made it challenging to carry on the Chinese tradition that emphasises reciprocal responsibilities across generations.

The coexistence of seniors' selfless devotion to their children's families, and acceptance of the compromised fulfilment of filial duties by the latter, demonstrates their pragmatic adjustment to changing generational relationships in their new environment. Through their strategic practices of Chinese cultural norms – that is, grandparents' obligation to help children but not necessarily adult children's obligation to care for their elders – these immigrant families have de facto become agents for the 're-creation and transformation of culture' (Vertovec, 2009, p 64). Regardless of their immigrant status and the country where they end up living, meanwhile, their relationships with their children's families in Canada and their subsequent multi-stranded connections with both China and Canada are integral to their later lives. The changing or new relationship between grandparents and grandchildren in the context of immigration suggests new insights into social organisations (for example, family and grandparenthood) that are usually considered in the context of a particular territorial space or geographical immobility.

The findings of this study also affirm the importance of translocality – defined as 'the emergence of multidirectional and overlapping networks created by migration that facilitate the circulation of resources, practices and ideas and thereby transform the particular localities they connect' (Greiner, 2011, p, 610) – for better understanding the spatial configuration of the family and the practice of transnational grandparenting in the contexts of skilled immigration and neoliberal care provision. On the one hand, grandparents' transnational childcare enables these immigrant families to gain 'flexibility' to mobilise care resources across generations and state borders; on the other hand, these transnational and multilocal connections across distance also 'structure locality off the ground' and influence people's activities, ideas and social interdependence 'in particular material contexts' (McKay and Brady, 2005, p 91). Despite the importance of transnational grandparenting for these immigrant families to tackle the 'care deficit', we also see the collapse of the global into the locality through such effects such as the fragmentation of the family, the rupture of generational reciprocity and the precariousness of grandparents' later lives.

In conclusion, I argue that transnational grandparenting should not be simplified as culture-informed grandparental relationships across borders; rather, it should also be viewed as comprising both transnational and translocal processes that are simultaneously shaping and being shaped by various familial, social, cultural, economic and political forces in both the host and home countries of international migrants. The transnational grandparenting under study also demonstrates the broader structural forces beyond cultural traditions, as well as cultural dynamics beyond those of neoliberal economic globalisation; it thus also provides an alternative narrative that has the potential to challenge both culturalised accounts of transnational grandparenting and economic-centric discourses on care and immigration. It is concluded that the exploration of the intersection of transnationalism and translocality can help to decipher the complex, dynamic relationships between mobility and locality and between cultural resiliency and structural inequalities embedded in the changing intergenerational relationships of immigrant families. The vulnerability being perpetuated in grandparents' new ageing trajectories also calls for a critical analysis of public policies that often have spillover effects across generations and nation states in this globalising world.

Acknowledgements

I wish to express my appreciation to Chinese seniors and skilled immigrant women who participated in this study and to the research assistants (Kayla Tessier, Liping Peng, Xiaoxin Ji, Xieqing Lin, Dan He, Winnie Lo, Mingwei Zhang and Huijing Yang) for their assistance at different stages of this research project. This work was carried out with the aid of the Social Sciences and Humanities Research Council Standard Research Grant, Canada. Some components of this chapter were also presented in my publications (2012–17) generated from this research project.

References

Appadurai, A. (1996) *Modernity at large: Cultural dimensions of globalization* (vol. 1), Minneapolis and London: University of Minnesota Press.

Aronson, J. and Neysmith, S. (2006) 'Obscuring the costs of home care: Restructuring at work', *Work, Employment and Society*, 20(1): 27–45.

Benz, A. (2014) 'Mobility, multilocality and translocal development: Changing livelihoods in the Karakoram', *Geographica Helvetica*, 69(4): 259–270.

Chen, H.M. and Lewis, D.C. (2016) 'A changing relationship: Visiting Chinese grandparents and their adult children in the United States', *Journal of Ethnographic & Qualitative Research*, 11(2): 87–98.

Chen, X. and Thorpe, S.X. (2015) 'Temporary families? the parent and grandparent sponsorship program and the neoliberal regime of immigration governance in Canada', *Migration, Mobility & Displacement*, 1(1): 67–80.

Cheung, C.K. and Kwan, Y.H. (2009) 'The erosion of filial piety by modernisation in Chinese Cities', *Ageing and Society*, 29(1): 179–198.

Chou, R.J. (2011) 'Filial piety by contract? The emergence, implementation, and implications of the "family support agreement" in China', *Gerontologist*, 51(1): 3–16.

Da, W.W. (2003) 'Transnational grandparenting: Child care arrangements among migrants from the People's Republic of China to Australia', *Journal of International Migration and Integration / Revue de l'integration et de la migration internationale*, 4(1): 79–103.

Desai, V., and Tye, M. (2009) 'Critically understanding Asian perspectives on ageing', *Third World Quarterly*, 30(5): 1007–1025.

Dirlik, A. (2005) 'Performing the world: Reality and representation in the making of world histor(ies)', *Journal of World History*, 16(4): 397–410.

Freitag, U. and von Oppen, A. (2009) 'Introduction: Translocality: An approach to connection and transfer in area studies', in U. Freitag and A. von Oppen (eds), *Translocality: The study of globalising processes from a Southern perspective* (vol. 4), Leiden: Brill, pp 1–21.

Friendly, M. (2009) 'Can Canada walk and chew gum? The state of child care in Canada in 2009', *Our Schools / Our Selves*, 18(3): 41–55.

Goh, E.C. (2009) 'Grandparents as childcare providers: An in-depth analysis of the case of Xiamen, China', *Journal of Aging Studies*, 23(1): 60–68.

Greiner, C. (2011) 'Migration, translocal networks and stratification in Namibia', *Africa: Journal of the International African Institute*, 81(4): 606–627.

Greiner, C. and Sakdapolrak, P. (2013) 'Translocality: Concepts, applications and emerging research perspectives', *Geography Compass*, 7(5): 373–384.

Greiner, C., Peth, S.A. and Sakdapolrak, P. (2015) 'Deciphering migration in the age of climate change. Towards an understanding of translocal relations in social-ecological systems', *Translocal Resilience Project Working Paper*, No. 2, Bonn, Germany: Department of Geography, University of Bonn, pp 1-15.

Hwang, E. (2008) 'Exploring aging-in-place among Chinese and Korean seniors in British Columbia, Canada', *Ageing International*, 32(3): 205–218.

Kauh, T. (1997) 'Intergenerational relations: Older Korean-Americans' experiences', *Journal of Cross-Cultural Gerontology*, 12: 245–271.

Lai, D.W.L. (2004) 'Depression among elderly Chinese-Canadian immigrants from mainland China', *Chinese Medical Journal*, 117(5): 677–683.

Lai, D.W.L., and Leonenko, W.L. (2007) 'Correlates of living alone among single elderly Chinese immigrants in Canada', *The International Journal of Aging and Human Development*, 65(2): 121–148.

Lamb, S. (2002) 'Intimacy in a transnational era: The remaking of aging among Indian Americans', *Diaspora: A Journal of Transnational Studies*, 11(3): 299–330.

Lan, P. (2002) 'Subcontracting filial piety: Elder care in ethnic Chinese immigrant families in California', *Journal of Family Issues*, 23: 812–835.

Lie, M.L. (2010) 'Across the oceans: childcare and grandparenting in UK Chinese and Bangladeshi households', *Journal of Ethnic and Migration Studies*, 36(9): 1425–1443.

Lieber, E., Nihira, K., and Mink, I.T. (2004) 'Filial piety, modernization, and the challenges of raising children for Chinese immigrants: Quantitative and qualitative evidence', *Ethos*, 32(3): 324–347.

Lunt, N. (2009) 'Older people within transnational families: The social policy implications', *International Journal of Social Welfare*, 18(3): 243–251.

Maher, J., Lindsay, J. and Franzway, S. (2008) 'Time, caring labour and social policy: Understanding the family time economy in contemporary families', *Work, Employment & Society*, 22(3): 547–558.

Man, G. (2002) 'Globalization and the erosion of the welfare state: Effects on Chinese women', *Canadian Women Studies*, 21/22 (4/1): 26–32.

McKay, D. and Brady, C. (2005) 'Practices of place-making: Globalisation and locality in the Philippines', *Asia Pacific Viewpoint*, 46(2): 89–103.

Mui, A.C. and Kang, S. (2006) 'Acculturation stress and depression among Asian immigrant elders', *Social Work*, 51(3): 243–255.

Nesteruk, O. and Marks, L. (2009) 'Grandparents across the ocean: Eastern European immigrants' struggle to maintain intergenerational relationships', *Journal of Comparative Family Studies*, 40: 77–95.

Ng, L. (2013) 'Translocal temporalities in Alexis Wright's Carpentaria', in M. Munkelt, M. Schmitz, M. Stein, and S. Stroh (eds) *Postcolonial translocations: Cultural representation and critical spatial thinking*, Leiden: Brill, pp 109–126.

Pieke, F.N. (2006) 'Editorial introduction: Community and identity in the new Chinese migration order', *Population, Space and Place*, 13(2): 81–94.

Sigad, L.I. and Eisikovits, R.A. (2013) 'Grandparenting across borders: American grandparents and their Israeli grandchildren in a transnational reality', *Journal of Aging Studies*, 27(4): 308–316.

Statistics Canada (2008) '2006 Census: Ethnic origin, visible minorities, place of work and mode of transportation'. Retrieved from http://www.statcan.gc.ca/daily-quotidien/080402/dq080402a-eng.htm

Stephen, V. (2013) 'Indian diasporic grandparents in Canada and Changing roles for grandparents across nations', in A. Singh (ed) *Indian diaspora: Voices of grandparents and grandparenting*, Rotterdam: Sense Publishers, pp 189–206.

Sun, K.C. (2012) 'Fashioning the reciprocal norms of elder care: A case of immigrants in the United States and their parents in Taiwan', *Journal of Family Issues*, 33(9): 1240–1271.

Sung, K. and Kim, M.H. (2002) 'The effects of the US public welfare system upon elderly Korean immigrants' independent living arrangements', *Journal of Poverty*, 6(4): 83–94.

Tsuda, T. (2012) 'Whatever happened to simultaneity? Transnational migration theory and dual engagement in sending and receiving countries', *Journal of Ethnic and Migration Studies*, 38(4): 631–649.

Vertovec, S. (2009) *Transnationalism*, New York: Routledge.

Wu, Z. and Hart, R. (2002) 'Social and health factors associated with support among elderly immigrants in Canada', *Research on Aging*, 24(4): 391–412.

Yeates, N. (2008) 'The idea of global social policy', in N. Yeates (ed) *Understanding global social policy*, Bristol: Policy Press, pp 1–24.

Yeates, N. (2012) 'Global care chains: A state-of-the-art review and future directions in care transnationalization research', *Global Networks*, 12(2): 135–154.

Zhan, H.J. and Montgomery, R.J. (2003) 'Gender and elder care in China: The influence of filial piety and structural constraints', *Gender & Society*, 17(2): 209–229.

Zhou, Y.R. (2012) 'Space, time, and self: Rethinking aging in the contexts of immigration and transnationalism', *Journal of Aging Studies*, 26(3): 232–242.

Zhou, Y.R. (2013a) 'Toward transnational care interdependence: Rethinking the relationships between care, immigration and social policy', *Global Social Policy*, 13(3): 280–298.

Zhou, Y.R. (2013b) 'Transnational aging: The impacts of adult children's immigration on their parents' later lives', *Transnational Social Review*, 3(1): 49–64.

Zhou, Y.R. (2015) 'Time, space and care: Rethinking transnational care from a temporal perspective', *Time & Society*, 24(2): 163–182.

Zhou, Y.R. (2017) 'The new aging trajectories of Chinese grandparents in Canada', in P. Dossa and C. Coe (eds) *Transnational aging and kin-work*, New Brunswick, NJ: Rutgers University Press, pp 43–60.

SEVEN

Transnational grandmother–grandchild relationships in the context of migration from Lithuania to Ireland

Dovile Vildaite

Introduction

Over the last two decades the east–west migration within the European Union (EU) has evoked a growing body of research on cross-national family networks, documenting new ways, forms and practices that these families generate to maintain familial ties across borders (King et al., 2014; Reynolds and Zontini, 2014; Ryan, 2011). The transnational migration approach has been adopted to reconceptualise and explore the range of contemporary migrant experiences, which are defined as lived across transnational borders, by forging and sustaining simultaneous multifaceted social relations that link together migrants' societies of origin and settlement (Glick Schiller et al., 1995; Levitt and Glick Schiller, 2004). This approach points to the significant changes that occur in family life when family members are scattered across borders. One of the key changes is that the transnational dimension transforms a number of everyday contexts not only for migrants but also for non-migrant family members, with the latter experiencing a transnational turn without the concurrent spatial mobility (Baldassar et al., 2007; Nedelcu, 2012). As a result, transnational migration is viewed as a process affecting both migrants and their non-migrant family members and respectively conceptualised as not an individual but a collective family matter, which is framed, planned and implemented in response to multiple negotiations occurring among family members (Carling, 2008; Levitt and Glick Schiller, 2004).

Despite steady international migration across the globe and numerous studies exploring family migration and changing structures of family lives, there is a dearth of research on the dynamics of the grandparent–grandchild relationship in transnational migrant families, and particularly on how both migrant grandchildren and their non-migrant grandparents experience and perceive intergenerational ties spanning national borders. Existing literature on the intergenerational relations in transnationally scattered families has focused predominantly on parent–children relationships (for example, Baldassar et al., 2007; King et al., 2014; Madianou and Miller, 2012), and only a handful of studies have explored the changing nature of grandparenting in the context of migration from the perspective of grandparents (Banks, 2009; Plaza, 2000; Sigad and Eisikovits, 2013). The findings of these studies highlighted the challenges that geographical and cultural distances posed to traditional and socially accepted grandparenting roles and responsibilities. Grandparents struggled with their redefined roles as grandparents yet were eager to develop new ways of maintaining relationships with their geographically and culturally distant grandchildren (Nesteruk and Marks, 2009; Sigad and Eisikovits, 2013).

Accounts and analysis of migrant grandchildren's experiences of their relationships with grandparents remaining in the country of origin are almost completely lacking in the literature. In qualitative migration research, some fragmentary accounts of their relationships with geographically distant grandparents are mentioned when exploring young migrants' engagement in transnational family practices and cross-border networks (for example, Moskal, 2015; Ní Laoire et al., 2011; Sime and Fox, 2015). In these studies, grandparents occasionally appear in young migrants' premigration memories when children were taken care of by their grandparents or other relatives (Moskal, 2015) or are referred to as significant transnational family members who are frequently brought up with respect to children's return visits or occasional contact maintained transnationally (Ní Laoire et al., 2011; Sime and Fox, 2015). While many studies have argued that physical distance hinders contact between grandparents and grandchildren, which in turn leads to decreased emotional bonds (for example, Harwood, 2000; Mueller and Elder, 2003), the absence of more in-depth analysis on grandparent–grandchild relationships maintained across national borders leaves unanswered questions as to what extent, and in what ways, migration affects these relationships and how the dynamics of intergenerational ties evolve after family migration.

The present chapter aims to address this gap in the literature by going beyond the nuclear family to examine the impact of transnational family migration on the relationships between Lithuanian migrant adolescents living in Ireland and their non-migrant grandmothers residing in Lithuania. Historically, the traditional role of grandparents (and especially grandmothers) in Eastern European families has been instrumental due to their active involvement in their children's and grandchildren's lives and frequent provision of grandchild care, along with financial, emotional and other types of support (Kraniauskienė and Gedvilaitė-Kordušienė, 2012; Łobodzińska, 1995; Robila, 2004). However, the increased flows of outward migration since the EU enlargement in 2004 resulted in long-term separation, disrupted family structures and reshaped traditional family practices. By integrating cross-generational perspectives and multi-sited methodology, this chapter contributes to the study of intergenerational relationships by providing a more nuanced understanding of how significant physical distance and long-time separation affect relationships, contact practices and perceived emotional ties between grandparents and grandchildren.

Context of the study

Following the EU enlargement in 2004, the UK and Ireland opened their labour markets to the eight 'new European' (accession) countries from Central and Eastern Europe, referred to as A8 (Favell, 2008), leading to unprecedented flows of east–west migration from the new member states. Over the first three years (that is, 2004–07) approximately 1.2 million A8 nationals moved to these countries, prompting migration scholars to define the new migration waves as 'the most important social and economic phenomena' shaping Europe in the 21st century (Pollard et al., 2008, p 7). Among these countries, Ireland and Lithuania stand out as particularly interesting cases – Lithuania representing one of the key sending countries and Ireland one of the major recipients of migration flows (Barrett, 2009). In addition, recent migration trends indicate that Ireland is among the key destination countries for Lithuanian migrants, outnumbered only by the UK (approximately 185,000 Lithuanians residing in the UK and 85,000 in Ireland in 2014 (Statistics Lithuania, 2014b)).

According to European Commission statistical data (EUROSTAT, 2012), Lithuania stands out as one of the countries most significantly affected by emigration since the EU enlargement. For example, it is estimated that Lithuania has lost 20% of its population since the early 1990s and nearly 14% of its population since 2004 (Statistics Lithuania, 2014a). Children and young people (up to the age of 19) constitute a sizeable proportion of all emigrants; their numbers peaked in 2007, when they constituted 23.7% of all Lithuanian migrants, and slightly decreased in 2013 to 19.5% of all Lithuanian migrants (Statistics Lithuania, 2013). In addition to a steadily decreasing population, Lithuania is home to one of the most rapidly ageing societies in Europe (EUROSTAT, 2012). From 2003 to 2013, the number of people aged 65 and older increased by 3% (from 512,200 to 542,200), and, in 2014, older people comprised 18.2% of the total population (Statistics Lithuania, 2014b). The sex ratio for this population shows that women comprise the majority of the older population (360,000 women compared to 183,000 men). In addition, recent research has shown that older people in Lithuania experience a particularly prominent indirect effect of emigration in their lives as substantial numbers of their adult children and grandchildren move abroad (Gedvilaitė-Kordušienė, 2015).

Research methods

The findings presented in this chapter build on data collected in three phases over an 18-month period (2012–14) in Ireland and Lithuania during the author's doctoral studies at Trinity College, Dublin. The broader research was a qualitative study of transnational youth and family migration, as experienced and interpreted by a sample of 25 Lithuanian migrants aged 14–18 living with their families in Ireland and ten of their grandmothers residing in Lithuania. A qualitative, multi-sited, multimethod approach including biographical–narrative interviews and semistructured interviews was used in this study.

The sample of 25 Lithuanian adolescents – male and female, aged 14–18 years – was recruited through Irish secondary schools and the Lithuanian community in Dublin by conducting a brief survey on their transnational connections with family remaining in Lithuania. The selection criteria for this sample was to select participants with a range of different migration experiences and diverse patterns of transnational social ties – ranging from weak or infrequent connections to strong or frequent connections to Lithuania. Following 25 biographical–narrative interviews with adolescent participants, 15 follow-up interviews were conducted with a smaller subsample of ten adolescents after a one-year break, five of them interviewed during their summer visits back in Lithuania. Additionally, ten grandmothers were recruited through the adolescent participants for semistructured interviews conducted in Lithuania.

In total, 50 interviews were carried out during the course of the project: 25 biographical–narrative interviews with migrant youth, 10 semistructured in-depth interviews with grandmothers in Lithuania and 15 semistructured follow-up interviews with young Lithuanian migrants, either in Lithuania or in Ireland. The interviews were audio-recorded and transcribed. Data were organised and analysed using descriptive thematic analysis and a framework approach using the qualitative data analysis software package NVivo 9. This chapter focuses on three themes that emerged from the interview data, namely:

1. the changing *nature* of grandmother–grandchild relationships, as perceived by both parties involved;
2. *practices* endorsed in maintaining intergenerational ties transnationally;
3. the key *factors* contributing to the grandmother–grandchild relationship in Lithuanian migrant families.

Each of these themes is elaborated and explored in the following sections, with accompanying illustrative examples drawn from the interview data.

Changing nature of grandmother–grandchild relationships

Three types of relationships maintained transnationally between intergenerational dyads emerged from data: 1) strong and/or enduring relationships; 2) weakening/fading relationships; and 3) minimal or nonexistent relationships. The first type of relationship was maintained by approximately half of the qualitative sample of young migrants and four of the ten grandmothers who felt that, despite increased distance, lack of regular contact and passing years, the emotional closeness and attachment remained the same. Although both grandchildren and grandmothers agreed that the frequency and *intensity* of contact had decreased, they believed that emotional attachment formed before migration did not weaken over years spent apart:

> 'Has our relationship changed? Well, with my grandma it hasn't changed a bit, because … we talk the same, everything is the same. The only thing is that I can't see her and touch her, you know. Of course I miss her, but our relationship is in no way different.' (Lukas, 17)

> 'We all live in different countries, all scattered across Europe but we're constantly in touch. They [grandchildren] text me on the phone: "Grandma, sign in [on Skype]!", and then I run quickly to chat with them.' (Grandmother Marija)

In addition, the data suggest that, for grandchildren, this type of relationship could be further segmented into two subtypes. First, five participants revealed that, regardless of physical distance and irregular face-to-face contact, their relationships with grandmothers evolved further into a more emotionally mature and mutually supportive connection. Sandra (17), for example, explained that she now sees her grandmother as a confidante, compared to her childhood years when she was "a little girl spoiled by grandmother". In addition, this subgroup of participants shared a common experience of being raised by, or growing up in close proximity to, their grandmothers, which participants described as the main reason for developing strong relationships with them in early childhood. As a result, the importance of remaining emotionally close, as well as efforts and desire to maintain regular and independent contact, were central in these participants' narratives.

The other subtype of relationship can be described as an 'enduring' relationship and refers to those relationships which, according to a subgroup of seven grandchildren, have not changed over time. Participants described these relationships as "the same", "warm" and "good", and spoke respectfully of their grandparents. Nevertheless, unlike previously discussed participants, this group was not raised by their grandparents and felt less emotionally attached to them. The enduring emotional bonds were facilitated by the close proximity (two participants reported their grandmothers had recently moved to Ireland) and the mediating role of parents in encouraging and maintaining the contact.

Seven out of 25 grandchildren in this study and six out of ten grandmothers believed their relationships had changed over time, resulting in less emotionally close connections. Adolescent participants in this subgroup, and their grandmothers in particular, attributed the growing emotional distance to geographical distance, time spent apart and diverging interests as grandchildren entered adolescence. The changing grandmother–grandchild relationships were also attributed to the lack of shared, everyday activities and knowledge of each other's daily lives:

> 'I used to see [grandparents] more often, almost every day, and I knew everything about their lives, we used to visit them all the time. And now, I don't know. The feeling is not the same, perhaps you feel less close? I don't know. Of course we try to keep in touch and all, but … I haven't

seen them in three years and that half an hour on Skype is not the same.' (Akvile, 15)

'I can feel that with my granddaughters, they are drifting away from me, and I understand, they have all their lives there, their friends and all the activities, I don't expect them to ... But still, it is the way it is, I can feel we have moved apart, perhaps when they were little they needed me more.' (Grandmother Beata)

These accounts offer support to previous studies that highlighted the importance of geographical proximity and frequency of contact as important influences on closeness in grandparent–grandchildren relationships (for instance Kivett, 1991; Ross et al., 2005). As noted by Ross and colleagues (2005), frequent interactions and shared daily routines and activities facilitate the formation of closeness and reciprocity, building a strong bond over time. The lack of these shared activities, infrequent face-to-face contact and insufficient quality time spent together has contributed to decreasing intimacy and emotional closeness, and even increased discomfort in grandparents' presence:

> DV: 'Has your relationship [with grandmother] changed since you moved to Ireland?'
>
> LINA: 'Um ... We grew apart more. For example, when I go back for holidays, and when I tell her things and I get really embarrassed, I don't know what to say, then I just look down and ... I don't know ... Somehow we talk less. But when I lived in Lithuania, we used to be really close, every day I remember we used to spend together because my mum had left [for Ireland] and I was only seven so I stayed with my grandma.'

For grandmothers, the diminishing intimacy and emotional bonds with grandchildren were perceived to contribute to overall emotional distress caused by family migration, as they were struggling to adjust to the changing role of grandmothers in their transnational families (see also King et al., 2014; Sigad and Eisikovits, 2013). Emotional distress caused by lack of involvement in their grandchildren's lives and a sense of alienation were particularly evident in the accounts of those grandmothers who had all their grandchildren living abroad or who had especially strong emotional attachments to their migrant grandchildren:

'We used to be very close, she grew up here and lived with me for a while, so our relationship used to be very close, but it's not the same now. … But I remember after she left [for Ireland] and then during the first summers [of return visits], we would part very painfully, it was hard for both of us. She would say: "Grandma, why can't I stay with you?". But then … Last summer she left without problems and I don't think there'll be any tears this time either.' (Grandmother Liucija)

Not all adolescent participants in this study reported maintaining (or having previously maintained) meaningful relationships with their grandparents, and six out of 25 participants described their relationships with their grandparents as minimal or completely absent. Remarkably, none of the participants felt that their migration was to blame for the minimal contact they had with their grandparents; rather, they attributed it to negative attitudes towards migration, which their grandparents endorsed: "We've never been close. And she is very much against emigration so …" (Indre, 17). In other cases, the lack of contact with grandparents was determined by parent–grandparent interactions and conflicts in the family. For example, Simas (17) explained that his nonexistent relationship with his maternal grandmother was a result of parent–grandparent conflict in the past: "There was this incident in our family and since then my parents don't really want to stay in touch with her [grandmother] so I haven't talked to her either".

Practices of 'keeping in touch'

As described in the transnational migration literature, cross-border relationships are typically sustained through regular telephone calls, emails, chatting online and, in most cases, personal visits (see Bacigalupe and Lambe, 2011; Baldassar et al., 2007; Madianou and Miller, 2012). Over the last decades, widespread use of information and communication technologies (ICTs) has generated a 'multiplicity of flows characterised by the simultaneity and intensity of transnational exchanges' (Nedelcu, 2012, p 1340). The findings of this study support existing literature by showing that, nowadays, transnational family networks are maintained through a variety of channels that can facilitate the continuous co-presence of migrants and their non-migrant family members despite physical distance and long-term separation.

Interview data with migrant adolescents highlighted the crucial importance of return trips to their country of origin in providing an opportunity to reconnect with places and people, and often to restore and solidify social relationships that were established prior to migration. Family obligations and extended family networks were thus identified as one of the main reasons for these visits. Participants explained they longed for summer trips to Lithuania and expressed feelings of both personal enjoyment and obligation regarding going back and visiting their relatives ("My grandma is so happy when we're back"; "We all miss each other so it's good to come back"). In addition, the attitudes and expectations of the extended family in Lithuania had a strong impact on the continuation and frequency of return visits, which provided an important setting for the restoration and consolidation of intergenerational ties.

Nevertheless, one of the central themes that emerged from the interviews was the changing nature of return visits – both in terms of frequency and the meaning attached to these visits. Affordable transportation options enabled young migrants to visit their 'left behind' families and friends more frequently than before, often leading to more recurrent yet shorter visits organised by their parents. The role of the middle generation in planning and arranging return visits was central, indicating one of the ways in which young migrants' parents mediated their transnational activities. For example, some study participants stressed how family visits to Lithuania grew shorter and/ or less frequent because of the parents' decision to spend their holidays in different – often more 'exotic' – locations:

'No, this summer we're not coming back, my parents want to go to Spain instead.' (Sandra, 17)

'At first she [daughter] would come back to Lithuania at least twice a year but then, you know, time has an impact [on their return visits] and then they started to choose trips to Spain, France and Egypt over the trips to Lithuania and they would say they don't have enough money to go both places, and that sometimes it's cheaper to go to those [other] places.' (Grandmother Ona)

In line with the growing literature on the use of technology in transnational families, participants' accounts pointed to the crucial importance of ICT (in particular, mobile phones, Skype and social networking sites) in facilitating the maintenance of transnational family relations and making instant connectivity a reality. Most participants were found to use various ICTs to keep in touch with each other, although the adoption of different ICTs was fluid, suggesting a gradual move from phone-based to computer-mediated communication. Invariably, the use of ICTs depended on the financial situation of the family, with the internet often prioritised as the most affordable and 'most giving' channel of communication (Madianou and Miller, 2012). Although the mobile phone was the first means used by both sides to maintain contact, internet usage has become far more common in recent years:

> 'At first when my daughter left ten years ago, we would talk on the phone but very rarely, she would just call to say she is well and to ask about us, that's it, it was incredibly expensive. But then when Jonas [grandson] left, there was already Skype back then, and we would chat on Skype at least twice a week, that's such a great thing that Skype is, such a helper for everyone [in keeping in touch]. Can you imagine the amount of money I would spend if there was no Skype?' (Grandmother Ona)

Interviews with grandchildren revealed that maintaining contact with extended family members was frequently viewed as parents' responsibility, and many grandchildren reported "occasionally joining" their parents in their virtual communication practices. Lina (14), for example, described how her mother used Skype to talk to Lina's grandmother "a few times a week", giving Lina an opportunity to also participate in these virtual meetings. In addition, many participants reported that they were aware and well informed about their family's lives in Lithuania through their parents' ongoing communication and transnational practices (see also Bacigalupe and Lambe, 2011; Haikkola, 2011).

The mediated nature of their contact with grandchildren and the brevity of conversations with them over ICTs were reiterated in grandmothers' accounts, pointing to the difficulty of reconnecting and/or building relationships with their grandchildren:

> 'I do talk sometimes with him [grandson], too. But he's always busy with his friends or computer. He walks by, waves "Hi grandma", and off he goes again!' (Grandmother Morta)

Overall, intergenerational contact in Lithuanian families in this study was predominantly maintained through the middle generation, occasional or regular connection over ICTs and during visits to Lithuania, which in most cases were reported to take place during the summer months.

Multiple factors shaping grandmother–grandchild relationships

A combination of several factors emerged from interview data to explain the complex and sometimes changing nature of grandparent–grandchildren relationships in this sample of transnational Lithuanian families. As participants' accounts suggest, there is rarely one explanatory factor but rather an interaction of diverse individual, familial and contextual influences from both the past (pre-migration) and present (post-migration) family dynamics. Apart from face-to face contact and shared activities, both of which are crucial in preserving emotional bonds (Monserud, 2010; Ross et al., 2005), the key influences determining the nature of grandmother–grandchild relationships in these transnational families included family history and the quality of grandmother–grandchild relationship prior to migration; individual perceptions of relationships and feelings of connectedness; perceptions of geographical distance and contact; a grandchild's embeddedness in social networks in Ireland; accessibility and usage of ICTs; the mediating role of parents; and the quality of the grandmother–parent relationship. In most participants' accounts, several of these elements intersected to explain the currently maintained relationships in the intergenerational dyads.

While participants attributed changes to and decreased quality of intergenerational bonds to the physical distance and restricted opportunities for quality contact ("distance is distance"), most accounts pointed to an interplay of different factors that could mitigate the impact of increased physical distance. For example, the quality of relationships, and particularly the emotional bond (or lack thereof) established between youth and grandparents in childhood, was often the central element that influenced the type of interactions and quality of their post-migration relationship. More importantly, adolescent participants who were partially raised by or grew up near their grandmothers typically maintained an independent relationship and fairly regular contact with their grandmothers *after* migration. This finding supports previous research, which has demonstrated that caregiving provided by grandparents or frequent and emotionally close relations with grandparent in childhood are associated with stronger relationships later in life (Brown, 2003; Monserud, 2010; Xu et al.,

2014). Even with less frequent face-to-face contact, both groups of participants described feeling emotionally close, which was often linked to the development of new ways of maintaining relationship via phone or Skype calls, emails and return visits.

Although some adolescents' narratives highlighted the crucial importance of pre-migration factors in shaping the development of intergenerational relationships, others cited their preoccupation with, or involvement in, their present lives in Ireland as a key determinant affecting their relationships with those in Lithuania. As evidenced in the cases discussed in previous sections, it was usually the combination of infrequent visits, years spent apart and engagement in new social networks that led to the subsequent loss of interest in their grandparents' lives. According to Monserud (2010), transitioning from one life-course stage to another (for example, childhood to adolescence) often necessitates renegotiation of the grandchild–grandparent relationship due to the new priorities and competing responsibilities in the grandchild's life. Furthermore, interview data suggested that, in adolescence, emotional intimacy with grandparents was perceived to decrease as peer relationships become more important. This was evident in the grandchildren's narratives where they spoke of the immediate family life in Ireland, local social circles, school and afterschool activities:

> 'I don't really have time, I'm busy with school and then afterschool singing, and preparation for exams and so on. But my mum usually talks to my grandma fairly often, and so there's no need for me really … When they are all talking on Skype, I say "Hi!" but then I go to my room to study, I don't really have time to stay and chat.' (Akvile, 15)

As suggested in Akvile's quote and reiterated in other participants' narratives, intergenerational bonds and contact were often influenced and mediated by the middle generation in numerous ways. For example, Simas's (17) story of the nonexistent relationship with his grandmother reflected the role that parents can have as 'gatekeepers' (Mueller and Elder, 2003) or a 'relational bridge' (Xu et al., 2014); that is, only permitting or facilitating grandmother–grandchild interactions when they themselves are emotionally close to the grandmother. In addition, mediated contact was particularly evident among adolescent participants who did not have an independent relationship with their grandparents:

'My mum is often telling me "Go and talk to your grandma!", so I do, but my mum is often telling her everything about me, she is always reporting on my life' (laughs). (Goda, 16)

Overall, participants' accounts pointed to a spectrum of diverse individual experiences of transnational contact, influenced and shaped by a number of intersecting pre- and post-migration factors. In addition, the data highlighted the prominence of a 'double mediation' occurring in transnational families, which suggests that contact between grandparents and their grandchildren in transnational families is often mediated by *both* parents *and* ICTs.

Discussion and conclusions

The findings presented in this chapter support previous studies that emphasise the negative effect of geographical distance on the quality of grandparent–grandchild relationships by curtailing opportunities for interactions (Bangerter and Waldron, 2014; Harwood, 2000). Nevertheless, data analysis of cross-generational perspectives revealed a more nuanced picture of grandmother–grandchild relationships in the context of transnational family migration, leading to several important theoretical insights.

First, the findings revealed a considerable diversity with regard to the nature of grandparent–grandchild relationships, suggesting there is neither a 'typical' nor a uniform experience of the intergenerational relationship in transnational families. Rather, participants' experiences of grandparent–grandchild relationships ranged from extremely emotionally close to one in which grandparents played a merely peripheral (or absent) role in their grandchildren's lives, with a number of participants reporting declining relations over time and distance. This finding contributes to the existing literature by demonstrating that, despite advancements in transportation and ICTs, the limited interactions that sometimes follow emigration can restrict the historically rich, meaningful and continuous intergenerational relations particularly common and valued in many Eastern European families (Nesteruk and Marks, 2009; Robila, 2004).

Second, both young migrants' and their grandmothers' narratives suggested the dynamic nature of intergenerational relations in Lithuanian transnational families were never determined by one single influence but rather were seen as contingent on a combination of individual, familial and contextual influences, often forged in the past and extending into the present. Importantly, the quality of the grandchild–grandmother relationship and emotional bonds established prior to the grandchild's migration were central factors in determining post-migration intergenerational bonds and both frequency and quality of contact. This offers support to previous research that pointed to the lingering effects of early experiences with grandparents on stronger intergenerational relationships later in life (Brown, 2003; Monserud, 2010; Xu et al., 2014). This finding thus highlights the crucial importance of investing in intergenerational relationships and establishing strong emotional bonds with grandchildren in their early lives to cushion the potentially detrimental influence of family migration.

Third, young participants' and their grandmothers' accounts pointed to the fact that long-distance family contact and communication patterns have been drastically transformed by the availability and affordability of modern communication channels and accessibility of air travel (also see Baldassar et al., 2007; Baldassar and Merla, 2014; Madianou and Miller, 2012). Among those intergenerational dyads that maintained regular and independent contact post-migration, the mobile phone, the internet and especially webcam calls facilitated sustaining the *same* levels of emotional closeness through experiences of 'virtual co-presence', regardless of the physical distance (Baldassar, 2008; Nedelcu, 2012). However, for most adolescent migrants, grandparent–grandchild contact was limited primarily to parent-mediated communication via ICTs and return visits during the summer breaks or major family holidays. These findings demonstrate that the role of parents as 'mediators' or 'relational bridges' (Kivett, 1991; Monserud, 2010; Xu et al., 2014) is particularly prominent in transnationally dispersed families, where grandchildren and grandparents have limited opportunities for face-to-face contact. For many participants in this study, the middle generation served as the *only* relational bridge linking emotional closeness between grandparents and grandchildren. In addition, the data suggest that return visits, which provide an opportunity to restore and strengthen extended family bonds, tend to become less regular and strongly dependent on family resources (such as time and finances).

This study is among the first to explore grandparent–grandchild ties in the context of transnational migration and thus offers several suggestions for future research. While the findings cannot be generalised to broader migrant populations, future research should aim to replicate and extend them across different migrant groups and in different cultural contexts. In addition, by acknowledging the central role of the middle generation in mediating and facilitating the grandparent–grandchild connection, this study highlights the need to take a three-generation approach (Hagestad, 2006) when studying intergenerational relationships in the transnational context. Furthermore, given that the key foci of this study were intergenerational relationships and perceived changes within them *throughout time*, a longitudinal approach should be employed in future studies. Finally, although transnational grandparenting in the present study was depicted as a particularly gendered process, wherein transnational family ties were maintained predominantly by grandmothers, future studies should explore grandfathers' participation in transnational family practices. So far, the male voice among non-migrant family members is particularly overlooked, leading to a portrayal of grandfathers as absent and nonexistent in transnational families.

Acknowledgements

The author acknowledges funding for this research project from the Irish Research Council through the Government of Ireland Postgraduate Scholarship. The ethical approval for the research project was granted by the Research Ethics Approval Committee of the School of Social Work and Social Policy (Trinity College, Dublin) in May 2012.

References

Bacigalupe, G. and Lambe, S. (2011) 'Virtual intimacy: Information communication technologies and transnational families in therapy', *Family Process*, 50(1): 12–26.

Baldassar, L. (2008) 'Missing kin and longing to be together: Emotions and the construction of copresence in transnational relationships', *Journal of Intercultural Studies*, 29(3): 247–266.

Baldassar, L. and Merla, L. (eds) (2014) *Transnational families, migration and the circulation of care: Understanding mobility and absence in family life*, New York: Routledge.

Baldassar, L, Baldock, C. and Wilding, R. (2007) *Families caring across borders: Migration, aging and transnational caregiving*, London: Palgrave Macmillan.

Bangerter, L.R. and Waldron, V.R. (2014) 'Turning points in long distance grandparent–grandchild relationships', *Journal of Aging Studies*, 29(1): 88–97.

Banks, S.P. (2009) 'Intergenerational ties across borders: Grandparenting narratives by expatriate retirees in Mexico', *Journal of Aging Studies*, 23(3): 178–87.

Barrett, A. (2009) *EU enlargement and Ireland's labour market*, Bonn: IZA.

Brown, L. (2003) 'Intergenerational influences of perceptions of current relationships with grandparents', *Journal of Intergenerational Relationships*, 1(1): 95–112.

Carling, J. (2008) 'The human dynamics of migrant transnationalism', *Ethnic and Racial Studies*, 31(8): 1452–1477.

EUROSTAT (2012) *Migrants in Europe: A statistical portrait of the first and second generation*, Luxembourg: European Commission.

Favell, A. (2008) 'The new face of east–west migration in Europe', *Journal of Ethnic and Migration Studies*, 34(5): 701–716.

Gedvilaitė-Kordušienė, M. (2015) 'Norms and care relationships in transnational families: The case of elderly parents left behind in Lithuania', *Baltic Journal of European Studies*, 2(19): 90–107.

Glick Schiller, N., Basch, L. and Blanc Szanton, C. (1995) 'From immigrant to transmigrant: Theorizing transnational migration', *Anthropological Quarterly*, 68(1): 48–63.

Hagestad, G.O. (2006) 'Transfers between grandparents and grandchildren: The importance of taking a three-generation perspective', *Zeitschrift für Familienforschung*, 18(1): 315–332.

Haikkola, L. (2011) 'Making connections: Second-generation children and the transnational field of relations', *Journal of Ethnic and Migration Studies*, 37(8): 1201–1217.

Harwood, J. (2000) 'Communication media use in the grandparent–grandchild relationship', *Journal of Communication*, 50(4): 56–78.

King, R., Cela, E/, Fokkema, T. and Vullnetari, J. (2014) 'The migration and well-being of the zero generation: Transgenerational care, grandparenting, and loneliness amongst Albanian older people', *Population, Space and Place*, 20(8): 728–738.

Kivett, V. (1991) 'The grandparent–grandchild connection', *Marriage and Family Review*, 16: 267–290.

Kraniauskienė S. and Gedvilaitė-Kordušienė, M. (2012) 'Kartų solidarumas Lietuvoje: Anūkų priežiūros įtaka senelių gerovei' [Grandparents' childcare support in Lithuania: Predictors and consequences for well-being], *Sociologija. Mintis ir veiksmas*, 2(31): 239–264.

Levitt, P. and Glick Schiller, N. (2004) 'Conceptualizing simultaneity: A transnational social field perspective on society', *International Migration Review*, 38(3): 1002–1039.

Łobodzińska, B. (ed) (1995) *Family, women, and employment in Central-Eastern Europe*, Westport: Greenwood Press.

Madianou, M. and Miller, D. (2012) *Migration and new media: Transnational families and polymedia*, London: Routledge.

Monserud, M. (2010) 'Continuity and change in grandchildren's closeness to grandparents: Consequences of changing intergenerational ties', *Marriage and Family Review*, 46(5): 366–388.

Moskal, M. (2015) '"When I think home I think family here and there": Translocal and social ideas of home in narratives of migrant children and young people', *Geoforum*, 58: 143–152.

Mueller, M. and Elder, G. (2003) 'Family contingencies across the generations: Grandparent–grandchild relationships in holistic perspective', *Journal of Marriage and the Family*, 65(2): 404–417.

Nedelcu, M. (2012) 'Migrants' new transnational habitus: Rethinking migration through a cosmopolitan lens in the digital age', *Journal of Ethnic and Migration Studies*, 38(9): 1339–1356.

Nesteruk, O. and Marks, L. (2009) 'Grandparents across the ocean: Eastern European immigrants' struggle to maintain intergenerational relationships', *Journal of Comparative Family Studies*, 40(3): 77–95.

Ní Laoire, C, Carpena-Mendez, F, Tyrrell, N. and White, A. (2011) *Childhood and migration in Europe: Portraits of mobility, identity and belonging in contemporary Ireland*, Surrey: Ashgate.

Plaza, D. (2000) 'Transnational grannies: The changing family responsibilities of elderly African Caribbean born women resident in Britain', *Social Indicators Research Journal*, 9(7): 180–201.

Pollard, N., Latorre, M. and Sriskandarajah, D. (2008) *Floodgates or turnstiles? Post-EU enlargement migration flows to (and from) the UK*, London: Institute for Public Policy Research.

Reynolds, T. and Zontini, E. (2014) 'Bringing transnational families from the margins to the centre of family studies in Britain', *Families, Relationships and Societies*, 3(2): 251–268.

Robila, M. (ed) (2004) *Families in Eastern Europe*, New York: Elsevier.

Ross, N., Hill, M., Sweeting, H. and Cunningham-Burley, S. (2005) *Grandparents and teen grandchildren: Exploring intergenerational relationships*, Glasgow: Centre for Research on Families and Relationships.

Ryan, L. (2011) 'Transnational relations: Family migration among recent Polish migrants in London', *International Migration*, 49(2): 80–103.

Sigad, L.I., and Eisikovits, R.A. (2013) 'Grandparenting across borders: American grandparents and their Israeli grandchildren in a transnational reality', *Journal of Aging Studies*, 27(4): 308–316.

Sime, D. and Fox, R. (2015) 'Home abroad: Eastern European children's family and peer relationships after migration', *Childhood*, 22(3): 377–393.

Statistics Lithuania (2013) *Lithuanian population by age: School-age population*, Vilnius: Statistics Lithuania.

Statistics Lithuania (2014a) *International migration of Lithuanian population*, Vilnius: Statistics Lithuania.

Statistics Lithuania (2014b) *Lithuanian population by age: Elderly population*, Vilnius: Statistics Lithuania.

Xu, L, Silverstein, M. and Chi, I. (2014) 'Emotional closeness between grandparents and grandchildren in rural China: The mediating role of the middle generation', *Journal of Intergenerational Relationships*, 12(3): 226–240.

PART 4
Gender, intersectionalities and grandparenting

The composition of grandparent childcare: gendered patterns in cross-national perspective

Lyn Craig, Myra Hamilton and Judith E. Brown

Introduction

Internationally, grandparents are important providers of childcare while their adult children participate in work and other activities. There is a growing body of literature that explores grandparents' experiences of providing childcare and the effects it has on their lives. This research indicates most grandparents enjoy caring for their grandchildren and derive many benefits for their health, wellbeing and family relationships (Goodfellow and Laverty, 2003; Ochiltree, 2006). But there can also be costs for grandparents. Lack of choice over their childcare responsibilities or particularly demanding childcare responsibilities (for example, long or nonstandard hours or lack of support from a partner) can have a negative effect on grandparents' wellbeing (Hamilton and Jenkins, 2015). Care responsibilities can also have an impact on grandparents' workforce participation, retirement decisions and incomes (Hamilton and Jenkins, 2015).

There is also an emerging body of literature that examines the characteristics of grandparent childcare providers and the prevalence and intensity of grandparent childcare; that is, how often they provide care and for how long (Craig and Jenkins, 2016; Glaser et al., 2013; Timonen and Arber, 2012). This literature suggests that the prevalence and intensity of childcare provision varies by country (Glaser et al., 2013; Herlofson and Hagestad, 2012) and according to patterns of employment participation, cultural and gender norms and values, and policy constellations (Glaser et al., 2013). Prevalence and intensity of grandparent childcare is shaped by both parental employment participation and mature-age employment participation. Research suggests there is a direct relationship between parental employment participation and grandparent childcare provision (Glaser et al., 2013;

Hamilton and Jenkins, 2015). In countries with higher participation rates among older people, the prevalence of regular grandparent childcare provision is lower (Glaser et al., 2013). Gender norms and values about work and familial care provision also shape the extent and intensity of grandparent childcare within countries (Glaser et al., 2013). Patterns in grandparental childcare also differ across policy contexts, with different constellations of work and family policies (Arber and Timonen, 2012; Ghysels, 2011; Glaser et al., 2013). Research is lacking, however, on the *composition* of grandparent childcare time and whether this varies across countries. Composition is important. If we are to understand grandparents' experience of childcare provision and the effects it has on their lives, we need to look beyond just how much care they are doing and how often to examine which care tasks they are doing. For example, routine physical care (such as feeding and bathing) or being responsible for regularly accompanying children to and from school are likely to be more demanding and time-constraining than other forms of care, such as supervising children while they play (Craig, 2006a). The composition of grandparents' caregiving is likely to affect their enjoyment of childcare, its impact on their health and wellbeing and the extent to which they can fit these tasks around their work, leisure and other commitments. As most grandparents who provide childcare are partnered (Glaser et al., 2013), how these tasks are distributed within couples matters.

In this chapter, we explore *how* grandparents spend time with their grandchildren in Australia, Korea, Italy and France. We explore how the distribution of childcare tasks compares across countries within the context of different patterns of employment participation, gender norms and policy constellations.

Composition of childcare

Childcare consists of a range of different tasks, some of which are more demanding than others. Research consistently shows that fathers spend more of their childcare time talking, reading, teaching, listening and playing with children than doing physical care tasks such as bathing, dressing, feeding, changing and putting children to bed (Baxter and Smart, 2011; Craig, 2006b; Hook and Wolfe, 2012). In couple families, this means mothers generally take more responsibility for the routine activities, centrally physical childcare and delivering children to school and activities on time. While fathers' predominantly talk-based childcare is less time-critical and easier to fit around their other commitments, mothers' mostly routine activities tend to need doing at particular times of day. While fathers are becoming more involved in routine activities, deep divisions persist (Craig et al., 2014).

But do gender differences in the division of childcare pertain for grandparents?

It may be that gender differences are deeply entrenched in the older generation after decades of gender-role separation (Martinengo et al., 2010). Or, among older couples who have withdrawn or partially withdrawn from the labour market, more equal time availability may create a more gender-equal distribution of tasks. Retired or semi-retired men whose employment precluded them from being closely involved in caring for their own children may use their time availability in later life to be more involved in the care of their grandchildren (Craig and Jenkins, 2016; Ghysels, 2011; Tarrant, 2012). While many men may still bring more economic resources into the household (as men usually have higher retirement savings than women), the concept of 'earning power' shifts once the members of a couple are no longer engaged in the labour market, and this may be less influential in shaping household negotiations about the distribution of unpaid tasks. Thus, it is possible that being at a later stage of the life course could *weaken* gender norms (Emslie et al., 2004; Tarrant, 2012) and facilitate the more equal distribution of care activities among grandparents than among parents.

Gender differences in the distribution of childcare tasks could also be narrower for grandparents than for parents because, across the parent–grandparent dyad, mothers continue to do most of the routine care for the child. If mothers continue to take primary responsibility for the routine care tasks then fathers, grandfathers and grandmothers are likely to spend less of their time on these tasks and more of their time on activities such as talking, listening and play (Craig and Jenkins, 2016). Indeed, a recent study of care composition in Australia found that, while gender differences were smaller between grandparents than between parents, this was because grandmothers spent a lower proportion of their time undertaking routine care tasks than mothers did. Grandfathers spent a much lower proportion of their time than grandmothers on routine childcare tasks (Craig and Jenkins, 2016). This chapter seeks to explore whether this pattern is reproduced across country contexts.

Care contexts

Australia, Italy, France and Korea have different patterns of employment participation, gender norms and policy constellations.

Australia

Australia is usually classified as a liberal welfare state characterised by a residual role of the state in providing support to parents. Childcare is subsidised by the state but mostly provided by the market, costs are high and coverage is comparatively low. There is a relatively limited paid parental leave scheme of 18 weeks at the minimum wage and a system of family support payments for mothers who stay at home.

Employment patterns in parent couples suggest a 'one and a half earner model' (Gerhard et al., 2005, p 136), with high rates of full-time employment and long working hours among men and high rates of part-time employment among women (Craig and Mullan, 2009). The mature-age employment rate (that is, the employment rate among those aged 55–64 years old) is relatively high (56.5%), with an effective age of labour market exit of 65 for men and 63 for women in 2014 (OECD, 2015).

Research suggests Australian families subscribe strongly to the idea that intensive family care for children is essential (Gray et al., 2008). Australian mothers and fathers spend the most daily time of any Organisation for Economic Co-operation and Development (OECD) country caring for children (Fisher and Robinson, 2010). The 'normative valorising of family care' means many Australian parents involve grandparents in the regular care of their children (Craig and Jenkins, 2016).

Australian grandparents play what Glaser and co-authors (2013) would describe as a 'middling role', characteristic of liberal welfare states, with moderate levels of participation in both intensive and occasional childcare. As a result, they are likely to be providing routine tasks at varying levels. The high rates of part-time work among mothers may mean mothers undertake most of the routine childcare tasks, and that therefore the demand for grandparents to perform routine tasks is lower than in countries where women tend to work full time and childcare provision by grandparents is intensive. While there is a clear gender disparity in the composition of care among Australian mothers and fathers, fathers devote a lot of time to childcare tasks compared with their OECD counterparts, which suggests a commitment to intensive childcare time (Craig and Mullan, 2011; Fisher and Robinson, 2010). It is possible that in later life, once time commitments of paid work are reduced, grandfathers may invest more heavily in routine care tasks, which could narrow gender gaps in care tasks between grandparents.

Italy

Italy is usually classified as a conservative European model of welfare state, characterised by an emphasis on a (male) breadwinner and an adherence to a traditional familialist approach to welfare provision (Esping-Andersen, 2002). Italy has a generous paid parental leave scheme of 22 weeks paid leave at 80% wage replacement followed by 11 months at 30% wage replacement (Del Boca, 2015). Italy has well-developed universal early childhood education and care services for children aged 3–6, which are widely used (Glaser et al., 2010). Childcare for children under three years old is publicly subsidised and mostly publicly operated. However, supply is limited and, as a result, parents of children this age often rely on grandparents (Del Boca, 2015; Glaser et al., 2010).

Employment among Italian women is well below the European Union (EU) average and part-time work is comparatively rare (Roland Berger et al., 2013a). Employment among older Italians is also low, with the effective age of labour market exit only 61 for men and women in 2014. There is an emphasis on the role of women in family care (Roland Berger et al., 2013a) and some stigma attached to mothers being employed (Del Boca, 2015). Although this culture is beginning to change, Italian women are more likely than others in the EU to leave work during childbearing years and the division of domestic labour is highly gendered (Del Boca, 2015).

Grandparents in Italy who provide childcare are likely to play an intensive role – very few provide 'occasional' childcare. Italy has among the highest rates of grandparents providing regular and intensive childcare – around 20% of grandparents who look after their grandchildren provide childcare 'almost daily' (Glaser et al., 2013). For this reason, Glaser et al. group Italy with the Southern European countries, where 'few part-time jobs, sparse institutional childcare and ungenerous in-kind family benefits, [mean that] more grandmothers provide intensive child care' (Glaser et al., 2013, p 71). The high proportion of grandparents providing intensive care is likely to result in grandparents providing a large amount of routine care. The strong maternalist culture in Italy is likely to result in much of the responsibility for these routine tasks falling to grandmothers.

Korea

Korea is classified as a liberal–familialist model of welfare state, as it combines high rates of participation in full-time work with a heavily gendered division of unpaid work. Korea has a strong tradition of relying on family, particularly women, to provide childcare (Kwon, 2005; Ochiai, 2009). Over the last two decades, Korean governments have invested in improving family policies, particularly access to childcare (Lee and Bauer, 2010). Korea has a publicly funded and privately provided system of childcare, with care for children aged 0–5 entirely subsidised by government (Chin et al., 2014). The Korean maternity leave scheme offers female employees 90 days paid leave and then a year of parental leave paid at a lower rate (Chin et al., 2014). A childrearing allowance provides a flat-rate benefit for low–income families with young children who do not use childcare (Chin et al., 2014).

Korea has very long full-time working hours (Kwon, 2005; Ochiai, 2009). Female participation rates are lower than the OECD average, but among those who do work the full-time rate is comparatively high. Korea has a high mature-age employment participation rate and a high effective age of labour market exit (73 for men and 71 for women in 2014).

Despite an increasing emphasis on work–family balance, Korea's high rates of full-time work (and low rates of part-time work) mean many mothers who return to work require intensive childcare. Recent research suggests that, while the proportion of Korean grandmothers who 'had provided childcare in the last year' was comparatively low (12%), those who did provide care did so for an average of 50 hours per week (Lee and Bauer, 2010). As in Italy, the high proportion of grandparents providing intensive care in Korea is likely to see them doing a large amount of routine care. Also like Italy, the strong maternalist culture in Korea is likely to see much of the responsibility for these routine tasks fall to grandmothers. Given the high average retirement age, grandparents in Korea have less time to develop new patterns of time use, which may lead to higher gender segregation in care tasks.

France

France shares some characteristics of conservative European and some of social democratic welfare states (Esping-Andersen, 2002). It has an employment-based system of social protection, in which social rights accrue to the male breadwinner, but combines this with support for women's paid work (Del Boca, 2015; Pfau-Effinger, 2005). France has a system of highly available and affordable subsidised childcare – both formal centre-based care and care by 'childminders' in the home. There are also generous paid maternity (16 weeks at 100% wage replacement) and parental (36 months at just over 40% wage replacement) leave schemes (Del Boca, 2015) and a generous system of family payments (Glaser et al., 2010).

Women's employment participation is higher than the EU average and their part-time employment sits at about the EU average (Roland Berger et al., 2013b). Mature-age employment is the lowest of the four countries in this study, with the effective age of labour market exit about 59 for men and 60 for women in 2014.

While France's family policies align quite closely with those of the social democratic countries, the social and cultural context differs. In the social democratic countries there is an 'egalitarian cultural image of the family', whereas in France the 'dominant model assigns responsibility for informal care work unilaterally to the woman' (Pfau-Effinger, 2005, p 334). The widely accessible formal childcare and generous parental leave systems mean grandparents are more likely to provide occasional than intensive care for grandchildren (Glaser et al., 2013). The result may be that, overall, grandparents in France do fewer routine care tasks; this may also mean the routine care tasks they do undertake are shared more equally between grandmothers and grandfathers.

Data and method

To explore how grandparents spend time with their grandchildren, we used time use surveys (TUS) of Australia (AUSTUS 2006), Korea (KTUS 2009), Italy (ITUS 2009) and France (TUS 2010) conducted by the national statistical agency of each country. Each contains representative samples of the respective country populations. All collected information through a self-completed time diary of activities performed over the full 24 hours of each surveyed day. The Australian, Korean and French TUS collected data over two days and the Italian TUS collected data for one day only.

Several issues arose in harmonising the four countries' data because demographic detail and activity coding were not identical. In the AUSTUS, grandparents were identified through a survey question: 'Do you have a grandchild under 15?' The Italian, Korean and French TUS had no specific indicator of grandparent status. Therefore, we used childcare behaviour as a proxy to identify grandparents. We selected respondents aged 55–75 who reported doing unpaid childcare on the diary day(s) and were not the child's own parent. This solution had limitations: we could not accurately identify all grandparents, only those who participated in unpaid childcare. However, our interest is in the gender composition of care, not the amount performed or how many grandparents do it. Our final sample consisted of 1,789 grandparents. A sample description is in Table 8.1.

The outcome variables are the specific activities that comprise childcare: **physical care**, including feeding, bathing, dressing and putting children to bed; **accompanying** children, including transporting children, waiting for or meeting children, ensuring their safety and handing them over to substitute carers; **talk-based care**, including reading, teaching, talking, listening and playing games with children; and **minding** children, including caring for children without active involvement, monitoring children, being an adult presence for children to turn to and supervising. All four surveys differentiate between these four broad activities but specific coding slightly differs. Due to the sample and coding differences we do not compare countries directly or conduct multivariate analysis but rather present descriptive summaries of gendered patterns within countries. Grandparents' mean daily minutes spent in each of the four dimensions of childcare are shown in Table 8.1. Our focus is the proportional composition of care in each country, so we use the amount of childcare only as a basis for calculating within-country shares. We present figures illustrating how each activity is proportionally distributed in two ways. First, we look at how the total of each type of care is shared between grandfathers and grandmothers. This is to show the gender distribution of each care type in each of the four countries. Second, we look at how the total childcare time of grandfathers and grandmothers is proportionally distributed across the four types of childcare. This is to compare, in each country, the gendered composition of care. Our aim is to examine whether and how grandmothers' and grandfathers' relative contribution differs across countries.

This study is subject to several limitations. As noted, we inferred grandparent status through childcare behaviour. There are also small sample sizes, especially for Italy, so we present descriptive analyses and can draw broad inferences only. Our cross-sectional data can only give a snapshot of grandparental childcare at a point in time. We do not know how many grandchildren are cared for and their ages. We also do not know how close the grandparents lived to their grandchildren or whether the grandparents were paternal or maternal – both factors that can affect the intensity of care (Condon et al., 2013; Ghysels, 2011). Notwithstanding these caveats, the study offers new insight into the gendered distribution of care in grandparenthood and how this differs cross-nationally.

Table 8.1: Sample description and mean time spent on each childcare activity

	Italy		Korea		Australia		France	
	M	F	M	F	M	F	M	F
No of diaries	37	45	195	445	197	377	326	644
No of people	37	45	144	303	150	269	295	546
Gender (%)	49.8	50.2	30.8	69.2	33.9	66.1	33.5	66.5
Age (mean)	57.0	58.0	63.9	63.6	61.0	58.2	62.1	62.6
(SD)	(6.3)	(6.3)	(5.2)	(5.6)	(9.8)	(9.7)	(5.0)	(5.2)
Employment status (%)								
Full time	54.7	14.8	35.1	13.6	39.3	14.5	15.6	16.0
Part time	4.6	13.9	15.4	12.7	9.8	29.1	4.3	4.3
Not employed	40.8	71.3	49.5	73.8	50.9	56.4	80.1	79.7
Care type (mean (SD), minutes per day)								
Physical	3.5	30.1	16.2	45.6	9.7	32.4	13.7	20.1
	(16.6)	(43.8)	(39.9)	(62.7)	(22.0)	(61.5)	(37.4)	(44.8)
Accompanying	29.6	12.9	15.8	18.8	19.2	20.4	22.5	12.2
	(26.1)	(24.4)	(40.8)	(37.5)	(33.1)	(33.2)	(42.8)	(26.3)
Talk-based	13.1	11.7	41.3	36.7	39.4	44.8	28.6	24.8
	(35.2)	(26.8)	(47.4)	(57.3)	(49.1)	(51.4)	(48.9)	(46.7)
Minding	12.1	14.2	18.9	23.3	23.7	25.6	17.7	41.8
	(34.5)	(29.6)	(36.1)	(45.0)	(69.8)	(54.9)	(43.7)	(73.3)
Total	58.3	68.8	92.2	124.4	92.0	123.2	82.5	98.9
	(52.1)	(66.2)	(91.0)	(117.5)	(86.7)	(99.6)	(71.2)	(87.2)

Note: M = Male; F = Female.

Results

Figure 8.1 illustrates the gender balance for grandparents within the total amount of each type of childcare. It shows what proportion of total childcare time within each category is done by grandfathers and what proportion by grandmothers. Some activities are more evenly distributed by gender than others. For example, a higher proportion of total physical care is performed by grandmothers than by grandfathers in all four countries, whereas in most of the countries, talk-based care is more evenly distributed by gender.

However, gender patterns are not the same in each country. Italy conformed to the aforementioned pattern, in that time spent on talk-based care was relatively equally distributed between grandmothers and grandfathers. Grandfathers contributed around 45% of the time spent supervising or minding children, suggesting time spent in this activity was also fairly equally distributed. However, in contrast, physical care was overwhelmingly performed by grandmothers. In Italy, the

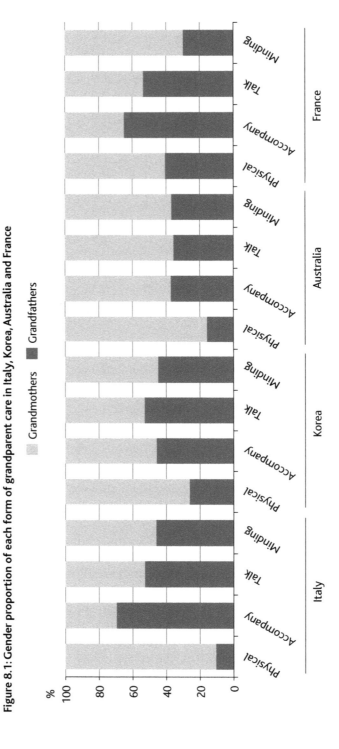

Figure 8.1: Gender proportion of each form of grandparent care in Italy, Korea, Australia and France

Grandmothers ■ Grandfathers

distribution of time spent on physical tasks was the most unequal of the four countries, with grandmothers providing 90% and grandfathers only 10%. The contribution to time spent accompanying a child was also substantially different for Italian grandmothers and grandfathers. Grandfathers spent about 70% of the total grandparental time allocated to accompanying and transporting children. One possibility is that Italian grandfathers may be delegated responsibility for taking children to and from school or day care; another is that there may be a disparity in holding a driver's licence among older cohorts of Italian men and women, although our small Italian sample means we cannot draw strong conclusions.

Patterns of childcare time for France were similar to Italy with some notable exceptions. Physical care in France was more equally distributed than in Italy, with French grandfathers contributing 41% of physical care. However, like in Italy, talk-based care was approximately evenly distributed between grandmothers and grandfathers. In France, grandfathers contributed around 30% of supervisory care and, as in Italy, men contributed a high proportion of the time devoted to accompanying and transporting children.

In Korea, similar to Italy and France, talk-based care was approximately evenly distributed between grandparents. Supervisory care was also fairly equally distributed and, in contrast to Italy and France, Korean grandfathers spent slightly *less* time accompanying children than did grandmothers. In Korea, the distribution of time spent on physical tasks was the most unequal of the four care tasks, with grandmothers providing 74% and grandfathers 26%. This was distributed more equally than in Italy but less equally than in France.

Australia has the most unequal distribution of care tasks between grandmothers and grandfathers. Australian grandfathers did a considerably lower proportion of talking and accompanying/transporting than Australian grandmothers. They also did a considerably lower proportion of talking and accompanying than their male counterparts in the three other countries. In Australia, grandfathers contributed around 37% of supervisory care compared with grandmothers' 63%, higher than France but lower than Italy and Korea. In Australia, grandmothers provided 84% and grandfathers 16% of physical care tasks, more equally distributed than in Italy but less equal than France and Korea.

Figure 8.2 cuts the data differently and presents a gender comparison of grandparents' own average childcare composition in each of the four countries. In Italy, physical care consumed the greatest proportion (around 44%) of grandmothers' care time. Accompanying a child and

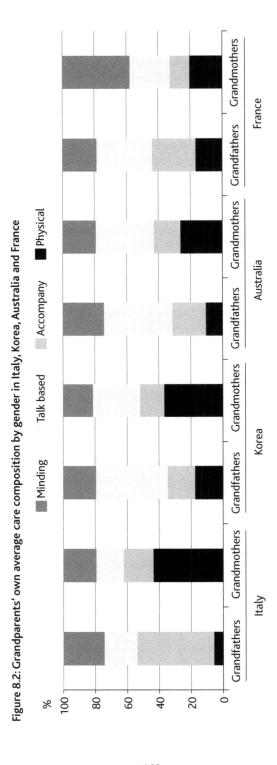

Figure 8.2: Grandparents' own average care composition by gender in Italy, Korea, Australia and France

talk-based tasks consumed around 17–19% of grandmothers' time. In contrast, Italian grandfathers spent less than 6% of their care time on physical tasks, just under 50% of their time accompanying a child and approximately 20% on talk-based care. Childminding occupied around 20% of both genders' childcare time.

Patterns were different in France. French grandmothers and grandfathers spent a relatively similar proportion of their care time (20% and 17% respectively) on physical care tasks. Grandmothers spent around 42% of their care time supervising children while grandfathers spent considerably less of their care time on this task (21%). Grandfathers spent more of their overall childcare time on talk-based and accompanying tasks than grandmothers did.

In Korea, patterns were like those in Italy. Korean grandmothers spent around 40% of their care time on physical care, around 15% accompanying a child, around 30% on talk-based care and almost 20% minding children. Korean grandfathers spent less of their care time on physical care (20%) but talk dominated their care time. Like in Italy, the proportion of total care devoted to childminding in Korea was relatively similar by gender, at 20%. However, unlike in Italy, relative time spent in accompanying a child was consistent (17%) across genders.

In Australia, like Korea, the gender gap in the proportion of physical care was approximately 15–20%, with grandmothers spending approximately 25% of their care time and grandfathers spending approximately 10% of their care time doing physical care tasks. However, in Australia, grandmothers and grandfathers spent a lower proportion of their overall care time doing physical care tasks than Korean grandparents did. Australian grandfathers spent relatively more of their time than Australian grandmothers on accompanying, talk-based and supervisory tasks, though the proportional gender differences in these three care types were not large.

Across all countries, men's care included relatively less physical care than women's care. The gender gap in the proportion of physical care was much narrower in France. In all countries except Italy, grandfathers reported that talk-based care took up the greatest proportion of their time. Relative time spent on childminding was the most consistent by gender, with the exception that French grandmothers reported a considerably higher proportion of supervisory care than grandmothers and grandfathers in the other three countries. Except for Italian and French grandfathers, who reported higher proportions, the relative time spent accompanying a child was also reasonably consistent (12–20%) across both genders.

Discussion and conclusion

Gender differences in how care activities were distributed were present in all four countries. The descriptive results in Figure 8.1 suggest that, in all countries, grandmothers do considerably more physical care tasks than grandfathers. This reflects patterns we see in the distribution of physical care tasks among parents (Craig 2006a; Craig et al., 2014).

But the *extent* of gender difference in the distribution of physical care varies across countries. France had the most equal apportionment of physical care tasks. This could be for several reasons. France is the only one of the four countries in which more grandmothers in the sample are employed than grandfathers. It is also the only country with fairly equal participation in full- and part-time work among grandfathers and grandmothers in the sample (see Table 8.1), so the time available for routine tasks is more equal. France's more widely accessible and generous formal childcare and parental leave schemes, which mean grandparents are less likely to provide intensive care (Glaser et al., 2013), may create a context in which grandparents are providing fewer physical care tasks in a more gender egalitarian policy context, leading to the more equal sharing of physical care tasks.

Physical care tasks are distributed less equally in Korea, Australia and Italy, where grandfathers undertake 18%, 11% and 6% of physical care tasks respectively. The Italian grandfathers in the sample have the highest levels of full-time work, followed by Australian and then Korean grandfathers, so it is possible that time availability plays a role. It could also partly be a function of social norms about the gendered distribution of care. In Korea and Italy, which exhibit familialist-style welfare states and social norms, we could expect a more gender-unequal distribution of care tasks. However, Australia has a liberal welfare model, higher levels of female participation in work and high time commitment of fathers to childcare compared with the OECD, yet grandparents share physical care tasks less equally than grandparents in Korea. One possible explanation for this is that in Australia – where a high proportion of mothers work part time – grandparents tend to play a middling role, whereas in Korea – where levels of part-time work are low – grandparents are more likely to undertake an intensive role and may be sharing what is a more demanding overall physical care task load more equally.

The distribution of the other three forms of care – accompanying, talking and minding – was more equal by gender. Except for Australia, grandfathers did roughly equal to or more than grandmothers when it came to accompanying grandchildren; for example, taking grandchildren to childcare. In Italy and France, grandfathers did considerably more of the accompanying care than grandmothers. This diverges from the patterns we see in the distribution of tasks among parents, where mothers tended to do a greater proportion of the accompanying than fathers (Craig, 2006b; Craig and Jenkins, 2016). This may be a result of grandfathers' greater availability for transporting children in the mornings and afternoons once they are no longer working or working more flexibly.

However, while French grandfathers in the sample have the lowest workforce participation (see Table 8.1), the grandfathers in the Italian sample (who are younger on average than the grandfathers in the other three countries) report the highest levels of full-time employment – and simultaneously, much higher levels of accompanying. This suggests factors other than time availability may be at play, but the small sample size makes it difficult to draw conclusions. Nonetheless, the increased participation of grandfathers in accompanying may contribute to narrower gender gaps in the distribution of care tasks among grandparents than among parents.

In all countries except Australia, grandfathers and grandmothers share talk-based tasks such as playing, reading and teaching close to equally. Minding is shared fairly equally between genders in Italy and Korea, but in Australia and France grandmothers do more minding than grandfathers. It is possible that in Australia and France, which have higher rates of part-time work, more of the care that grandmothers do is secondary care while their daughters or daughters-in-law are present or absent for short periods, so minding makes up a greater proportion of their overall care time.

It appears that in Italy and Korea – the two countries in which low rates of part-time work and poor access to childcare are likely to see grandparents play what Glaser et al. (2013) describe as a more 'intensive role' – grandparents are undertaking more routine care (physical and accompanying) as a proportion of their overall childcare. They are also undertaking more physical care as a proportion of their own overall childcare compared with grandparents in France, where a strong public childcare system means grandparents are more likely to provide what Glaser et al. (2013) describe as 'occasional' childcare, and Australia, where grandparents play what Glaser et al. (2013) would describe as a 'middling role', with moderate levels of participation in both intensive and occasional childcare.

But while in some countries grandparents in general spend a higher proportion of their care in routine tasks, the way it is distributed between grandmothers and grandfathers varies and is shaped by a range of factors. For grandfathers in Italy, Korea and Australia, more of their childcare consists of time-flexible activities such as talking, reading, listening and play, whereas for grandmothers in these countries more of their time is spent doing routine tasks. In France, grandmothers spend a greater proportion of their care time doing physical care tasks than grandfathers. However, it is the only country in which grandfathers spend a higher proportion of their care time on overall routine tasks (physical and accompanying care combined) than grandmothers. Routine tasks are likely to be more demanding and time-constraining than supervising or playing (Craig, 2006b), so it is grandmothers in Italy, Korea and Australia whose caring tasks are more likely to affect their enjoyment of childcare and impact on their health and wellbeing, work, leisure and other commitments.

In conclusion, this study reveals the way in which gender differences in the distribution of childcare tasks persist across generations in different country contexts. Across all four countries, grandmothers do more physical care tasks than grandfathers, suggesting that even when less constrained by time spent at work, gender norms in the distribution of care tasks persist into grandparenthood. Existing research has found that a country's institutional context can shape the prevalence of grandparent childcare provision and how much care grandparents are providing (Glaser et al., 2013). This study suggests that a country's institutional context also has the potential to shape the *types* of childcare tasks that grandparents undertake, and the **reproduction of gendered patterns of childcare across generations**. In countries with policies or cultures that support mothers to combine work and care, such as Australia and France, grandmothers do less routine care as a proportion of their overall childcare. Where there is little support for mothers to combine work and care, and grandparents are likely to assume more 'intensive' (Glaser et al., 2013) childcare responsibilities, grandmothers are spending much more of their childcare time in routine care – especially physical care tasks. This suggests that the care tasks carried out by mothers and by grandmothers are intertwined, as the two generations manage employment and childcare in different institutional contexts.

References

Arber, S. and Timonen, V. (eds) (2012) *Contemporary grandparenting: Changing family relationships in global contexts*, Bristol: Policy Press.

Baxter, J. and Smart, D. (2011) 'Fathering in Australia among couple families with young children', Occasional Paper no. 37, Canberra: Department of Families, Housing, Community Services and Indigenous Affairs.

Chin, M., Lee, J., Lee, S., Son, S. and Sung, M. (2014) 'Family policy in South Korea: Development, implementation, and evaluation', in M. Robila (ed) *Handbook of family policies across the globe*, New York: Springer, pp 305–318.

Condon, J., Corkindale, C., Luszcz, M. and Gamble, E. (2013) 'The Australian first-time grandparents' study: Time spent with the grandchild and its predictors', *Australasian Journal on Ageing*, 32(1): 21–27.

Craig, L. (2006a) 'Children and the revolution: a time-diary analysis of the impact of motherhood on daily workload', *Journal of Sociology*, 42(2): 125–143.

Craig, L. (2006b) 'Does father care mean fathers share? A comparison of how mothers and fathers in intact families spend time with children', *Gender & Society*, 20(2): 259–281.

Craig, L. and Jenkins, B. (2016) 'The composition of parents' and grandparents' childcare time: Gender and generational patterns in activity, multitasking and co-presence', *Ageing and Society*, 36(4): 785–810.

Craig, L. and Mullan, K. (2009) 'The Policeman and the part-time sales assistant: Household labour supply, family time and subjective time pressure in Australia 1997–2006', *Journal of Comparative Family Studies*, 40(4): 545–560.

Craig, L. and Mullan, K. (2011) 'How mothers and fathers share childcare: A cross-national time-diary comparison', *American Sociological Review*, 76(6): 834–861.

Craig, L., Powell, A. and Smyth, C. (2014) 'Towards intensive parenting? Changes in the composition and determinants of mothers and fathers' time with children 1992–2006', *British Journal of Sociology*, 65(3): 555–579.

Del Boca, D. (2015) *Child care arrangements and labor supply*. IDB Working Paper Series no. IDB-WP-569, Washington DC: Inter-American Development Bank.

Emslie, C., Hunt, K. and O'Brien, R. (2004) 'Masculinities in older men: A qualitative study in the west of Scotland', *The Journal of Men's Studies*, 23(3): 207–225.

Esping-Andersen, E. (2002) 'Towards the good society once again', in G. Esping-Andersen, D. Gallie, A. Hemerijck and J. Myles (eds) *Why we need a new welfare state*, Oxford: Oxford University Press, pp 1–25.

Fisher, K. and Robinson, J. (2010) *Daily routines in 22 countries: Diary evidence of average daily time spent in thirty activities*. Oxford: Centre for Time Use Research, University of Oxford.

Gerhard, U., Knijn, T., and Weckwert, A. (2005) 'Women's particpation in European labour markets', in U. Gerhard, T. Knijn and A. Weckwert (eds) *Working mothers in Europe: A comparison of policies and practices*, Cheltenham: Edward Elgar, pp 122–143.

Ghysels, J. (2011) *The provision of informal childcare by European grandparents: Constraints versus selective preferences*, CSB Working Paper 11/08, Antwerp: Herman Deleeck Centre for Social Policy, University of Antwerp.

Glaser, K., Montserrat, E., Waginger, U., Price, D., Stuchbury, R. and Tinker, A. (2010) *Grandparenting in Europe*, London: Grandparents Plus.

Glaser, K., Price, D., Di Gessa, G., Montserrat, E. and Tinker, A. (2013) *Grandparenting in Europe: Family policy and grandparents' role in providing child care*. London: Grandparent Plus.

Goodfellow, J. and Laverty, J. (2003) *Grandcaring: Insights into grandparents' experiences as regular child care providers*, Sydney: University of Western Sydney.

Gray, M., Baxter, J. and Alexander, M. (2008) 'Parent-only care: a child care choice for working couple families?', *Family Matters*, 79: 42–49.

Hamilton, M. and Jenkins, B. (2015) *Grandparent childcare and labour market participation in Australia*, SPRC Report 14/2015, Melbourne: National Seniors Australia.

Herlofson, K., and Hagestad, G. (2012) 'Transformations in the role of grandparents across welfare states', in S. Arber and V. Timonen (eds) *Contemporary grandparenting: Changing family relationships in global contexts edited*, Bristol: Policy Press, pp 27–49.

Hook, J. and Wolfe, C. (2012) 'New fathers? Residential fathers' time with children in four countries', *Journal of Family Issues*, 33(4): 415–450.

Kwon, H.-J. (2005) *Transforming the developmental welfare states in East Asia*, New York: Palgrave Macmillan.

Lee, J. and Bauer, J. (2010) 'Profiles of grandmothers providing child care to their grandchildren in South Korea', *Journal of Comparative Family Studies*, 41(3): 455–475

Martinengo, G., Jacob, J. and Hill, J. (2010) 'Gender and the work–family interface: Exploring differences across the family life course', *Journal of Family Issues* 31(10): 1363–1390.

Ochiai, E. (2009) 'Care diamonds and welfare regimes in East and South-East Asian societies: Bridging family and welfare sociology', *International Journal of Japanese Sociology*, 18(1): 60–78.

Ochiltree, G. (2006) *The changing role of grandparents*. Australian Family Relationships Clearinghouse briefing no. 2., Melbourne: Australian Institute of Family Studies.

OECD (2015) 'Ageing and employment policies'. Available at: http://www.oecd.org/employment/ageingandemploymentpolicies.htm.

Pfau-Effinger, B. (2005) 'Welfare state policies and the development of care arrangements', *European Societies*, 7(2): 321–347.

Roland Berger Strategy Consultants GmbH and ergo Unternehmenskommunikation GmbH & Co. KG (2013a) *The current situation of gender equality in Italy: Country profile*. Report prepared for the European Commission, Directorate-General Justice, Unit D2 (Gender Equality). Available at: http://ec.europa.eu/justice/gender-equality/files/epo_campaign/131203_country_profile_italy.pdf.

Roland Berger Strategy Consultants GmbH and ergo Unternehmenskommunikation GmbH & Co. KG (2013b) *The current situation of gender equality in France: Country profile*. Report prepared for the European Commission, Directorate-General Justice, Unit D2 (Gender Equality). Available at: http://ec.europa.eu/justice/gender-equality/files/epo_campaign/131203_country-profile_france.pdf.

Tarrant, A. (2012) 'Grandfathering: The construction of new identities and masculinities', in S. Arber and V. Timonen (eds) *Contemporary grandparenting: Changing family relationships in global contexts*, Bristol: Policy Press, pp 181 –201.

Timonen, V. and Arber, S. (2012) 'Introduction: A new look at grandparenting', in S. Arber and V. Timonen (eds) *Contemporary Grandparenting: Changing family relationships in global contexts*, Bristol: Policy Press, pp 1–27.

NINE

Class-based grandfathering practices in Finland

Hanna Ojala and Ilkka Pietilä

Introduction

For decades, a great deal of research on grandparenting has focused on grandmothers. They have been thought of – either explicitly or implicitly – as the principal grandparents, whereas grandfathers have been largely seen as 'peripheral figures' in the lives of grandchildren and family life in general (Mann, 2007, pp 281–2). Recently, there has emerged a burgeoning interest in grandfathering in contemporary family research. Population ageing increases the time span for grandparenthood, which today can last several decades. Therefore, grandparenting has become a much more common practice for older men, too.

Recent qualitative research (for example, Mann et al., 2016; Mann and Leeson, 2010; Roberto et al., 2001; Sorensen and Cooper, 2010; Tarrant, 2012, 2013) on grandfathers' own perspectives has aimed to depart from the image of grandfathers as distant heads of family, assistants to grandmothers and entertainers rather than caregivers – ideas that were prominent in earlier research. This shift towards viewing grandfathers as active, independent and gendered actors instead of mere auxiliaries to grandmothers has also underlined the importance of studying heterogeneity among grandfathers and the intersecting factors behind it. Grandfatherhood and men's grandparenting practices are shaped by both intergenerational relations and processes related to class, place, age, generation, grandchildren's age and marital status, among other factors. Furthermore, societal structures such as welfare state systems and how society supports families (especially women through provision or financing of childcare) impact on expectations regarding grandparenthood and grandparenting practices, and thus on cultural norms.

In this chapter, our focus is on class-based features of grandfathering in the context of a Nordic welfare state. Based on face-to-face,

171

open-ended interviews with 17 Finnish working- and middle-class grandfathers aged 50 years and over, we explore how these men talk about their relationships with their grandchildren, their grandfathering practices and grandfatherhood, and how these descriptions are structured by class cultures and models of class-based masculinities.

Contemporary dynamics of grandfathering

Grandfatherhood has been considered to include paradoxical features (Davidson et al., 2003, pp 178–9). On the one hand, grandfatherhood is an opportunity for men to form new and close relationships with children in the family. Especially grandsons are thought to provide men with an access to emotionality, and to create closeness that men rarely experienced with their own children as fathers due to working long hours (Davidson et al., 2003, p 179; Sorensen and Cooper, 2010, p 132). Thus, becoming a grandfather potentially allows men to adopt more nurturing, softer masculine identities and, as Tarrant (2013, p 205) states, grandfatherhood therefore has a transformative potential in producing multiplicity in masculinities. Grandchildren can also be seen to offer an opportunity for men to be active and fit and to get out of the house (Tarrant, 2014, p 247); thus, grandfathering enables an arena for active and successful ageing (Mann et al., 2016, p 606).

On the other hand, grandfatherhood – and especially grandfathering practices concerning intimate care work (such as nappy changing) – has been seen to be in potential conflict with traditional masculinities (Tarrant, 2012). A nurturing grandfatherhood has therefore been called 'alternative' (Mann, 2007) or 'nonhegemonic' (Bartholomaeus and Tarrant, 2015), and has led researchers to explore how men renegotiate these new family opportunities in relation to their masculine identities (Mann et al., 2016). This line of thinking has also contributed to interpretations that grandfathers' emphasis on outdoor activities and fun-seeking with their grandchildren relates to reaffirmation or reproduction of traditional masculinities (Tarrant, 2014, p 246), which reinforces traditional views of active grandfatherhood as a threat to the truly masculine self. Tarrant (2013, p 201; 2014, p 247) also found that, for some men, becoming a grandfather was deemed a marker of old age and therefore not a straightforwardly positive life event.

Research on grandfatherhood has, to a large extent, approached the early stages of becoming a grandfather and focused on activities that grandfathers engage in with relatively small grandchildren. There has been a special interest in whether grandfathers engage in nurturing small grandchildren or in more traditional instrumental tasks (such as accompanying grandchildren to appointments, playing together, educating and taking them out to do various activities). Part of this increasing interest in grandfathering practices with small children relates to changes in younger men's roles in parenting, which have evolved towards more active and participative fatherhood and, in turn, gradually changed expectations of grandfatherhood. Mann and Leeson (2010, p 238) conceptualise this as 'a new grandfatherhood', by which they refer to equal sharing of the practical and emotional work associated with family life with grandchildren, as well as the emergence of 'new' norms of grandfatherhood that accentuate nurturing and mentoring (Mann, 2007, p 289). Previous research thus highlights that cultural conceptions and norms of masculinity and gendered division of work are the key constituents of the social imaginary of grandfatherhood.

Intergenerational relations – that is, father(-in-law)–son/daughter(-in-law) – play an important role in the construction of grandparenthood. These relations may change; for instance, due to divorce (Timonen and Doyle, 2012). Geographical proximity or distance may also affect intergenerational relations and men's opportunities to perform their grandfatherhood. Although it would be easy to assume geographical distance weakens intergenerational relations, empirical studies have also reported contradictory findings. Roberto and co-authors (2001, pp 422–3) found that despite geographical distance and infrequent contact with grandchildren, grandfathers saw relationships as positive and meaningful. Sorensen and Cooper's (2010, p 128) study also showed that distance alone did not interfere intergenerational contact, and vice versa: close proximity did not automatically mean active involvement.

Mann (2007, p 284) argues that grandfathering practices also depend on the extent to which grandparents want to maintain independence in later life. However, willingness to stay independent is not only an individual choice but also depends on structural factors, such as class. In their Irish study, McGarrigle and colleagues (2018) found that, in the higher socioeconomic groups, grandparents were more strongly oriented to their own leisure time activities and grandchild care was construed as a choice that had to fit in with other priorities. Gauthier (2002, p 303) calls these sorts of grandparents the 'specialists'. They have less frequent contact with grandchildren and have a more limited and specific role, such as facilitating their grandchildren's participation in school and leisure activities. The 'educational subcontractors', which are found mainly among the working-to-middle classes, tend to act as part-time 'replacement parents'. They often live nearby and their activities are centred on the domestic sphere (Gauthier, 2002, pp 300–2). As McGarrigle and colleagues (2018) show, the lower socioeconomic groups have less scope to refuse intensive grandchild care because of structural pressures. This is because grandparental childcare is mostly needed to allow (lone) mothers' participation in the labour market; due to the mothers' weaker economic position, they would struggle to pay for childcare.

Variations in welfare state arrangements, particularly public investments in childcare, mean that the frequency and intensity of support needed from grandparents vary. Based on a survey carried out in 11 European countries, Igel and Szydlik (2011, p 221) argue that strong welfare state arrangements motivate grandparents to offer their time to younger family generations and to take care of sporadic tasks. In a Scandinavian survey, 60% of respondents reported taking care of grandchildren 'regularly' or 'occasionally', compared to continental and Southern Europe where less than 50% stated they were engaged in grandchild care (Herlofson and Hagestad, 2012). Both Herlofson and Hagestad (2012) and Igel and Szydlik (2011) attribute this difference to the role of public institutions that provide time-consuming and intensive childcare.

For instance, in Finland (one of the Nordic welfare states) the state offers paid maternity, paternity and parental leave and a child homecare allowance (for parents of children under the age of three). There is also universal and subsidised public day care available for children under primary school age. Thus, the Nordic welfare state provides a wide range of social services, which on the one hand generate jobs for (predominantly) women and on the other facilitate women's employment by relieving them of the responsibility for family care (Esping-Andersen, 1990). Women's participation in paid work is thus not dependent on childcare provided by grandparents. Therefore, the Nordic welfare state has been called 'woman-friendly' (Borchorst and Siim, 2002). Moreover, we can also see it as 'third age friendly' because it supports grandparents' chances to choose the level of intensity of their participation in grandchildren's lives (Herlofson and Hagestad, 2012). As a result, a larger proportion of Nordic grandparents are involved, but in a less intensive way than their Southern European counterparts.

Based on taxation and free public education (following the 'one school for all' ideology), among other mechanisms, the Nordic welfare states have also reduced income differences and balanced the class structure and class transmission in society (Anttonen, 2002). Compared to Anglo-American liberal or Southern European conservative welfare state systems, there are no clearly visible class differences in grandparents' participation in childcare in Finland. In the first place, in Finnish culture (unlike, for instance, British culture: see Devine et al., 2005; Skeggs, 2004), class is not a common shorthand concept for categorising people and there are no major public debates concerning class. People's neighbourhoods or clothing are not necessarily simple means of identifying persons of different classes. Nonetheless, people are certainly able to locate themselves in terms of their class position and their income inevitably has an effect on their lifestyles, such as hobbies and travelling. Class therefore shapes people's practices and values, and thus structures the ways in which men experience and interpret their grandfatherhood.

Materials and methods

This study is based on face-to-face open-ended interviews with 17 middle- and working-class Finnish grandfathers aged 50 and over. Social class is here imputed largely on the basis of occupation: ten of the interviewed men were metalworkers and seven were engineers. As a traditional, manual, industrial and male-dominated occupation, metalworkers represent vocationally educated working-class men. Engineers, in turn, are more highly educated (Master of Science and/or PhD) and work as professionals in the field of technology, and thus represent middle-class men. All men were Caucasian and heterosexual; six were employed and 11 retired; 11 were either married or co-habitants and one was divorced and single. Grandchildren were aged from newborn to young adults. Some men had also step-grandchildren as a result of remarriage or re-partnering. One man had great-grandchildren.

The data analysed is a part of a larger qualitative longitudinal study on men's ageing (MANage study). The overall topic of the original (in 2010 and 2011) and follow-up (in 2017) interviews was men's ageing and included several themes, ranging from family life, intergenerational relations and social relationships to health-related behaviours, psychosocial wellbeing, ageing employees' position in the labour market and finally retirement as a period of change in a man's life. An interview guide was used flexibly to allow for free discussion of topics that respondents themselves considered relevant. All interviews were digitally recorded with signed informed consent from the interviewees, transcribed verbatim by a professional transcription service and validated by the study investigators to ensure accurate and complete transcription. All names used in the data excerpts are pseudonyms.

Based on multiple readings of the transcripts, we used an open coding process to generate a comprehensive list of themes (for instance, descriptions of intergenerational relations, feelings pertaining to grandfatherhood and descriptions of activities with grandchildren) in the data. For the current analysis, we separately reread the coded data in the light of social class, focusing on men's descriptions of their grandfatherhood and how they spend time with their grandchildren. The analyses led us to note that class-based cultures matter in men's grandfathering practices and that grandchildren's age has a central effect on how the class difference appears. At the next stage of the analysis, we approached men's descriptions from a discursive perspective (see, for instance, Wetherell and Edley, 1999) with a focus on how class-based cultural knowledge and gendered ways of talking shape men's interpretations of grandfathering.

Classless but gendered pride: grandfathering with small children

In line with previous research (see Mann and Leeson, 2010; Tarrant, 2012), all our interviewees emphasised the joy and pride of being a grandfather, particularly when they thought about grandfatherhood on a general and somewhat abstract level. When they considered it from the perspective of everyday life and practices, their talk included different tones as well. Jarmo, a 58-year-old metalworker and grandfather of 1- and 5-year-old children, sounds happy and proud of becoming a grandfather – but his account involves more diverse tones when he talks about the changes grandfatherhood has brought about in his life. On the one hand, he emphasises his willingness to care for the child, even more than his own daughter. On the other hand, however, he describes his new tasks using expressions that could be taken to have negative connotations and to refer to some care tasks as somewhat unpleasant duties:

> INTERVIEWER: 'Well, what kind of a change was [becoming a grandfather] in your life, or did you think about it as a change?'
> JARMO: 'Well, it was certainly a change in the sense that … Especially now you almost every week have to be involved in those jobs with the grandchild. This is because the parents of the child work shifts, and

particularly [son-in-law], he works in [transportation company], in shifts. Like again on Thursday I must take the girl to the indoor ice rink. And as there's two children, then another, the younger one, is brought for grandma's care, of course, and then I take them [short laughter], the mother and the girl to do some skating. So [grandfatherhood] surely has given me these kinds of jobs. But it certainly also changes your way of thinking. Like she [granddaughter] is often a more important child than your own child. And unfortunately, sort of you take more care of her like than of your own [child]. I suppose it's because she's certainly not around every day and it's lucky that she isn't. Like they're anyway such energetic little creatures that a man of this age could hardly [bursts in laughter] run after her for several days!'

INTERVIEWER: 'Yeah. What are the other things you do sort of together with this 5-year-old, in addition to skating?'

JARMO: 'It's certainly ... well ... I can't really say like what it is that we really do. It's like she is there and we take care of her, and it's such sort of everyday stuff.'

The excerpt above features typical examples of men's descriptions of their everyday grandfathering practices. First, it highlights the taken-for-granted nature of the gendered division of care work with the younger grandchildren. Second, men often found it difficult to explicitly describe how they spent time with their younger grandchildren; most of them emphasised the frequency rather than content of time spent with grandchildren. Third, in many interviewees' accounts, joy and pride of being a grandfather was accompanied with notions of increased number of tasks related to grandchildren, and thus to some extent feelings of lost freedom.

The gendered division of care work with small grandchildren also meant that grandparents whose grandchildren lived nearby, in particular, spent time with grandchildren separately from each other. For example, 66-year-old engineer Mauri's wife retired earlier than him, and has created her own routine for care work with small grandchildren while Mauri has continued working. As Mauri's wife normally goes to her grandchildren's home to look after them, Mauri's contact with his grandchildren is sometimes limited to short meetings when he picks up his wife to bring her back home. It is worth noting, however, that Mauri does not find this kind of a division of work in any way problematic.

In our interviews, the gendered characteristics of care work with young grandchildren appeared similarly among both the metalworkers and the engineers. The gendered division of grandparenting practices was agreed on throughout our sample (see also Mann and Leeson, 2010) independently of interviewees' age and class. Grandmothers were seen as the primary carers of small grandchildren. In describing their grandparenting practices with school-aged grandchildren, men still underlined the primary role of the grandmother as the coordinator of grandparenting activities – grandmothers kept in contact with grandchildren, agreed on schedules, divided the tasks, remembered the grandchildren's birthdays and bought the gifts. Therefore, if grandfathering practices are seen from the perspective of care work with small children, the grandfathers indeed seem to play an auxiliary role in childcare. This underlines James Bates' (2009, p 336) notion that there is a weak and undefined societal expectation for grandfathers to be involved in the care of grandchildren compared to grandmothers. However, the older the grandchildren grew, the more grandfathers participated in daily activities and were able to describe these activities in detail.

Class-based functions of grandfathering

Particularly those grandfathers whose grandchildren lived in the same town described their relationships with school-aged grandchildren in terms of habitual everyday practices that included, among others, taking the children to their hobbies and spending afternoons after kindergarten or school with them. Similarly to grandfathers in the study by Mann and co-authors (2016), our interviewees wanted to "step in", "be there" and even be "far more involved". However, in contrast to Mann et al. (2016), both metalworkers and engineers in our study largely described their grandparenting in terms of support for their *own* children and did not so much emphasise their willingness to spend time with their grandchildren. One often-described practice was grandchildren going from school and kindergarten to their grandparents' home and spending the afternoon there. This shortened the time the children spent alone or outside their home but also helped the parents' everyday lives by decreasing their pressures to pick up the children from kindergarten on time and go directly home from work. When children got ill, grandparents often took over childcare while parents were at work. In this sense they acted in accordance with the role of 'family savers' (Herlofson and Hagestad, 2012) – in keeping with the Nordic childcare model, where grandparents are needed to enable normal family routines (especially parental employment) in 'emergencies', such as sickness, that the public childcare and school system do not cater for.

Summer holidays represented a similar opportunity for grandparents to help their children balance the requirements regarding work and family issues. Parents with regular full-time jobs have substantially shorter vacations than schoolchildren (around four weeks' vacation compared to two-and-a-half months' summer holidays from school in Finland), and grandparents played an important role in filling the care gaps during the summer. This had a particularly important meaning for grandparents who were more geographically distant from their grandchildren, who had a chance to spend longer periods with their grandchildren; for instance, at a summer cottage. Some of our interviewees also said that, by taking care of their grandchildren, they wanted to provide their own children with additional free time for their hobbies and relationships. Again, this explicit statement of 'service' for their adult children can be traced back to the firmly established dual-breadwinner model in Finland. This model would have been the majority experience among grandparents, too, as Finnish women's labour market participation rates have been high since the Second World War. Thus, there is perhaps the kind of awareness of pressures faced by dual-earner families that is not present among older generations in many other European countries, where women's labour market rates have historically been much lower.

Although our interviewees generally described their grandparenting in very similar ways, there were certain notable differences between the engineers and the metalworkers. These differences related to which kinds of demands their adult children's work set for grandparental childcare. Although some metalworkers' children had difficulties arranging childcare due to shift work, most often their work was clearly tied up with certain local places. The engineers' children more often had various expert positions in large companies, which required travelling, and the work did not only take place in an office or other particular physical work environment. These grandfathers were aware of the requirements that work set for their children and saw their role in supporting their children's families by offering their time resources. Hannes (a 66-year-old retired engineer) describes grandparenting with reference to his daughter's and her husband's strenuous work:

> '[Taking care of] grandchildren takes a lot of time, 'cause
> I have always driven them a lot. And my daughter's family
> lives close to us. Today, young people are anyway, those

in their forties, they both work in companies. And they are very strained. So in a way that's it, like [helping them makes] you feel useful. ... Like parents are bloody strained with their work. When another travels abroad and another is strained with work, so then it's like our [grandparents'] role to be involved.'

Hannes describes his grandparenting as a response to tightening pressures that his daughters' generation experiences in work. It is therefore worth noting that, although Hannes mentions practical reasons for childcare, there is simultaneously an emotional level in his talk. He refers several times to how his grandchildren's parents are 'strained' with work, thereby suggesting that grandparenting in his case is not only about practical issues related to time schedules but also a matter of emotional support for adult children. Ilmari, a 68-year-old engineer, talks about his grandfathering in a similar vein:

'[The grandchild] is on the third grade. ... He goes to [name of school] which is half a kilometre from us. Like one morning he came to our place before he went to school at nine o'clock, and then came back again after school. And then we go through, do the homework. It's because the father, he works for [large global information and communication technologies (ICT) company]. And sort of, his work is such that as they operate around the globe so in the evenings there are often various teleconferences so that ... And our daughter works in a pharmacy now as a pharmacist. So we in a way help them.'

Ilmari's account highlights that, in middle-class jobs, work is typically not restricted to office hours. In addition, travelling and global business require employees to readily adapt their everyday lives to schedules in different time zones and be available around the clock. Because public childcare services are not available for these families outside normal office hours, in middle-class families, grandparenting practices are often structured by the ways in which global business operates.

Class-based lives and practices with grown-up grandchildren

Asko, a 65-year-old metalworker, has spent a lot of time with his six grandchildren (who all live close to him), particularly since he retired. One of his traditions was to organise 'summer Olympics' for his grandchildren, where all of them had a chance to participate and win an 'Olympic' medal. When re-interviewed in 2017, Asko (then 72 years old) points out that nowadays the oldest grandchildren are adults; he says one of his grandsons, who is going into military service, would hardly get a day off from the army to take part in his grandfather's Olympics. Therefore, Asko concludes that grandparents need to adapt joint activities to grandchildren's age. Alongside grandchildren's age, Asko also notes that ICT changes the ways in which grandparents can communicate with their grandchildren:

> ASKO: 'Nowadays it's like, they have mobiles and computers. The wife has a computer, so one of them [grandchild] plays with that while another uses a mobile. And that's how they spend time.'
> INTERVIEWER: 'Yeah, so it's like if you want to have a chat with them, you need to deliberately...'
> ASKO: 'Yes, but they surely [obey you] when you say that now it's time for a small break. I've cooked for them, and they have taken part in that. [I have told them that] come on and learn some skills so that you won't be totally helpless when you live alone, and the youngsters don't even know how to cook. And then we have cooked together. I've given them tasks and watched that from aside. They certainly make the salads and roast the steaks, no problem. We have done this together.'

Men's grandparenting, particularly with school-aged or older grandchildren, typically revolves around concrete doing, such as fishing or sports. In addition to this, Asko's story of how he cooks with his grandchildren includes an aspect featured by many of our working-class interviewees: teaching practical skills to the next generation, most often with particular attention being paid to educating grandsons. Many metalworkers described interaction of generations in the contexts of manual work requiring specific knowledge and skills, such as car repairs and small-scale construction works. In an earlier interview (2010), Asko told the interviewer about the construction work he had been doing with his cousins and their families, and proudly concluded that the older participants still have important knowledge and skills they can teach to younger generations. In the same manner, in the previous excerpt Asko notes that as a grandfather he can help his grandchildren to learn cooking skills, which are vital for independent adult life.

Engineers had similar stories of delivering skills and knowledge – particularly to their children, but sometimes also to their grandchildren. This delivery of skills and knowledge had certain class-based characteristics. Some of the engineers had given their children career tips and 'coached' them at an early stage of their careers. Sometimes this kind of assistance took different forms and extended to cover not only children but also grandchildren. In his earlier interview (2011), Ilmari told the interviewer about a group of families he and his wife have had as friends for many years. These friends are mostly Ilmari's previous colleagues:

> 'Then we have these, based on work connections we have had a certain bunch of people with whom we have, let's say for more than 30 years we have regularly been in touch, like with their families. And now the children and grandchildren, some children have sort of already mutually networked, and partly grandchildren too. So like it continues, this networking, already in the third generation.'

Our interviewees' stories about their adult grandchildren represented features that pointed to not only personal continuity between the generations but also reproduction of class-based values, skills and lifestyles. 'Networking' among professionals can be seen as one such practice. As many of the engineers' children worked in the fields of technology and business, this kind of networking can be seen as a practice that increases younger generations' social capital and provides them with important contacts for their future occupational life. A notable feature of networking is that it does not include any particularly gendered aspects. In comparison, the metalworkers' grandfathering practices often included clearly gendered features, including the delivery of not only skills and knowledge but also values, ideals and lifestyles, mostly related to physical work. A recurrent context in these descriptions was the summer cottage (many Finns have a second home in the countryside, often quite modest and perhaps lacking in some modern conveniences), where male generations cooperated in undertaking physical labour, such as logging or chopping firewood.

Antti, a 70-year-old retired metalworker, was interviewed first in 2010. At the time, one of his sons had five sons; these grandsons (aged 20–30) assisted Antti and his wife in many physical tasks, particularly at their summer cottage. As Antti started to have physical limitations, his grandsons offered him a substantial work reserve and Antti proudly took the position of an instructor allocating tasks for the next generations of men. On a personal level, this gave Antti a chance to maintain a respected masculine position in the family despite his weakening physical ability. From the perspective of generations, the practice of joint physical work in a place where generations gather can also be seen as a reproduction of working-class masculinity, whereby older generations act as examples of masculine working-class respectability (Skeggs, 2004). When interviewed again in 2017, Antti was 77 years old and had five great-grandchildren. He still occasionally spends 'a few days' at his son's house in a rural area and helps the son with logging and similar tasks. As his grandsons also gather there to help their father, Antti's son's house is a site where three, or even four, generations of men collectively engage in physical work.

Masculine working-class cultures are strongly tied to local communities (McDowell, 2003). In our sample of interviewees, metalworkers' children and their families most often lived relatively close to grandfathers. Among engineers there was substantially more variation; some of the engineers' children and grandchildren lived in the same neighbourhood while others lived in other towns, other countries or even other continents. As discussed, the engineers' children often had middle-class jobs that involved travelling. All this means that, although grandparents tried to support their children with childcare, some did not necessarily have a chance spend leisure time and vacations with their children's families. Hannes, who referred to his daughter's and her husband's 'strenuous work' earlier, says he has to take care of all manual labour at the summer cottage alone because his children and son-in-law are so busy. When the interviewer suggests it might be easier to get some help from them in the summer, Hannes responds that they are always busy, even during vacations. Lack of support in manual work makes Hannes feels sad about the future of his summer cottage, a place that has a profound meaning for him:

> 'If I think about my son and my son-in-law, they are capable but they are so loaded with work. And then grandchildren, they have their own lives. So these jobs I now do, they will all be gone. Someone will take care of them, maybe, in a different way, or just won't bother to do them.'

The 'strenuous work' of middle-class children may require active support in childcare from grandparents. Ironically, a busy lifestyle – both in work and outside – is a barrier to reciprocity between generations. Hannes does not only feel sorry for the heavy jobs that will not get done after he is not able to do them; he also feels sad about a rupture in the chain of generations, as in his case the younger generations do not seem to share the same joy Hannes feels about the heavy manual work at the summer cottage. Therefore, he does not see continuity of his generation-based lifestyle in the future.

Discussion and conclusions

Roberto and colleagues (2001, p 423) point out that intergenerational relations and family practices are continually reshaped throughout the life course. Our study shows that grandchildren's age plays an important role in men's description of their grandfathering practices. For example, men's accounts of grandmothers having the primary responsibility for care mainly relate to the context of caring for small children. Men's independent role in their grandchildren's lives increases when the children grow older. Further research on men's grandfathering experiences and practices should therefore take note of the temporal context in which grandfathering practices take place.

Our study also shows that class differences in grandfathering practices are similarly dependent on grandchildren's age. Practices with young grandchildren are based on their needs for basic care, independently of (grand)parents' class position. When grandchildren grow older, the class-based cultural differences become more visible in what grandfathers do with their grandchildren, so that working-class grandfathers tend to provide their grandchildren with practical skills (such as cooking, hunting or car repairs) whereas middle-class grandfathers are inclined to focus on increasing their grandchildren's social capital (for instance, through supporting their schoolwork and networking).

Although our analysis is based on a small sample, the class-based grandfathering practices appear to be systematic. Among working-class men, these practices revolve around raising grandchildren in collaboration with their own sons and in the context of relatively tight family connections, where the geographical distance between generations is often small. Logging wood and other forms of physical labour are typically conducted as joint projects of three or even four generations of men. An essential feature of working-class grandfathering is therefore raising children together with the middle generation, with a special emphasis on creating continuity between men's generations (grandfather–son–grandson). Middle-class men's grandfathering practices are based on their purpose of supporting and promoting their own children's careers by taking responsibility for care work with grandchildren. A grandparenting practice that May and co-authors (2012) call 'being there but not interfering' thus seems be a particularly middle-class feature in our sample.

In this chapter, we have focused on how men do their grandparenting. It could be claimed that there are indeed certain gendered ways of doing grandfathering, which focus on playing, sports and leaving 'dirty' care work for grandmothers. Class nevertheless has major effects on how grandfathers spend their time with grandchildren. It is worth keeping in mind that our results are shaped by certain national characteristics that have their roots in history. In Finland, urbanisation took place relatively late (in the 1960s–70s); people's connection to rural places and lifestyles (mainly via summer cottages) is therefore strong, especially among the older generations. This is a plausible reason why men often describe their activities with grandchildren in terms of physical work, and highlights the intersectionality of masculinity, where class, generation and national histories and cultures shape the values, motives and purposes that men have regarding their grandfathering.

Our small-scale qualitative study yields further insight into concepts developed in earlier studies regarding the welfare state and grandparenthood (see Herlofson and Hagestad, 2012; Igel and Szydlik, 2011). In the context of the Nordic welfare state, grandparents are a backup resource or 'family savers'. Depending on grandparents' standpoint, the Nordic welfare state's universal day-care access either lowers the threshold for grandparents' participation in caring for their grandchildren, by making it easier to use the time resources for care in the afternoons and taking care of their hobbies, or limits grandparents' involvement to short-term occasions.

However, our study also shows that the Nordic welfare state is not flexible enough to meet the needs of many middle-class families, whose work demands are set by global enterprises. Day-care services only cover normal office hours, and therefore middle generations working in multi-sited global businesses need help from grandparents. In this sense, the notion from Anglo-American research that points to grandparents' important role in rendering possible working-class (or low-waged) women's paid work does not fully apply to Nordic welfare states. Rather, it could be claimed that it is the welfare state that facilitates Finnish working-class women's paid labour (through heavily subsidised childcare), whereas grandparents' support is most needed for middle-class mothers and fathers in dual-earner households with heavy employment-related pressures.

References

Anttonen, A. (2002) 'Universalism and social policy. A Nordic–feminist revaluation', *NORA: Nordic Journal of Feminist and Gender Research*, 10(2): 71–80.

Bartholomaeus, C. and Tarrant, A. (2015) 'Masculinities at the margins of "middle adulthood": What a consideration of young age and old age offers masculinities theorizing', *Men and Masculinities*, 19(4): 1–19.

Bates, J.S. (2009) 'Generative grandfathering: A conceptual framework for nurturing grandchildren', *Marriage and Family Review*, 45(4): 331–352.

Borchorst, A. and Siim, B. (2002) 'The women-friendly welfare state revisited', *NORA: Nordic Journal of Feminist and Gender Research*, 10(2): 90–98.

Davidson, K., Daly, T. and Arber, S. (2003) 'Exploring the social worlds of older men', in S. Arber, K. Davidson and J. Ginn (eds) *Gender and ageing: Changing roles and relationships*, Maidenhead: Open University Press, pp 168–185.

Devine, F., Savage, M., Scott, J. and Crompton, R. (eds) (2005) *Rethinking class: Culture, identities and lifestyles*, Basingstoke: Palgrave MacMillan.

Esping-Andersen, G. (1990) *The three worlds of welfare capitalism*, Cambridge: Polity Press.

Gauthier, A. (2002) 'The role of grandparents', *Current Sociology*, 50(2): 295–307.

Herlofson, K. and Hagestad, G.O. (2012) 'Transformations in the role of grandparents across welfare states', in S. Arber and V. Timonen (eds) *Contemporary grandparenting: Changing family relationships in global contexts*, Bristol: Policy Press, pp 27–49.

Igel, C. and Szydlik, M. (2011) 'Grandchild care and welfare state arrangements in Europe', *Journal of European Social Policy*, 21(3): 210–224.

Mann, R. (2007) 'Out of the shadows? Grandfatherhood, age and masculinities', *Journal of Aging Studies*, 21(4): 281–291.

Mann, R. and Leeson, G. (2010) 'Grandfathers in contemporary families in Britain. Evidence from qualitative research', *Journal of Intergenerational Relationships*, 8(3): 234–248.

Mann, R., Tarrant, A. and Leeson, G.W. (2016) 'Grandfatherhood: Shifting masculinities in later life', *Sociology*, 50(3): 594–610.

May, V., Mason, J. and Clarke, L. (2012) 'Being there yet not interfering: The paradoxes of grandparenting', in S. Arber and V. Timonen (eds) *Contemporary grandparenting: Changing family relationships in global contexts*, Bristol: Policy Press, pp 139–158.

McDowell, L. (2003) *Redundant masculinities? Employment change and white working class youth*, Malden: Blackwell.

McGarrigle, C.A., Timonen, V. and Layte, R. (2018) 'Choice and constraint in the negotiation of the grandparent role: A mixed-methods study', *Gerontology and Geriatric Medicine*, DOI: 10.1177/2333721417750944.

Roberto, K.A., Allen, K.R. and Blieszner, R. (2001) 'Grandfathers' perceptions and expectations of relationships with their adult grandchildren', *Journal of Family Issues*, 22(4): 407–426.

Skeggs, B. (2004) *Class, self, culture*, London: Routledge.

Sorensen, P. and Cooper, N.J. (2010) 'Reshaping the family man: A grounded theory study of the meaning of grandfatherhood', *The Journal of Men's Studies*, 18(2): 117–136.

Tarrant, A. (2012) 'Grandfathering: The construction of new identities and masculinities', in S. Arber and V. Timonen (eds) *Contemporary grandparenting: Changing family relationships in global contexts*, Bristol: Policy Press, pp 181–201.

Tarrant, A. (2013) 'Grandfathering as spatio-temporal practice: Conceptualizing performances of ageing masculinities in contemporary familial carescapes', *Social and Cultural Geography*, 14(2): 192–210.

Tarrant, A. (2014) 'Domestic ageing masculinities and grandfathering', in A. Gorman-Murray and P. Hopkins (eds) *Masculinities and Place*, Farnham: Ashgate, pp 241–254.

Timonen, V. and Doyle, M. (2012) 'Grandparental agency after adult children's divorce', in S. Arber and V. Timonen (eds) *Contemporary grandparenting: Changing family relationships in global contexts*, Bristol: Policy Press, pp 159–180.

Wetherell, M. and Edley, N. (1999) 'Negotiating hegemonic masculinity: Imaginary positions and psycho-discursive practices', *Feminism and Psychology*, 9(3): 335–356.

TEN

Grandfamilies in the United States: an intersectional analysis

Megan L. Dolbin-MacNab and April L. Few-Demo

Historically, grandparents have served as important sources of instrumental and emotional support to their children and grandchildren (Uhlenberg and Cheuk, 2010). The nature and extent of the support provided by grandparents to younger generations varies widely across global contexts and is influenced by sociopolitical forces, including economic opportunities, immigration, urban migration, disease epidemics and armed conflicts, as well as cultural traditions of grandparent involvement (Dolbin-MacNab and Yancura, 2018). Specific family circumstances such as intergenerational solidarity and family crises are also relevant to understanding grandparents' involvement in their families (Dolbin-MacNab and Yancura, 2018). Serving as a surrogate parent to one's grandchildren reflects one of the most intensive degrees of grandparent involvement in family life. In this chapter, these grandparents will be referred to as **grandparents raising grandchildren**, and their families as **grandfamilies**.

In the United States, approximately 2.6 million grandparents are raising 2.5 million or 3% of all children (Annie E. Casey Foundation Kids Count Data Center, 2016; Ellis and Simmons, 2014). Approximately one third of these grandparents are living in **skipped generation** households, meaning they are raising their grandchildren in a home without the grandchild's parents (Ellis and Simmons, 2014). While the remaining grandparents may co-reside with one or both of the grandchildren's parents, typically the grandchild's mother, these grandparents are often functioning as parental figures and supporting their grandchildren financially (Baker and Mutchler, 2010). Raising grandchildren is often a long-term caregiving arrangement: 39% of grandparents have raised their grandchildren for at least five years (Ellis and Simmons, 2014). Finally, United States grandparents raise their grandchildren both formally and informally; grandparents raising grandchildren formally do so within the context of the child welfare system or have established a legal relationship, such as custody, guardianship or adoption, with their grandchildren (Generations United, 2016). The vast majority of grandparents in the United States, however, are raising their grandchildren informally; there are 26 children in informal caregiving arrangements for every one child living in a formal arrangement (Generations United, 2015). These informal caregiving arrangements create barriers to grandparents' ability to access support services through the government, enrol their grandchildren in school and/or obtain medical care (Generations United, 2015).

Discussions of factors contributing to the formation of grandfamilies in the United States primarily focus on parental difficulties and stressful family events that prevent parents from adequately caring for their children. These include parental abuse and neglect, substance abuse, physical or mental illness, incarceration, adolescent pregnancy, death, deportation and military deployment (Hayslip and Kaminski, 2005). Of these contributing factors, parental substance abuse has historically been noted as being one of the most significant. In the 1980s and 1990s, attention centred on the impact of the crack cocaine epidemic, while more recent discussions have focused on the detrimental effects of the opioid epidemic (Generations United, 2016; Minkler and Roe, 1993). Grandparents also form multigenerational households and/or assume responsibility for their grandchildren to cope with economic distress (for example, parental unemployment: Livingston and Parker, 2010). Cultural traditions of familism and grandparent involvement in the care of younger generations – even in the absence of parental difficulties (Goodman and Silverstein, 2002) – and federal and state child welfare policies that encourage the placement of children with relatives (42 USC § 671(a)(19); Social Security Administration, 2017) further contribute to grandparents raising their grandchildren. In considering the multitude of factors that contribute to the development of grandfamilies, it should be noted that these factors tend to overlap, accumulate and intersect in complex ways.

Data from the 2010 United States Census and the 2012 American Community Survey reveal that grandparents raising grandchildren in the United States are a diverse population. That said, these grandparents are disproportionately more likely to be women, living in poverty, single, younger and less educated than grandparents who do not live their grandchildren (Ellis and Simmons, 2014). Minority ethnic groups are also more likely to be raising their grandchildren than other grandparents (Ellis and Simmons, 2014; Livingston and Parker, 2010). Despite these patterns in grandparents' social identities, which will be detailed later in this chapter, what is often neglected is a critical evaluation of the ways in which grandparents' multiple social identities (for example, 'race', ethnicity, class, gender and age), and the larger social structures in which they are embedded, interact to shape grandparents' experiences and wellbeing. Limited attention has also been given to why some grandparents are more or less resilient, despite their histories of trauma and experiences of cumulative inequality (Ferraro and Shippee, 2009; Hayslip and Smith, 2013; Lee et al., 2015). Overall, the literature on grandfamilies could benefit from greater consideration of how much of the discourse and research on grandparents raising grandchildren has been situated in dominant, yet often pathologising, western, white, male and middle-class perspectives (Few, 2007; West, 1982).

To promote reflection and deepen the understanding of grandfamilies in the United States, this chapter uses the theoretical framework of **intersectionality** (Crenshaw, 1993) to provide a critical analysis of grandparents raising grandchildren. Intersectionality captures how individuals' multiple social identities may overlap and/or conflict with one another, and how these identities are embedded within historical and cultural contexts that privilege some social identities over others (Crenshaw, 1993; Few-Demo, 2014; Greenwood, 2008). This results in differential opportunities that promote inequality, marginalisation and oppression (Few-Demo, 2014). By examining grandfamilies through an intersectional lens, we illuminate the complex nature of grandparents' individual experiences as well as the complexity of their interactions with larger social and institutional forces (Few-Demo, 2014). In doing so, we also offer recommendations for research, policy and practice that account for the social inequalities experienced by many grandparents raising grandchildren, for the purposes of improving their own wellbeing as well as that of their grandchildren.

Social identities of grandparents raising grandchildren

Grandparents raising grandchildren in the United States are a heterogeneous population. However, as noted previously, United States Census data reveal that certain social identities are disproportionately represented within the population. In this section, we offer a demographic portrait of grandparents raising grandchildren in the United States while also highlighting key interconnections among their various social identities.

Social identities relevant to grandparents raising grandchildren include gender, age and ability. In line with societal expectations of women as caregivers (Bozalek and Hooyman, 2012), approximately 64% of grandparents raising grandchildren are grandmothers (Ellis and Simmons, 2014). Grandfathers may be involved as part of two-grandparent households, but few (only 6%) grandfathers are solely responsible for the care of their grandchildren (Ellis and Simmons, 2014; United States Census Bureau, 2015). Age is another important consideration when understanding grandfamilies, as it may be relevant to grandparents' health status, disability status and ability to engage in the labour force. Estimates suggest that 39% of grandparents are 60 years of age or older (United States Census Bureau, 2015), which lends support to findings from the 1998–2008 Health and Retirement Study that younger grandparents are more likely to begin and remain raising grandchildren (Luo et al., 2012). Finally, with regard to ability, approximately 26% of grandparents have a disability that may impact their capacity to care for their grandchildren as well as seek and obtain employment, support services and other resources (Generations United, 2015).

'Race' and Hispanic origin have long been noted as key demographic characteristics relevant to the heterogeneity of grandparents raising grandchildren. The United States Census reports the following percentages of adults over the age of 30 who are living with their grandchildren: white non-Hispanic (2.6%), Asian (5.9%), Black (5.9%), Hispanic (7.2%), American Indian/Alaskan Native (7.5%) and Native Hawaiian/Pacific Islander (10.6%) (Ellis and Simmons, 2014). Of these co-resident grandparents, the following proportions are responsible for raising their grandchildren: Asian (15.3%), Native Hawaiian/Pacific Islander (30.4%), Hispanic (30.9%), white non-Hispanic (43.2%), Black (47.6%), and American Indian/Alaskan Native (54.0%) (Ellis and Simmons, 2014). In addition to prevalence, 'race' and Hispanic origin have also been linked to length of caregiving, household structure and grandparent wellbeing. Long-term care arrangements of five years or more are most common among Asian and Native Hawaiian/Pacific Islander grandparents and least common among Hispanic and white non-Hispanic grandparents (Ellis and Simmons, 2014). In terms of household structure, Luo and colleagues (2012) found that African American grandparents were more likely than Hispanic or white grandparents to initiate and maintain skipped generation households, while Hispanic grandparents were more likely to enter and maintain multigenerational households. Goodman and Silverstein (2002) linked grandparents' wellbeing to family structure; African American grandparents had the greatest wellbeing in skipped generation (vs. co-parenting) arrangements, after controlling for stress associated with parental problems, while Latino grandparents had the highest levels of wellbeing in co-parenting (multigenerational) arrangements. There were no differences in white grandparents' wellbeing based on family structure, a finding attributed to both custodial and co-parenting arrangements being in contrast with white grandparents' cultural preferences for a companionate grandparent role (Goodman and Silverstein, 2002). Recent studies continue to examine grandparents from a variety of racial and ethnic groups, often focusing on unique aspects of their experiences, service needs and demographic comparisons to other groups of grandparents (see Fuller-Thomson and Minkler, 2005, 2007; Mendoza et al., 2017; Whitley and Fuller-Thomson, 2017; Yancura, 2013). Much more information is needed about these groups of grandparents, particularly information about within-group variation (such as class variation within racial groups) in grandparents' experiences, resources and needs.

The prevalence of grandfamilies also varies geographically, though these variations primarily reflect differing concentrations of grandparents based on 'race' and Hispanic origin. Of all the adults in the United States over the age of 30, the highest proportion of those who live with their grandchildren reside in the west (4.3%), followed by the south (4.2%), northeast (3.2%) and Midwest (2.9%) (Ellis and Simmons, 2014). Among these co-resident grandparents, there is variation in the proportion who are also responsible for their grandchildren: 45.1% in the south, 41.5% in the Midwest and 31.6% and 31.4% in the northeast and the west respectively (Ellis and Simmons, 2014). Grandparents living in the south and Midwest are most likely to be younger than 60 and to be raising their grandchildren in a skipped generation home. Grandparents in the south are also the most likely to be living in poverty (24.1%) (Ellis and Simmons, 2014). Additionally, as close to half of everyone living in rural areas lives in the south (United States Census Bureau, 2017b), urban–rural residence is a related social identity. While much of the literature has focused on grandparents living in urban communities, there has been an increase in studies of grandfamilies living in rural areas. Evidence from these studies suggests that rural grandparents raising grandchildren experience poverty, limited community resources and loss of formal and informal supports (Crowther et al., 2014; Robinson et al., 2000).

Finally, with regard to socioeconomic status, grandfamilies often experience significant financial difficulties. Approximately one in five or 22% of all grandparents raising grandchildren have incomes below the poverty line, which was approximately US$15,000 for a family of two in 2011 (Ellis and Simmons, 2014; Livingston and Parker, 2010; United States Census Bureau, 2017a). This is despite the fact that 56.7% of grandparents raising grandchildren participate in the labour force (United States Census Bureau, 2015). Additionally, socioeconomic distress is not equally distributed; African American children being raised by grandparents are most likely to be living in poverty, followed by Hispanic and white children (Baker et al., 2008). Poverty rates also vary with household structure, with households involving single grandmothers and no parents having the highest (48%) poverty rates followed by households with single grandmothers and one parent (usually mothers; 33%) (Ellis and Simmons, 2014). Two-grandparent-headed households were also less likely to be experiencing poverty than households headed by single grandmothers (Ellis and Simmons, 2014).

Intersectionality

Intersectionality theory, as applied to grandfamilies, is essentially concerned with how grandparents' multiple social identities and their 'associated systems of representation' are historically and contextually situated (Crenshaw, 1993). Intersectionality also emphasises how the intersections of grandparents' social identities can result in identities and allegiances that conflict with one another (Yuval-Davis, 2006). Finally, intersectionality theory emphasises the ways in which sociostructural systems of oppression influence how grandparents' social identities are socially located or 'situated' as empowered and/ or disempowered in comparison to others (Greenwood, 2008). Thus, the lived experiences of grandparents raising grandchildren are shaped by the interaction of their various social identities with systems of oppression over time. For example, a poor, African American, lesbian, older grandmother raising grandchildren may find she has to negotiate classism, racism, homophobia, ageism and sexism simultaneously throughout her lifespan. She also may experience that a specific social identity (such as 'race') or a combination of social identities (for example, 'race' × gender × sexual orientation) may be more salient or visible in certain contexts than in others. For grandparents raising grandchildren, dominant discourses about the reasons they are raising their grandchildren and their family structure also intersect with their other social identities (for instance, how a poor, single, immigrant Latina grandmother raising a grandchild due to parental substance abuse might be viewed in comparison to an affluent, married, white grandmother raising a grandchild due to parental death from cancer) in ways that may further contribute to some grandparents' disempowerment. Thus, intersectionality can be conceptualised as being 'simultaneously political, symbolic, categorical, relational, and locational' (Few-Demo, 2014, p 171). For the purposes of this chapter, however, we focus on Crenshaw's (1993) political and symbolic approaches to examining intersectionality, which include representational, structural and political intersectionality.

Representational intersectionality

Crenshaw (1993) wrote about **representational intersectionality** as observing the ways cultural constructions of racial and ethnic minority women influence the framing and priorities of political agendas and creation of laws to discriminate against racial and ethnic minority groups. The ways in which specific groups are depicted symbolically in online and paper media are cultural constructions. This symbolic imagery, which creates a narrative about characteristics of a specific group, may be demeaning or empowering. The analysis of representational intersectionality concerns who has control over the production of these narratives and who does not, as well as how these narratives inform policies, interventions and institutions.

Grandparents raising grandchildren in the United States are subject to personal- and family-level cultural constructions that may result in demeaning and disempowering societal narratives. On the family level, narratives are shaped by western, white, middle-class, heteronormative assumptions about the primacy of the traditional nuclear family structure, bionormativity, or emphasis given to biologically related parents and children, parental responsibility for childrearing, single-generation households, grandparent non-interference and companionate models of grandparenting (Dolbin-MacNab, 2015; Yancura et al., 2016). These assumptions result in grandparents raising grandchildren often being portrayed culturally and politically as suffering and sacrificing everything to become 'silent saviours' or 'heroes' (Hayslip et al., 2013). While grandparents' lives are profoundly impacted by raising their grandchildren and they do make enormous personal sacrifices to provide their grandchildren with safe and stable homes, these portrayals are potentially disempowering in that they fail to account for grandparent resilience (Hayslip and Smith, 2013), families with cultural traditions of multigenerational households and grandmother involvement in childcare – regardless of parental difficulties (Goodman and Silverstein, 2002) – and cultural expectations of women as family caregivers (Bozalek and Hooyman, 2012). Thus, the existing narratives do not fully capture the complexity of grandparents' experiences and the varied personal and structural factors contributing to the caregiving arrangement.

The reasons that grandfamilies form may also contribute to oppressive cultural constructions. Research suggests that grandparents raising grandchildren are viewed more negatively when the reasons for raising their grandchildren are socially unacceptable (for example, drug abuse, child abuse/neglect or incarceration vs. death or job loss) or defined as being preventable or within the grandparent's control (Hayslip et al., 2009, 2013). Assumptions that grandparents have somehow failed as parents and will continue poor parenting practices are also common (Hayslip et al., 2009). Together, these constructions may drive demeaning narratives that grandparents are unable to provide adequate care for their grandchildren and/or are responsible for their circumstances (Dolbin-MacNab, 2015).

On the personal level, grandparents raising grandchildren are often viewed through cultural narratives shaped by ageism, classism, sexism and racism. Ageism may result in grandparents being viewed as too old to be raising children, incompetent, interpersonally difficult and physically or cognitively impaired (Nelson, 2002). Classist narratives blame grandparents living in poverty for their circumstances and view them as being unmotivated, not trying to help themselves, having poor family values and draining societal resources by purposefully staying on welfare (Lichter and Crowley, 2002). That said, while these biased assumptions are even held by those living in poverty (Lichter and Crowley, 2002), Black, Latino and college-educated white respondents tend to hold more favourable views of poverty (Lauter, 2016). This variation in perspectives on poverty serves as an important reminder of the variation in the cultural narratives associated with various social identities yet the tendency of particular narratives to be dominant, which results in the marginalisation and oppression of specific populations.

Sexist narratives rooted in expectations that women should (and want to) be responsible for the care of family members, despite the potential negative economic and personal consequences (Bozalek and Hooyman, 2012), result in grandmothers going unrecognised for their efforts and grandfathers being virtually ignored. Sexist narratives can also result in assumptions that grandparents 'don't mind' raising their grandchildren or will automatically assume responsibility for them. In fact, grandmothers often feel a sense of obligation when it comes to raising their grandchildren (Hayslip and Kaminski, 2005), suggesting the possibility that grandmothers may also internalise dominant narratives about the roles and responsibilities of women in families. Finally, sexism combines with pervasive racism to result in narratives that portray minority ethnic grandmothers as negligent parents, self-sacrificing nurturers or powerful matriarchs who emasculate men in their families (Collins, 1991; Guy-Sheftall, 1995). While perceived discrimination related to any one of these social identities can be detrimental to one's physical and mental health (Pascoe and Richman, 2009), the accumulation of these disempowering narratives across multiple social identities further marginalises and oppresses grandparents and compromises their wellbeing.

Even cultural constructions of the grandparent role itself reflect oppressive cultural constructions related to gender, age, class and 'race'. For instance, in a study examining the portrayal of grandparents in children's literature over a 20-year period, Crawford and Bhattacharya (2014) found that grandparents are depicted in ageist and sexist ways (for example, grandmothers are shown wearing dresses and aprons, with their grey hair worn in a bun). Though the racial and ethnic diversity of the grandparents depicted improved over time, most grandparents were still white and depictions of minority ethnic grandparents reflected stereotypical, traditional images of grandmothers or only emphasised the grandparents' cultural backgrounds. Two thirds of the few books about grandparents raising grandchildren featured minority ethnic families. One of the other books about grandfamilies featured a poor white family living in the rural south.

There is growing evidence that disempowering and oppressive cultural constructions associated with grandfamilies influence grandparents' utilisation of support services. Grandparents may not seek services, or may receive poorer quality services, due to insensitive or discriminatory treatment by professionals (Berrick et al., 1994). Studies also suggest that professionals lack an understanding of grandfamilies, take a judgmental stance or interact with grandparents in ways that communicate the various disempowering narratives outlined previously (Gibson, 2002; Gladstone et al., 2009; O'Hora and Dolbin-MacNab, 2015). As a result, grandparents may experience microaggressions, including micro-assaults (discrimination), micro-invalidations (nullification of experience) and micro-insults (insensitivity) (Yancura et al., 2016). Since grandparents frequently interact with multiple service providers across multiple contexts (teachers, case workers, medical providers and so on), micro-aggressions and discriminatory treatment can accumulate and result in compromised health and self-esteem (Nadal et al., 2014; Ong et al., 2013; Yancura et al., 2016).

Representational intersectionality may even be reflected in the topics selected for intervention. While many grandparents may benefit from parent training and interventions that promote resilience and positive coping (Hayslip and Kaminski, 2005), it is worth acknowledging that focusing on these issues also reflects dominant cultural constructions about grandparents' inability to parent and manage their circumstances. Indeed, there is evidence that some grandparents do not perceive themselves as needing assistance with parenting (Dolbin-MacNab, 2006), and many grandparents are highly resilient (Hayslip and Smith, 2013) despite experiencing significant challenges and histories of marginalisation and disadvantage. Federal and state policies regarding assistance, too, may reflect representational intersectionality and will be addressed in the next section.

Structural intersectionality

Structural intersectionality concerns how political, economic, representational and institutional forms of discrimination and domination shape the opportunities and constraints experienced by specific individuals and groups (Crenshaw, 1993). Examining structural intersectionality requires inquiring about how various social systems of oppression, such as heteronormativity, colonialism and capitalism, are indoctrinated and reproduced structurally through legitimised means (for instance, family policies, culturally based ideologies and civil, criminal, immigration and international laws) to privilege or oppress individuals and groups on the basis of their specific social identities.

The very reasons that grandparents raise their grandchildren reflect oppressive, yet structurally legitimised, social systems related to the intersections of 'race', gender, age and class. First, racial disparities related to education, employment and socioeconomic status, and the intersections of these social systems, can make it difficult for African American, Hispanic and other minority ethnic parents to support themselves and their children (Baker et al., 2008; House and Williams, 2000). In grandfamilies, the intergenerational nature of these disparities also means certain subgroups of grandfamilies carry significant cumulative disadvantage. Additionally, the increased incarceration of women, including a disproportionately large number of African American women, results in women needing to rely on their parents (often their mothers) to care for their children (Baker et al., 2008; Mauer, 2013).

Even under these circumstances, grandparents raising grandchildren provide an important safety net for society. Estimates suggest that grandparents save United States taxpayers approximately US$4 billion each year by keeping their grandchildren out of the foster care system (Generations United, 2015). Nevertheless, as a policy issue, grandparents raising grandchildren continues to be overlooked in the

United States, reflecting the dominant ideologies of individualism, self-reliance, family responsibility for its members and governmental non-interference into family affairs (Baker et al., 2008; Luo et al., 2012). As a result, 'most policies in the United States are designed to serve the vulnerable at the point at which family and individual resources have been exhausted' (Baker et al., 2008, p 5). These policies also neglect the majority of grandparents whose grandchildren are not involved in the child welfare system (Beltran, 2014), as well as families that do not view the permanent placement of the grandchild with the grandparent as the goal (Kropf and Kolomer, 2004). Restrictive eligibility requirements that effectively block some groups of grandparents from obtaining resources and support services (Baker et al., 2008) further marginalise this population.

There are several federal and state policy initiatives with specific implications for grandfamilies, though they are not widely available and may not adequately address grandparents' varied needs (Beltran, 2014; Generations United, 2015). For those grandparents without legal custody or guardianship, educational and medical consent laws have facilitated grandparents' ability to obtain services, though only 52% and 34% of states have medical and education consent laws respectively (Generations United, 2015). The National Caregiver Support programme allows states to allot up to 10% of the federal funds they receive for services for grandparents raising grandchildren, but only 14% of states use their full allotment (Generations United, 2015). Finally, Temporary Assistance to Needy Families (TANF), which is often the only form of financial support available to grandfamilies (Beltran, 2014), offers family and child-only grants. However, TANF benefits are seriously underutilised by otherwise eligible grandfamilies due to a number of restrictive requirements, such as time-limited benefits, work requirements and consideration of the caregiver's assets when determining eligibility for child-only grants (Beltran, 2014; Generations United, 2015). These restrictions mean some of the most marginalised yet most in need grandparents are unable to access these critical resources.

Collectively, these policies reflect several aspects of structural intersectionality. For example, states' low implementation rate of the policies underscores the relative invisibility of grandfamilies and the ongoing oppression of marginalised social identities in the United States. Additionally, TANF work restrictions as they intersect with immigration status, language barriers, ability and disparities related to education and employment make it virtually impossible for some grandparents to obtain support for their families. There is even evidence that 'a larger share of African American people in a state's population is generally associated with less generous [cash benefits] and more restrictive [TANF] policies' (Hahn et al., 2017, p 23). When combined with the history of institutions exploiting racial and ethnic minorities and other marginalised populations (Collins, 1991; Crenshaw, 1993; Crenshaw et al., 1995), as well as discriminatory treatment by professionals (Dolbin-MacNab, 2015; Gibson 2002), it is not surprising that grandparents with oppressed social identities underutilise available services and that resources tend to be lacking (Baker et al., 2008; Crowther et al., 2014).

A final policy with significant implications for grandfamilies is the Federal Fostering Connections to Success and Increasing Adoptions Act of 2008, which focuses on children in the child welfare system (Social Security Administration, 2017). It delineates a preference for placement of children with relatives, if possible, and requires states to notify relatives when a child enters into foster care, to make efforts to place siblings in the same household and to 'waive non-safety-related foster care licensing standards for relatives' (Beltran, 2014, p 60; Social Security Administration, 2017). While there is significant evidence that placement with relatives helps maintain cultural, family and community connections, and is associated with better outcomes for children (Generations United, 2016; Kropf and Kolomer, 2004), from a structural intersectionality perspective, this approach still perpetuates dominant values of family responsibility for its members (Baker et al., 2008; Luo et al., 2012). Furthermore, given that African American and Native American children are overrepresented within the child welfare system (Child Welfare Information Gateway, 2016) and that grandparents receive less benefits than nonrelative foster parents (Baker et al., 2008), already-marginalised grandparents are the most likely to be impacted by these policies. Finally, from a macro perspective, the emphasis on relative placements can be viewed as reducing the burden on the child welfare system by shifting the burden of care to individuals and families (Kropf and Kolomer, 2004).

Political intersectionality

Crenshaw (1993) conceptualised **political intersectionality** as the examination of the ways in which traditional feminist and antiracist politics have contributed to the marginalisation of racial and ethnic minority women. Political intersectionality focuses on the importance of examining variation within and across groups. To analyse political intersectionality among grandparents raising grandchildren, it is necessary to consider how a specific minority group of grandparents is situated within at least two or more subordinated groups, as well as how this particular group of grandparents experiences discrimination due to conflicting political agendas based on their social identities.

Political intersectionality has not been an overt part of the discourse on grandfamilies. Generally, political advocacy on the federal and state levels has emphasised advancing legislation designed to help grandparents obtain needed resources and financial supports (such as TANF payments and creation of kinship navigator programmes) and decision-making authority for their grandchildren (for example, educational and medical consent laws) (Beltran, 2014; Generations United, 2015). Ostensibly, these efforts have focused on securing resources for the entirety of the population of grandparents raising grandchildren; however, closer inspection reveals that grandparents raising their grandchildren outside the child welfare system, specifically those who do not have legal custody of their grandchildren, are unable to obtain these benefits (Baker et al., 2008). This emphasis on formal caregiving uniquely jeopardises certain groups of grandparents, namely African American grandparents, who may elect not to seek custody of their grandchildren due to cultural traditions of taking in children (which have been shaped by slavery and post-Reconstruction patterns of migration: Baker et al., 2008; Burton, 1992) and distrust of governmental intrusion into family affairs stemming from a long history of oppression (Kropf and Kolomer, 2004). It may also uniquely jeopardise grandparents who are immigrants and those who lack the financial resources to pursue a legal relationship with their grandchildren. Thus, not all grandparents equally benefit from advocacy and policy efforts.

Implications and conclusion

Although grandfamilies in the United States are highly diverse, grandparents raising grandchildren are disproportionately likely to be women, racial and ethnic minorities and living in poverty (Ellis and Simmons, 2014; Livingston and Parker, 2010). Intersectionality theory (Crenshaw, 1993; Few-Demo, 2014) provides a valuable framework for deepening the understanding of grandfamilies by examining how grandparents' social identities interact with each other and with dominant systems of oppression over time to result in differential opportunities that promote inequality, marginalisation and oppression of subgroups of grandparents. By considering structural, political and representational intersectionality (Crenshaw, 1993), the current analysis revealed that oppressive discourses related to age, gender, 'race' and class are relevant to understanding the needs of grandfamilies. Even the family structure itself can be a basis for marginalisation. Our analysis also revealed how social systems of oppression are reproduced structurally through federal and state policies that, while designed to be supportive, may further oppress and disempower grandparents with specific social identities.

Given that grandfamilies are some of the most vulnerable families in the United States, the most important implication of this analysis is the need for ongoing critical discourse about how grandparents raising grandchildren are embedded within cultural contexts and social structures that may disempower and marginalise them and their efforts on behalf of their families. Research implications include the need to examine within-group variation and probe the subtleties of the intersections among grandparents' various social identities (such as class and 'race', as more affluent grandparents would be in a better position to access resources), ideally using nationally representative datasets. It would also behove researchers studying diverse groups of grandparents to be explicit and contextualise their findings historically, culturally, socially and politically. Research on how aspects of representational and structural intersectionality, including societal attitudes and social policies, impact the health and wellbeing of specific groups of grandparents raising grandchildren is also needed. Implications for practice include the need for practitioners to become deeply educated about grandfamilies and to engage in critical self-reflection about their biases and assumptions so they are not communicated via micro-aggressions or in other disempowering and oppressive ways (Dolbin-MacNab, 2015; Yancura et al., 2016). Practitioners would also benefit from incorporating diverse grandparent voices into their intervention and advocacy efforts so as to avoid speaking for the population or silencing certain subgroups. Finally, from a policy perspective, federal and state policies must avoid formulaic approaches that ignore entire subgroups of grandparents raising grandchildren, fail to account for the diversity in grandfamilies or force grandparents into dominant cultural constructions of family structure and functioning. In addition, policies that aim to reduce the educational, economic, criminal and child welfare disparities that contribute to the formation of grandfamilies are critical to improving the overall health and wellbeing of millions of grandparents, parents and children.

Grandparents around the world have long been key resources to their families (Uhlenberg and Cheuk, 2010). In the United States, grandparents raising grandchildren provide an important safety net for families who have been historically and systematically disempowered, marginalised and oppressed on the basis of any number of social identities. Embracing intersectionality (Crenshaw, 1993; Few-Demo, 2014) as a lens through which to view grandfamilies requires going beyond the provision of resources or the creation of supportive policies. What is needed are critical conversations about the historical and contemporary patterns of oppression that result in grandparents fulfilling a caregiving role within their families, explicit consideration of those grandparents who are often rendered invisible and subsequent societal-level efforts by those in power to reshape deeply rooted dominant narratives and social structures that further marginalise grandfamilies. By working to confront and reduce disparities and cumulative disadvantage associated with 'race', class, gender and age, grandfamilies may be better positioned to thrive.

References

Annie E. Casey Foundation Kids Count Data Center (2016) *Children in kinship care (2013–2015)*, Baltimore, MD: Annie E. Casey Foundation. Available at: http://datacenter.kidscount.org/data/tables/7172-children-in-kinship-care?loc=1&loct=1#detailed/1/any/false/1491,1443/any/14207,14208.

Baker, L. and Mutchler, J. (2010) 'Poverty and material hardship in grandparent-headed households', *Journal of Marriage and Family*, 72(4): 947–962.

Baker, L., Silverstein, M. and Putney, N. (2008) 'Grandparents raising grandchildren in the United States: Changing family forms, stagnant social policies', *Journal of Sociology and Social Policy*, 27(7): 53–69.

Beltran, A. (2014) 'Policy update: Federal and state legislation to support grandfamilies', *Grandfamilies*, 1(1): 56–73.

Berrick, J., Barth, R. and Needall, B. (1994) 'A comparison of kinship foster homes and foster family homes: Implications for kinship foster care as family preservation', *Children and Youth Services Review*, 16(1–2): 33–63.

Bozalek, V. and Hooyman, N. (2012) 'Ageing and intergenerational care: Critical/political ethics of care and feminist gerontology perspectives', *Agenda*, 26(4): 37–47.

Burton, L. (1992) 'Black grandparents rearing children of drug-addicted parents: stressors, outcomes and social service needs', *The Gerontologist*, 32(6): 744–751.

Child Welfare Information Gateway (2016) *Racial disproportionality and disparity in child welfare*, Washington DC: US Department of Health and Human Services Children's Bureau. Available at: https://www.childwelfare.gov/pubPDFs/racial_disproportionality.pdf.

Collins, P. (1991) *Black feminist thought: Knowledge, consciousness, and the politics of empowerment*, London: Routledge.

Crawford, P. and Bhattacharya, S. (2014) 'Grand images: Exploring images of grandparents in picture books', *Journal of Research in Childhood Education*, 28(1): 128–144.

Crenshaw, K. (1993) 'Demarginalizing the interaction of race and sex: A Black feminist critique of antidiscrimination doctrine, feminist theory, and anti-racist politics', in D. Weisburg (ed) *Feminist legal theory: Foundations*, Philadelphia, PA: Temple University Press, pp 383–411.

Crenshaw, K., Gotanda, N., Peller, G. and Thomas, K. (1995) *Critical race theory: The key writings that formed a movement*, New York: The New Press.

Crowther, M., Ford, C. and Peterson, T. (2014) 'A qualitative examination of barriers for urban and rural custodial grandparents', *Journal of Intergenerational Relationships*, 12(3): 207–226.

Dolbin-MacNab, M. (2006) 'Just like raising your own? Grandmothers' perceptions of parenting a second time around', *Family Relations*, 55(5): 564–575.

Dolbin-MacNab, M. (2015) 'Critical self-reflection questions for professionals who work with grandfamilies', *Grandfamilies*, 2(1): 139–159.

Dolbin-MacNab, M. and Yancura, L. (2018) 'International perspectives on grandparents raising grandchildren: Contextual considerations for advancing global discourse', *The International Journal of Aging and Human Development*, 86(1): 3–33.

Ellis, R. and Simmons, T. (2014) *Coresident grandparents and their grandchildren: 2012*, Washington DC: United States Census Bureau. Available at: https://www.census.gov/content/dam/Census/library/publications/2014/demo/p20-576.pdf.

Ferraro, K. and Shippee, T. (2009) 'Aging and cumulative inequality: How does inequality get under the skin', *The Gerontologist*, 49(3): 333–343.

Few, A. (2007) 'Integrating Black consciousness and critical race feminism into family studies research', *Journal of Family Issues*, 28(4): 452–473.

Few-Demo, A. (2014) 'Intersectionality as the "new" critical approach in feminist family studies: Evolving racial/ethnic feminisms and critical race theories', *Journal of Family Theory and Review*, 6(2): 169–183.

Fuller-Thomson, E. and Minkler, M. (2005) 'American Indian/Alaska Native grandparents raising grandchildren: Findings from the Census 2000 supplemental survey', *Social Work*, 50(2): 131–139.

Fuller-Thomson, E. and Minkler, M. (2007) 'Mexican American grandparents raising grandchildren: Findings from the Census 2000 American Community Survey', *Families in Society*, 88(4): 567–574.

Generations United (2015) *The state of grandfamilies in America*, Washington DC: Generations United. Available at: http://www.gu.org/LinkClick.aspx?fileticket=nv03BXVlGAI%3d&tabid=157&mid=606.

Generations United (2016) *Raising the children of the opioid epidemic: Solutions and support for grandfamilies*. Washington DC: Generations United. Available at: http://www.gu.org/Portals/0/documents/Reports/16-Report-State_of_Grandfamiles.pdf.

Gibson, P. (2002) 'Barriers, lessons learned, and helpful hints: Grandmother caregivers talk about service utilization', *Journal of Gerontological Social Work*, 39(4): 55–74.

Gladstone, J., Brown, R. and Fitzgerald, K. (2009) 'Grandparents raising their grandchildren: Tensions, service needs and involvement with child welfare agencies', *The International Journal of Aging and Human Development*, 69(1): 55–78.

Goodman, C. and Silverstein, M. (2002) 'Grandparents raising grandchildren: Family structure and well-being in culturally diverse families', *The Gerontologist*, 42(5): 676–689.

Greenwood, R. (2008) 'Intersectional political consciousness: Appreciation for intragroup differences and solidarity in diverse groups', *Psychology of Women Quarterly*, 32(1): 36–47.

Guy-Sheftall, B. (1995) *Words of fire: An anthology of African-American feminist thought*, New York: The New Press.

Hahn, H., Aron, L., Lou, C., Pratt, E. and Okoli, A. (2017) *Why does cash welfare depend on where your live? How and why state TANF programs vary*, Washington DC: Urban Institute.

Hayslip, B., Glover, R., Harris, B., Miltenberger, P., Baird, A. and Kaminski, P. (2009) 'Perceptions of custodial grandparents among young adults', *Journal of Intergenerational Relationships*, 7(2–3): 209–224.

Hayslip, B., Herrington, R., Glover, R. and Pollard, S. (2013) 'Assessing attitudes toward grandparents raising their grandchildren', *Journal of Intergenerational Relationships*, 11(4): 1–24.

Hayslip, B. and Kaminski, P. (2005) 'Grandparents raising their grandchildren: A review of the literature and suggestions for practice', *The Gerontologist*, 45(2): 262–269.

Hayslip, B. and Smith, G. (eds) (2013) *Resilient grandparent caregivers: A strengths-based perspective*, New York: Routledge.

House, J. and Williams, D. (2000). 'Understanding and reducing socioeconomic and racial/ethnic disparities in health', in B. Smedley and S. Syme (eds) *Promoting health: Interventions strategies from social and behavioral research*, Washington DC: National Academy Press, pp 81–124.

Kropf, N. and Kolomer, S. (2004) 'Grandparents raising grandchildren: A diverse population', *Journal of Human Behavior in the Social Environment*, 9(4): 65–83.

Lauter, D. (2016) 'How do Americans view poverty? Many blue-collar whites, key to Trump, criticize poor people as lazy and content to stay on welfare', *Los Angeles Times*, 14 August. Available at: http://www.latimes.com/projects/la-na-pol-poverty-poll/#chapter1.

Lee, Y., Blitz, L. and Srnka, M. (2015). 'Trauma and resiliency in grandparent-headed multigenerational families', *Families in Society*, 96(2): 116–124.

Lichter, D. and Crowley, M. (2002) *Poverty in America: Beyond welfare reform*, Washington DC: Population Reference Bureau. Available at: http://www.prb.org/Publications/Reports/2002/PovertyinAmericaBeyondWelfareReformPDF106MB.aspx.

Livingston, G. and Parker, K. (2010) *Since the start of the great recession, more children raised by grandparents*. Washington DC: Pew Research Center. Available at: http://www.pewsocialtrends.org/2010/09/09/since-the-start-of-the-great-recession-more-children-raised-by-grandparents/.

Luo, Y., LaPierre, T., Hughes, M. and Waite, L. (2012) 'Grandparents providing care to grandchildren: A population-based study of continuity and change', *Journal of Family Issues*, 33(9): 1143–1167.

Mauer, M. (2013) *The changing racial dynamics of women's incarceration*, Washington DC: The Sentencing Project.

Mendoza, A., Fruhauf, C., Bundy-Fazioli, K. and Weil, J. (2017) 'Understanding Latino grandparents raising grandchildren through a bioecological lens', *The International Journal of Aging and Human Development*. DOI: 10.1177/0091415017702907.

Minkler, M. and Roe, K. (1993) *Grandmothers as caregivers: Raising children of the crack cocaine epidemic*, Newbury Park, CA: Sage.

Nadal, K., Griffin, K., Wong, Y., Hamit, S. and Rasmus, M. (2014) 'The impact of racial micro-aggressions on mental health: Counseling implications for clients of color', *Journal of Counseling and Development*, 92(1): 57–66.

Nelson, T. (ed) (2002) *Ageism: Stereotyping and prejudice against older persons*, Cambridge, MA: MIT Press.

O'Hora, K. and Dolbin-MacNab, M. (2015) 'Practice recommendations for mental health professionals: Perspectives from grandparents and their adolescent grandchildren', *Grandfamilies*, 1(2): 97–137.

Ong, A., Burrow, A., Fuller-Rowell, T., Ja, N. and Sue, D. (2013) 'Racial micro-aggressions and daily well-being among Asian Americans', *Journal of Counseling Psychology*, 60(2): 188–199.

Pascoe, E. and Richman, L. (2009) 'Perceived discrimination and health: A meta-analytic review', *Psychological Bulletin*, 135(4): 531–554.

Robinson, M., Kropf, N. and Myers, L. (2000) 'Grandparents raising grandchildren in rural communities', *Journal of Mental Health and Aging*, 6(4): 353–365.

Social Security Administration (2017) *State plan for foster care and adoption assistance*, Washington DC: Social Security Administration. Available at: https://www.ssa.gov/OP_Home/ssact/title04/0471.htm#ft228.

Uhlenberg, P. and Cheuk, M. (2010) 'The significance of grandparents to grandchildren: an international perspective', in D. Dannefer and C. Phillipson (eds) *The Sage handbook of social gerontology*, Thousand Oaks, CA: Sage, pp 457–448.

United States Census Bureau (2015) *Grandparents: 2015 American Community Survey 1-year estimates*, Washington DC: United States Census Bureau. Available at: https://factfinder.census.gov/faces/tableservices/jsf/pages/productview.xhtml?src=bkmk.

United States Census Bureau (2017a) *Poverty thresholds*, Washington DC: United States Census Bureau. Available at: https://www.census.gov/data/tables/time-series/demo/income-poverty/historical-poverty-thresholds.html.

United States Census Bureau (2017b) *Rural America*, Washington DC: United States Census Bureau. Available at: https://storymaps.geo.census.gov/arcgis/apps/MapSeries/index.html?appid=9e459da9327b4c7e9a1248cb65ad942a.

West, C. (1982) *Prophesy deliverance! An Afro-American revolutionary Christianity*, Philadelphia, PA: Westminster Press.

Whitley, D. and Fuller-Thomson, E. (2017) 'African-American solo grandparents raising grandchildren: A representative profile of their health status', *Journal of Community Health*, 42(2): 312–323.

Yancura, L. (2013) 'Justifications for caregiving in white, Asian American, and Native Hawaiian grandparents raising grandchildren', *The Journals of Gerontology, Series B: Psychological Sciences and Social Sciences*, 68(1): 139–144.

Yancura, L., Fruhauf, C. and Greenwood-Junkermeier, H. (2016) 'Recognizing microaggressions: A framework for helping grandfamilies', *Grandfamilies*, 3(1): 106–121.

Yuval-Davis, N. (2006) 'Intersectionality and feminist politics', *European Journal of Women's Studies*, 13(3): 193–209.

PART 5
Grandparental roles, agency and influence

How grandparents influence the religiosity of their grandchildren: a mixed-methods study of three-generation families in the United States

Vern L. Bengtson and Merril Silverstein

Introduction

How values such as religion are communicated and transmitted across generations is important for understanding the linkage between family-level processes and macro-societal change. Surveys have shown historical declines in the centrality of religious affiliation in the United States, particularly in the past three decades (Pew Forum on Religious and Public Life, 2015). However, we know relatively little about how religious orientations are (or are not) reproduced within family lineages or about the complex, often poignant emotional issues that surface within families about religion. In this study, we take a mixed-methods and within-family approach to identify the distinctive processes by which religiosity is, or is not, passed down from grandparents to subsequent generations.

During the past half-century, historical forces have significantly altered the cultural landscape of society in the US, weakening the social institutions that mediate between individuals and the larger society. Frequently mentioned among these are organised religion and the family (Putnam, 2000). Cultural trends such as increased individualism, the growing influence of mass and digital media and the proliferation of non-traditional families caused by divorce and remarriage have been described as weakening the traditional role of older generations as agents of socialisation for younger generations (Bellah et al., 1985; Cherlin, 2009; Putnam, 2000; Putnam and Campbell, 2010). Polls show that participation in religious activities, such as service attendance, has declined in recent years, and people –

younger people in particular – are less likely to affiliate with a religious institution than in the past several decades (Pew Forum on Religious and Public Life, 2012, 2015).

Based on the life-course perspective and a theoretical model of intergenerational solidarity, we use qualitative and quantitative data from a longitudinal study of multigenerational families and apply a mixed-methods approach to examine the religious influence of grandparents on descending generations. Following the literature on intergenerational transmission of values (Schönpflug, 2001), we conceptualise intergenerational influence as the extent to which religious beliefs and values are transmitted and passed on to children and grandchildren. We analyse quantitative survey data to describe common patterns in the progression of religious intensity from grandparents to their adult children and grandchildren, and then use qualitative data from in-depth interviews to gain a deeper understanding of the processes or mechanisms of cross-generational religious influence of grandparents.

Background

The changing cultural scene: families and religion

Significant changes have occurred in both religious culture and families over the past four decades in the United States. Historically, the United States has been a highly churchgoing nation; church involvement particularly increased following the Second World War, hitting a peak in the mid-1950s (Chaves, 2011; Wuthnow, 1988). But the economic prosperity and stability of the 1950s was followed by cultural changes in the 1960s, when the first wave of baby-boomer youth became involved in protests challenging the politics and values of their elders, creating what appeared to be a 'generation gap' between the values of young adults and their middle-aged parents (Bengtson, 1970). In later decades, sociologists began describing an increasing secularisation of society, prompting public discourse about the role of religion in education, politics and mass communication (Bellah et al., 1985; Hout and Fischer, 2002; Wuthnow, 1978).

Most recently there has been a remarkable increase in the numbers of 'nones' in the United States – those who say they have no religious affiliation. In 2014, the unaffiliated represented more than one third of millennials, who are defined as the cohort born 1981–1996, in the US adult population – a proportion more than double that of baby boomers (Pew Forum on Religious and Public Life, 2015). At the same time, it must be recognised that today's young adults exhibit more diverse and diffuse religious practices and beliefs than preceding generations (Chaves, 2011; Smith and Denton, 2005; Smith and Snell, 2009; Wuthnow, 2007). Based on such evidence, it might be expected that religious continuity between youth and their parents and grandparents would have declined over recent decades.

Along with changes in the religious environment, families have changed over the past half-century in ways that have been linked to a decline in influence by older generations. Increased rates of divorce and remarriage are often cited as reasons for the fragility of contemporary families that threatens their effective functioning (Popenoe, 1993). Given the substantial changes that have occurred in culture and religion in the US over the past few decades, social critics have concluded that parents and grandparents have less moral and religious influence over children and grandchildren than in the past (Arnett, 2004; Putnam and Campbell, 2010).

In sum, there have been significant changes in religious culture in recent decades as well as significant changes in families in the US. Many young adults engage in a diverse array of religious expression, with a substantial portion having no religious identity. Moreover, traditional family structures have changed for many, with uncertain consequences for intergenerational transmission patterns. Based on this trend, one might expect cohort change toward greater secularism to render inconsequential any attempt by older generations to influence the religiosity of their young adult children and grandchildren.

The increasing importance of grandparents

At the same time, however, another development over the past four decades has been the increasing importance of grandparents in family life in the US (Bengtson, 2001). Generation Xers and millennials will have had greater involvement with their grandparents than any previous generation of grandchildren in US history (King and Elder, 1999; Mueller and Elder, 2003; Uhlenberg, 2005). More grandparents today are involved in and contributing to their grandchildren's development, resulting in cross-generational influence beyond what many contemporary observers anticipated (AARP, 2012; Birditt et al., 2012; Geurts et al., 2009; Swartz, 2009).

Grandparent contact, support and involvement with grandchildren are high in the US these days (Goyer, 2012). Over 50% of grandparents report seeing a grandchild at least once a week, and another 25% report seeing a grandchild every few weeks; 68% talk with a grandchild by telephone at least once a week and 26% say they communicate weekly by email, text or Skype. Nearly 60% feel they play a 'very important role' in the lives of grandchildren (Lampkin, 2012). A majority of US grandparents today are significantly invested in the religious socialisation of grandchildren, as seen from nationally representative surveys. In a 2009 survey, 67% of grandparents reported they had discussed religion and spirituality with their grandchildren and 47% said they had attended religious services with grandchildren recently (Lampkin 2012). This compares to 60% of grandparents who attended religious services with grandchildren over a one-year period a decade earlier (Silverstein and Marenco, 2001).

Several reasons can be cited as to why grandparents are likely to be more influential today than in the past. First, increased life expectancy has resulted in the growing availability of grandparents and the opportunity of grandchildren to share a greater proportion of their lives with grandparents; in 2005, 95% of 20-year-olds and almost 79% of 30-year-olds in the US had at least one grandparent alive (Uhlenberg, 2005, 2009). Second, due to fertility declines today's grandparents have fewer grandchildren than previous generations, reducing competition among grandchildren for the attention of grandparents. Third, more grandparents today are retired and thus have more opportunity to interact with and lend support to their grandchildren. With a majority of mothers with young children in the labour force, and with the growing number of single-parent households, more grandparents have been providing care for grandchildren than ever before (AARP, 2012; US Census, 2009).

For these reasons, a significant number of grandparents today play an important role in the lives of their grandchildren – more so than in previous decades. Thus, it is not surprising that a majority of grandchildren report being emotionally close to their grandparents as well as sharing similar views and values – including religious values – with them (AARP, 2012; Copen and Silverstein, 2008; Min et al., 2012). However, we know virtually nothing about the patterns and processes of grandparents' direct and indirect influence on grandchildren, particularly in the realm of values and religion. On the one hand, the evidence reviewed above suggests that the opportunity for grandparental involvement and influence may be significant, resulting in intergenerational continuity. On the other hand, macrosocial cultural trends involving an increase in secularisation and decline in religiosity may suggest otherwise. This is the focus of the analyses in this chapter: how grandparents are involved in the transmission of religiosity across generations, and how successful or unsuccessful their efforts have been, in the context of significant social and cultural change over recent decades.

Theoretical framework

The **life-course perspective** provides a useful paradigmatic orientation that highlights the interconnections of individual religious development, cohort trends and family influence (Elder et al., 2003). For our purposes, there are two key dimensions of this perspective. The first concerns the importance of historical contexts in shaping individual lives. To understand value transmission across generations requires that we consider social and cultural changes over recent decades, such as increased secularism and its unique impact on successive generations of family members. The second key principle is 'linked lives', referring to the interdependence of developmental outcomes over time. As individuals grow up, their development is tied in various ways to the lives of others in their immediate social network (Mueller and Elder, 2003). From this perspective, children's religious identities, beliefs and practices develop in ways that are linked to both their parents' and grandparents' religious identities, beliefs and practices.

A related theoretical perspective is the **intergenerational solidarity** model, which theorises relations between generations in the family as a multidimensional composite of interactions, emotions, expectations and conflicts (Bengtson et al., 2002; Silverstein et al.,1997). Primary among these dimensions is **affectual solidarity**, conceptualised as emotional closeness between generational partners. Previous research has indicated that parental warmth is particularly enabling in enhancing intergenerational transmission of values (Bengtson, 2013; Michaleski and Shackelford, 2005; Min et al., 2012; Monserud, 2008). Thus, the religious dimension in the 'linked lives' of grandparents, parents and grandchildren may be more powerful in relationships characterised by high affectional solidarity, producing greater continuity in religiosity across generations.

Research questions and hypotheses

Building on existing research literature concerning the cross-generational transmission of religious beliefs and practices, we employ a mixed-methods approach to examine the following general questions:

1. How has religious intensity changed across three generations, and how are patterns of multigenerational continuity and discontinuity manifested?
2. What processes can be identified in grandparents' attempts at religious influence, and in what ways are these efforts successful or unsuccessful in fostering intergenerational continuity in religious intensity?
3. How does the quality of the relationship – emotional closeness between grandchildren and grandparents – influence whether religiosity is passed down the generations?

Method

Sample

Respondents for both qualitative and quantitative analyses were drawn from the Longitudinal Study of Generations (LSOG), a study of over 3,000 respondents from 357 three- and four-generation families originally fielded in 1971. We use quantitative data from 1971, 1988 and 2005 waves of measurement (see Feng et al., 2006, for sample details) and in-depth interview data collected in 2005–06 (see Bengtson, 2013, for details).

Analytic approach

We take a mixed-methods approach, using two complementary analytic strategies that uniquely add to our understanding of grandparents' role in religious transmission across multiple generations in the family. First, we use longitudinal survey data to assess intergenerational continuity and discontinuity in religious intensity over a 34-year period, with the goals of identifying common patterns of change in religious intensity across generations and the role played by emotional closeness in maintaining religious stability. Second, we use in-depth data from intensive interviews of a subsample of multigenerational families that elucidate how, and the conditions under which, grandparents are enhanced or inhibited in their ability to transmit their religious traditions to younger generations. It is important to note that each strategy treats three-generation family lineages as the primary units of analysis.

Quantitative analysis of survey data

To chart patterns of change and stability in religiosity across generations, we use 34 years of survey data from the LSOG and examine the degree to which late-adolescent and young adult grandchildren maintained the religious intensity of their grandparents and parents. Reports from grandparents were taken from the 1971 survey, parents' reports from the 1988 survey and grandchildren's reports from the 2005 survey. This staggered generational design incorporates historical change in religious affiliation into the model, maximises standardisation on life stage across generations and avoids the exclusion of grandparents who died over the course of the study. Table 11.1 shows the sample structure and descriptive information for each generation in the analysis.

Generalised religiosity is assessed in the survey with the following measure of religious intensity: 'Regardless of whether you attend religious services, do you consider yourself to be *not at all religious, somewhat religious, pretty religious, or very religious?*'

To measure affectual solidarity between grandchildren and grandparents, we use an additive scale comprised of three questions asked of grandchildren about their relationship with surviving grandmothers (GM) and grandfathers (GF): 'How close do you feel to your (GM/GF)?', 'How much affection do you have for your (GM/GF)?' and 'How is communication between you and your (GM/GF)?' Because our interest is in the early influences of grandparents, we use assessments when grandchildren were younger than 18 years of age. This method captures 48% of relationships with grandparents. For the remainder of grandchildren (including 64 grandchildren with missing data), we use information from G3 parents who reported the amount of contact with *their* parents in 1985 or 1988 to impute affectual solidarity. With these imputations supplementing direct observations, 81% of all relationships with grandparents are included in the analysis.

Table 11.1: Description of sample by generation

Generation	Year of measurement	Mean age (SD)	Mean religious intensity (SD)	N
Grandmothers	1971	43.06 (4.48)	3.07 (0.78)	424
Grandfathers	1971	45.98 (5.23)	2.90 (0.87)	350
Mothers	1988	36.92 (2.82)	2.76 (0.97)	276
Fathers	1988	36.53 (2.80)	2.73 (0.93)	156
Granddaughters	2005	28.31 (5.20)	2.40 (1.01)	281
Grandsons	2005	27.73 (5.48)	2.24 (1.08)	219

A dummy variable indicating whether the imputation was made serves as a control variable in multivariate analyses.

Analytic strategy

To assess multigenerational patterns of religious intensity, we estimated a Latent Markov Model (LMM) with a latent mixture component using Latent GOLD 5.0 statistical software (Vermunt and Magidson, 2013). LMM is typically used to describe patterns of intra-individual change but lends itself well to the sequencing of different individuals linked across generations within the same family lineages. Triads headed by grandmothers and triads headed by grandfathers are analysed separately, and gender of parents and grandchildren are entered as control variables. Robust standard errors are estimated to account for family dependencies in the data. The procedure uses Full Information Maximum Likelihood estimation to account for missing data.

Mean values of religious intensity are shown for grandparents, parents and grandchildren by gender in Table 11.1. Religious intensity follows predictable generational cohort pattern, with the oldest generation expressing the strongest intensity and the youngest generation expressing the weakest intensity. Gender patterns were also manifest, with women expressing stronger religious intensity than men in each generation.

In estimating the LMM model, we first determined the optimal number of latent states of religious intensity to classify respondents based on their level of intensity. Second, we determined the optimal number of latent classes that describe triadic patterns in state membership across generations so that families can be classified. In determining the number of states and classes, we tested increasing numbers of each until the Bayesian Information Criterion statistic failed to diminish, the log-likelihood fit was close to non-significance and a satisfactorily interpretable set of classes was obtained.

For both grandmother- and grandfather-headed triads, a two-state model best fit the data based on these criteria. The conditional probabilities from this model revealed two religious states: one characterised by strong religious intensity (either somewhat or very religious) and the other by weak religious intensity (either not very or not at all religious).

Classifying triads into meaningful patterns of generational change, we found that a three-class model fit the data reasonably well for both grandmother- and grandfather-headed triads. These three classes are described for grandmother-headed triads in Figure 11.1 based on the

Figure 11.1: Per cent of grandmother-headed triads with high religious intensity

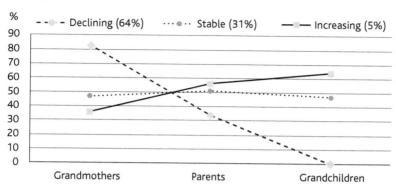

probability of being in the stronger religious intensity group. The prevalence of each class is described in the legend with a descriptive label. The first class for grandmother-headed triads is characterised by declining religiosity (64%). The next most common class shows stable religiosity (31%). The third class demonstrates modestly increasing religiosity (5%).

The results for grandfather-headed triads are shown in Figure 11.2. The general class structure was similar to that found among grandmother-headed triads but the distribution of classes is different. While the declining religiosity class forms the largest group (52%), the prevalence is lower than that for grandmother-headed triads. The increasing religiosity class (25%) formed the next largest group, followed by the stable religiosity class (23%) – representations different from those found among grandmother-headed triads.

Figure 11.2: Per cent of grandfather-headed triads with high religious intensity

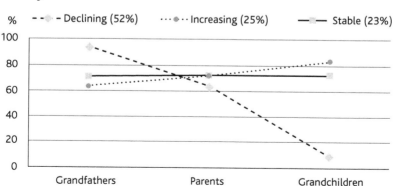

Next, we sought to discover whether affectual solidarity between grandchildren and grandparents was associated with particular patterns of religious change. We estimated logistic regression models predicting the likelihood of being in the declining religiosity class relative to the stable and strengthening classes combined. Due to similarity in the measurement model between triads headed by grandmothers and triads headed by grandfathers, we pool the two groups.

We also tested this model on the subset of triads in which grandparents identified with commonly observed religious denominations – mainline Protestants, evangelical Protestants, Catholics, Jews and Mormons – to determine whether any effect of emotional closeness on religious continuity is a function of denominational differences. Robust standard errors adjusted significance tests for family clustering.

The results shown in the first equation of Table 11.2 indicate that emotional solidarity with grandparents reduces the likelihood of

Table 11.2: Logistic regression predicting declining religious intensity vs. stable/increasing religious intensity in intergenerational triads with grandmothers and grandfathers pooled

Predictors	Full triad sample (n=817) Odds ratio	robust CI	Triads in which grandparent expressed religious preference (n=575) Odds ratio	robust CI
Grandmother (vs. grandfather)	2.00***	1.51–2.63	2.70***	1.77–4.11
Granddaughter (vs. grandson)	0.85	0.56–1.28	1.15	0.67–1.99
Grandmother * granddaughter	0.69*	0.50–0.96	0.41***	0.25–0.69
Mother (vs. father)	1.24	0.78–1.96	0.86	0.50–1.49
Age grandchild	1.02	0.98–1.07	0.98	0.93–1.04
Emotional closeness to grandparent	0.92*	0.85–0.99	0.89*	0.80–1.00
Imputation dummy	1.32	0.76–2.32	1.54	0.73–3.23
Religious denomination of grandparent (vs. mainstream Protestant)				
Evangelical Protestant			0.75	0.37–1.56
Catholic			1.48	0.77–2.84
Jewish			2.38	0.81–7.00
Mormon			0.12***	0.44–0.32
Constant	1.33	0.74–2.07	6.07	0.81–5.63
Wald χ^2	29.54***		46.01***	
Df	7		11	
Pseudo R^2	0.02		0.11	

*p<0.05, ** p<0.01, ***p<0.001

intergenerational religious decline. Religious stability/strengthening is enhanced when grandchildren's past relationships with grandparents were emotionally close. Religious decline is also less common in triads consisting of grandmothers, particularly when grandmothers are paired with granddaughters. When we control for religious denomination (see Table 11.2, second equation), we found that Mormons are significantly less likely than mainline Protestants to be in the declining class. Affectual solidarity continues to be a significant predictor with denomination controlled.

Qualitative analysis of interview data

Participants and procedures

The goal of the qualitative study was to gain a more in-depth understanding of how religious values and traditions are maintained across generations in some families but not others. We conducted interviews with 156 family members from 25 of the 356 multigenerational families drawn from the LSOG panel. Selected families reflected a variety of religious and ethnic backgrounds (for details of the sample selection, see Bengtson, 2013).

The interview schedule covered family relationships; mental and physical health; the subjects' perceptions of God, religion and spirituality; experiences with religious transmission; and efforts of older generations to pass on these practices and beliefs to younger ones. The interviews averaged 90 minutes, varying from 45 minutes to almost 3 hours. We used the ATLAS.ti qualitative data analysis software to assist in the coding process. Transcribed interviews were coded using a grounded inductive analytical approach to identify common themes across interviews; these were used as lenses through which to view data from each family member in developing family case studies. We then shifted from an individual level of analysis to a family level and created family case studies that included all family members of each generation. For this portion of the analysis, our intent is to provide a rich description of families that exemplify each of the three types of family lineages identified in the quantitative typology.

Religious stability across generations

The first pattern evident was families in which religious affiliation and beliefs are shared over three, four and five generations. In these families, grandparents supported parents' efforts to socialise their children to religious ideologies and talked about their wish to pass on their faith to their grandchildren.

One example of this type is the Wilsons, a family of evangelical Protestants. When grandmother Carolyn was asked about the greatest influence in her religious development, she said: "[It was my] grandparents' influence. We just grew up with that belief. So it has just been our way of life." Carolyn's granddaughter (G4), Susan, described the pattern of family religious influence in subsequent generations:

> 'We all play a part. Like, right now, my mom teaches her grandkids, my son and my sister's sons. She'll tell them about why [we love and follow Jesus]. Then their aunts, like my sisters, will all add things to it. So we're all active in that. We're all into it.'

From great-grandparents to grandmother Carolyn and on to her children and grandchildren, the Wilsons' story is one of religious continuity. Intergenerational religious momentum is maintained by grandparents and parents telling and retelling religious stories and maxims. There is remarkable similarity across generations in how they describe God, focusing on a sense of personal relationship. David (G1) said: "God is a person to me." His grandson, Ken (G3), said: "He's a personal God … You can relate to Him; you can talk to Him … [T]he Holy Spirit is the personal side that comes and dwells in us." Ken talked about his grandparents' example and what they taught him: "It just all boils down to that relationship with Jesus Christ. That's the main thing they passed down [to us] and everything springs from there."

In looking for explanations concerning such strong multigenerational continuity across families like the Wilsons, we found two things that were prominent: the consistent example in religious practice and beliefs (**role modelling**) of the older generations, and the warmth and affirmation (affectual solidarity) that characterised intergenerational relationships. These observations support the intergenerational solidarity model described at the beginning of this chapter. Each generation in the Wilson family mentioned the warmth and support of the older generation as a factor that enhanced their faith – and religious continuity across generations.

Religious decline across generations

The most common pattern found in the quantitative analysis was religious decline. The qualitative results reveal this type of family among grandparents who either were not involved or were unsuccessful in socialising children and grandchildren to their religious beliefs and practices.

The Jacksons are a family in which grandparents have had little to do with their grandchildren's religious training. When asked what she learned from her grandparents about religion, Myrna (G1) replied: "Not a great deal. We just grew [up] by ourselves." Similarly, Myrna seems to have had little impact on her own grandchildren's religiosity. Myrna's granddaughter, Karen (G3), said about religion:

> 'That was just one subject that wasn't brought up, wasn't talked about, because there were too many different beliefs, I guess ... If I did believe something, it was best to just keep it quiet, keep it to yourself to avoid coming under attack for believing or not.'

Relationships in this family were characterised by a degree of emotional detachment with grandparents.

In an unsuccessful attempt to influence her family, Gladys Sanchez (G1) is a devout Catholic who would very much like all her family to follow in her Catholic faith, but some of her great-grandchildren have not been baptised – a situation she finds to be quite distressing and adversely affecting the quality of her relationship with her adult grandchildren. Speaking about her granddaughter Natasha, she laments:

> 'They don't baptise their kids ... I told them, it's not right. Natasha's mother [Gladys's daughter, grandmother to the children in question] should tell them, why they don't baptise? I wish I could get one of the [boys], and just take them to be baptised. Maybe I'll do it myself.'

Religious strengthening across generations

A less common type of family is where the grandchild followed the grandparent's religious commitment, sometimes in a stronger form. Shari Sabelli (G3) said she had an "extremely close" relationship with her grandfather, Leo (G1), in the context of a difficult childhood. They lived in the same neighborhood, allowing for regular interaction that served as a source of stability during her mother's frequent hospitalisations and her parents' divorce. Shari recalls taking comfort in the predictable routine of attending Catholic mass with her grandfather:

'It meant we were all going to be in the same place together. My grandfather always had a carnation in his lapel. We sat in the same seats. It was predictable. And most of what was going on in my family life just wasn't predictable.'

She says the closeness of their relationship contributed to her grandfather's influence on her religious values:

'My Grandpa Leo ... influenced me, because I saw him living [his Catholic faith]. He didn't just go to church or talk about it; he lived the tenets of the faith. He was wonderful. He was like a rock for me. You know, when everything was going bad, he was the rock.'

Shari's cousin, Nina (G3), is also in our sample. She too talks about her close relationship with their grandfather. Nina says Leo is responsible for the important role religion plays in her life today. This contrasts with the emotional distance she felt from her own father. A warm and affirming grandfather, Leo was highly involved in the lives of his grandchildren and played an important role in their religious development. The close bonds he developed with his grandchildren compensated for the solidarity that was missing in their emotionally distant relationships with their parents.

Another example of religious strengthening was reported by Norman Bernstein (G2) and his grandchildren. He said it has become his goal to maintain the family's Orthodox Jewish traditions for his grandchildren. Norman's efforts appear to have paid off; his granddaughter, Rachel (G4), today attends synagogue services regularly. She recalls religious holidays she spent with her grandfather as a child:

'I remember going to temple with my grandma and my grandpa and walking with them because it was a holiday and they only walked to temple. They were Orthodox so I had to sit with my grandma and my grandpa sat with my brother, and I always remember just really enjoying being with them on that holiday.'

Another grandchild, Grant (G4), ages 28, said he felt "extremely close" to his grandfather and attends synagogue services on a regular basis.

Discussion

This study used a mixed-methods approach to examine family dynamics in religious continuity and discontinuity across grandparents, parents and grandchildren. By focusing on the religiosity of individuals in three linked generations, we treated the family lineage as an arena of interaction and mutual influence. Qualitative and quantitative analyses provided unique but complementary vantage points from which to view both the patterns and the processes by which religion is transmitted (or not transmitted) from grandparents to descending generations. Further, because the United States represents a religious outlier among western countries, intergenerational transmission of religiosity – and grandparents' involvement – represents a particularly salient family dynamic.

We found that the largest category of religious change consisted of multigenerational triads exhibiting *declines* in religious intensity, representing about two thirds of grandmother-headed and half of grandfather-headed triads; the greater drop for grandmother-headed triads was partially due to relatively stronger religiosity among grandmothers. However, significant numbers of both types of intergenerational triads – more than a quarter of each – were *stable* in their religious intensity, and about one quarter of grandfather-headed triads showed *increasing* religious intensity through the generations. Thus, there is significant heterogeneity in religious patterns, with a sizable proportion characterised by generational continuity and even strengthening religious intensity.

Our predictive models revealed that emotional closeness between grandchildren and grandparents enhanced intergenerational religious continuity or inhibited its decline. This effect persisted even when controlling for grandparents' religious denomination, suggesting that this finding transcends the boundaries of particular religious dogmas and borders on something universal. The qualitative analysis was instructive for understanding in greater depth the general patterns characterised by the survey data. Warmth and intimacy was a theme repeated in the qualitative narratives of those continuing the religious traditions of their grandparents. As these examples suggest, family continuity – or discontinuity – in religion is often linked to grandparental intervention and the capacity of grandparents to forge strong emotional ties to their grandchildren. When grandparents had conflicted relationships with children or grandchildren and there was low intergenerational solidarity, we saw fewer examples of intergenerational continuity.

Synthesising the qualitative and quantitative analyses, we find considerable consistency in the results. Both sets of analyses found that religious continuity between grandparents and grandchildren was strongest when grandchild–grandparent relations were emotionally close. One conclusion we draw is that the emotional component of intergenerational relationships serves as a facilitator of the transmission process. Nevertheless, we must be careful to acknowledge that religious reproduction and religious drift across generations may be reasons why some relationships were close and others were not. The narratives point to retrospective accounts of fondness for grandparents that grew out of shared religious experiences and rituals.

In the qualitative data, we found evidence that grandparents' efforts to transmit their religious orientations to their descendants were sometimes not successful – a finding consistent with evidence from the quantitative data that continuous religious decline represented the most common intergenerational pattern. Yet it would be a mistake to paint all families as secularising through generational time, as a significant minority of families in our quantitative analysis exhibited religious stability or strengthening. Further, the qualitative findings showed that even when grandparents didn't fully reproduce their religious orientations in their children and grandchildren, they often conveyed elements of religiosity – such as rituals or a diffuse sense of spirituality – through the generations.

One contribution of this study is the extension of intergenerational socialisation to include the contribution of grandparents. It provides support for the life-course perspective's sociological framework, which has emphasised how social contexts influence individual development. Particularly useful is the concept from the life-course perspective of **linked lives** – operationalised as grandparents' religious influence in the context of intergenerational solidarity. From the narratives, we see how grandparents modelling their religious beliefs and practices for their grandchildren, coupled with grandchildren's reminiscences of warm, affirming grandparenting during their youth, have led to the internalisation and passing on of those beliefs and practices across the generations.

A second contribution is to remind family scholars of the salience of religion and spirituality as a source of social and moral connection in families emanating from the grandparents' generation. There is something about values and religion that 'sticks around' families over generations, which we call **intergenerational momentum**. In our qualitative data, we see that the legacy of grandparents, great-grandparents and even great-great-grandparents can live on, long after

226

they have passed away, in the stories families tell about them. The quantitative analysis identified these families as characterised by stable or increasing religious intensity. Evidence of intergenerational religious momentum may be surprising to some researchers who have focused only on the 'decline' in religion.

Conclusion

Our data suggest that passing down religious values was a goal that many grandparents were willing to invest considerable time and effort into, and that grandparents were articulate about maintaining intergenerational momentum – transmitting to younger generations the spiritual values and religious practices they had found to be so valuable in their own lives. However, even when grandparents are successful at transmitting certain aspects of their religious traditions to subsequent generations, religious identities may still follow a path toward greater secularisation, as our quantitative data suggest.

The results of this study indicate that families are diversified in their capacity to pass on religion through the generations. On the one hand, we observed in both qualitative and quantitative analyses considerable amounts of discontinuity in religious orientations across three generations. On the other hand, many families exhibited continuity and have retained considerable moral and religious influence over several generations. Whether grandparents – most of whom will be in better health and with more financial resources than grandparents in the past – will be more influential in future cohorts remains an open question (Bengtson, 2013; Kemp, 2007; Swartz, 2009). It is possible that the strong trend toward secularisation in the United States – at a rate now comparable to Western Europe (Voas and Chaves, 2016) – will render grandparents less effective in reproducing their religious orientations across younger generations.

Future research may do well to examine the consequences when transmission does not occur in more orthodox religions. In earlier research, we found that sharp religious divergences interrupt intergenerational continuity and can be a source of great pain to devout parents and grandparents (Bengtson, 2013). Processes of religious socialisation that lead to failure – to blocked intergenerational momentum – are as important to study as those that lead to outcomes desired by grandparents and parents.

Based on this study, it can be expected that many, if not most, religious grandparents will continue to transmit moral and religious values across generations in some form, while others will see their youth following the historical trend toward secularism or unconventional religious expression. This diversification is part and parcel of what some scholars have called the emergent independence of young adults from the influence of their older family members (Arnett, 2004; Rosenfeld and Kim, 2005). Whether the overall strength of intergenerational transmission from grandparents will decline, plateau or perhaps increase awaits future research, but it seems certain that the salience of religion as a source of intergenerational cohesion – or tension – will remain well into the 21st century.

Acknowledgement

This research was supported by a grant from the John Templeton Foundation.

References

AARP. (2012) *Insights and spending habits of modern grandparents*, Washington DC: AARP Research and Strategic Analysis.

Arnett, J. (2004) *Emerging adulthood: The winding road from the late teens through the twenties*, New York: Oxford University Press.

Bellah, R.N., Madsen, R., Sullivan, W.M., Swidler, A. and Tipton, S.M. (1985) *Habits of the heart: Individualism and commitment in American life*, New York: Harper and Row.

Bengtson, V.L. (1970) 'The generation gap: A review and typology of social–psychological perspectives', *Youth and Society*, 2, 7–32.

Bengtson, V.L. (2001) 'Beyond the nuclear family: The increasing importance of multigenerational relationships in American society', *Journal of Marriage and Family* 63(1): 1–16.

Bengtson, V.L. (2013) *Families and faith: How religion is passed down across generations*, Oxford: Oxford University Press.

Bengtson, V.L., Giarrusso, R., Mabry, J.B. and Silverstein, M. (2002) 'Solidarity, conflict, and ambivalence: Complementary or competing perspectives on intergenerational relationships?', *Journal of Marriage and the Family*, 64: 568–576.

Birditt, K.S., Tighe, L.A., Fingerman, K.L. and Zarit, S.H. (2012) 'Intergenerational relationship quality across three generations', *Journal of Gerontology, Psychological Sciences and Social Sciences*, 67: 627–638.

Chaves, M.A. (2011) *American religion: Contemporary trends*. Princeton, NJ: Princeton and Oxford.

Cherlin, A.J. (2009) *The marriage-go-round: The state of marriage and the family in America today*. New York: Alfred A. Knopf.

Copen, C.A. and Silverstein, M. (2008) 'Intergenerational transmission of religious beliefs to young adults: Do grandmothers matter?', *Journal of Contemporary Family Studies*, 38: 497–510.

Elder, G.H., Jr., Johnson, M.K. and Crosnoe, R. (2003) 'The emergence and development of life course theory', in J.T. Mortimer and M. Shanahan (eds), *Handbook of the life course*, New York: Kluwer Academic/Plenum Publishers, pp 3–19.

Feng, D., Silverstein, M., Giarrusso, R., McArdle, J. and Bengtson, V.L. (2006) 'Attrition of older parents in a three-decade study of multigenerational families', *Journals of Gerontology: Social Science*, 61: S343–S328.

Geurts, T., Poortman, A., van Tilburg, T. and Dykstra, P.A. (2009) 'Contact between grandchildren and their grandparents in early adulthood', *Journal of Family Issues*, 30: 1698–1713.

Goyer, A. (2012) *Study: Grandparents give 'til it hurts. Generations United: Grandparents investing in grandchildren: The MetLife Study on how grandparents share their time, values and money.* Available at: http://blog.aarp.org/2012/09/08/amy-goyer-grandparents-financial-gifts.

Hout, M. and Fischer, C.S. (2002) 'Why more Americans have no religious preference: Politics and generations', *American Sociological Review*, 65: 165–190.

Kemp, C. (2007) 'Grandparent–grandchild ties: Reflections on continuity and change across three generations', *Journal of Family Issues*, 28: 855–879.

King, V. and Elder, Jr, G. H. (1999) 'Are religious grandparents more involved grandparents?', *Journal of Gerontology: Social Sciences*, 54: S317–S328.

Lampkin, C.L. (2012) *Insights and spending habits of modern grandparents*, Washington, DC: AARP: Research and Strategic Analysis. Available at: http://www.aarp.org/research.

Michaleski, R.L. and Shackelford, T.K. (2005) 'Grandparental investment as a function of relational uncertainty and emotional closeness with parents', *Human Nature*, 16: 293–305.

Min, J., Silverstein, M. and Lendon, J.P. (2012) 'Intergenerational transmission of value over the family life course', *Advances in Life Course Research*, 17: 112–120.

Monserud, M.A. (2008) 'Intergenerational relationships and affectual solidarity between grandparents and young adults', *Journal of Marriage and Family*, 70: 182–195.

Mueller, M.M. and Elder, Jr., G.H. (2003) 'Family contingencies across the generations: Grandparent–grandchild relationships in holistic perspective', *Journal of Marriage and Family*, 65: 404–417.

Pew Forum on Religion and Public Life (2012) '"Nones" on the rise: One-in-five adults have no religious affiliation.' Available at: http:/pewforum.org/Unaffiliated/nones-on-the rise.aspx.

Pew Forum on Religion and Public Life. (2015) *US public becoming less religious*. Washington DC: Pew Research Center. Available at: http://pewforum.org/reports.

Popenoe, D. (1993) 'American family decline, 1960-1990: A review and appraisal', *Journal of Marriage and the Family*, 55(3): 527–542.

Putnam, R.D. (2000) *Bowling alone: The collapse and revival of American community*. New York: Simon and Schuster.

Putnam, R.D. and Campbell, D. (2010) *American grace: How religion divides and unites us*. New York: Simon and Schuster.

Rosenfeld, M.J. and Kim, B.S. (2005) 'The independence of young adults and the rise of interracial and same-sex unions', *American Sociological Review*, 70(4): 541–562.

Schönpflug, U. (2001) 'Intergenerational transmission of values the role of transmission belts', *Journal of Cross-Cultural Psychology*, 32(2): 174–185.

Silverstein, M., Bengtson, V.L. and Lawton, L. (1997) 'Intergenerational solidarity and the structure of adult child–parent relationships in American families', *American Journal of Sociology*, 103: 429–460.

Silverstein, M. and Marenco, A. (2001) 'How Americans enact the grandparent role', *Journal of Family Issues*, 22: 493–522.

Smith, C. and Denton, M. (2005) *Soul searching: The religious and spiritual lives of American teenagers*, New York: Oxford University Press.

Smith, C. and Snell, P. (2009) *Souls in transition: The religious and spiritual lives of emerging adults*, New York: Oxford University Press.

Swartz, T.T. (2009) 'Intergenerational family relationships in adulthood: Patterns, variations, and implications in the contemporary United States', *Annual Review of Sociology*, 35: 191–212.

Uhlenberg, P.R. (2005) 'Historical forces shaping grandparent–grandchild relationships: Demography and beyond', in M. Silverstein (ed) *Intergenerational relations across time and place*, New York: Springer, pp 77–97.

Uhlenberg, P.R. (2009) 'Children in an aging society', *The Journals of Gerontology, Series B: Psychological Sciences and Social Sciences*, 64B: 489–496.

US Bureau of the Census (2009) 'Grandparents as caregivers'. Available at: http://www.census.gov/newsroom/releases/archives/facts_for_features_special_editions/cb11-ff17.html.

Vermunt, J.K. and Magidson, J. (2013) *Latent GOLD 5.0 Upgrade Manual*, Belmont, MA: Statistical Innovations Inc.

Voas, D. and Chaves, M. (2016) 'Is the United States a counterexample to the secularization thesis?', *American Journal of Sociology*, 121(5): 1517–1556.

Wuthnow, R. (1978) *Experimentation in American religion*, Berkeley and Los Angeles, CA: University of California Press.

Wuthnow, R. (1988) *The restructuring of American religion: Society and faith since World War II*, Princeton, NJ: Princeton University Press.

Wuthnow, R. (2007) *After the baby boomers: How twenty- and thirty-somethings are shaping the future of American religion*, Princeton, NJ: Princeton University Press.

TWELVE

Can Chinese grandparents say no? A comparison of grandmothers in two Asian cities

Esther C.L. Goh and Sheng-li Wang

Introduction

This chapter interrogates two dominant research constructs found in studies on Chinese grandparents providing childcare to grandchildren, namely **cultural obligation** and **intergenerational reciprocity** (Chen, 2006; Fei, 1982, 1992; Wu and Sun, 2003). The prominence of these two constructs could be attributed to their relationship to the Confucian value of filial piety, which governed family relationships in China for thousands of years. In the Confucian system, both the roles and duties of family members are connected through mutual interdependence over the life course (Hwang, 1999). Chinese grandparents are portrayed as 'enjoying family happiness' and caregiving is considered as a willing exchange for the help they receive from their children because Chinese grandparents tend to consider the welfare of the family, particularly their desire to *chuan zhong jie dai* (maintain the family line), before their own interests (Chen, 2006; Fei, 1982, 1992; Low and Goh, 2015). Research findings tend to report positive physical and mental health outcomes for grandparents caring for grandchildren (Guo et al., 2008; Chen et al., 2011), alluding to grandchild care as contributing towards intergenerational solidarity and intergenerational reciprocal caregiving.

Notwithstanding their popularity and contributions, we question whether cultural obligation and intergenerational reciprocity have unwittingly silenced the diverse voices of Chinese older persons with regards to grandchild care. Recent studies have begun to report insights into intergenerational tension in Asian families, particularly highlighting the challenges faced by grandparents who provide informal childcare (Goh, 2009; Goh et al., 2016; Low and Goh, 2015; Teo et al., 2006; Xu et al., 2017). These tensions were felt acutely, particularly by grandmothers, as the task of intensive and hands-on grandchild care provision falls overwhelmingly on women – hence our focus on grandmothers in this chapter. We agree with Timonen and Doyle (2012) that grandparental agency has remained an underappreciated and undertheorised aspect of grandparenting. That is, instead of examining the provision of childcare as Chinese grandmothers' response to cultural obligations and contributing to enhanced intergenerational reciprocity, grandmothers should be viewed as strategic agents who actively shape their relationships with adult children and grandchildren through generating different types of connections with them, in which providing childcare could be one of the agentic decisions. To explicate and theorise grandmothers as active agents, this chapter utilises social relational theory (SRT), which treats parents and children as equally agentic in their relationships to address the question: 'Can Chinese grandparents say "no" to providing grandchild care?'. This chapter reports on two groups of grandmothers, (1) those who provide informal childcare to grandchildren and (2) those who do not, to unpack potential differences between the agentic expressions of these two groups of Chinese grandmothers.

Grandmothers as active agents

Existing gerontological theories tend to conceptualise grandparents as passive, operating under pressures from lineage, gender, economic and social structural forces that leave the older persons without alternatives (Pierce and Timonen, 2010; Timonen and Doyle, 2012). Challenging the intergenerational solidarity perspective, Connidis and McMullin (2002) proposed using the **sociological ambivalence** framework to examine how social structural forces collide with individual agency of older persons in negotiating relationships with their adult daughters. While we acknowledge sociological ambivalence for highlighting the centrality of agency, this theory does not provide the concrete tools to guide researchers in explicating, identifying and measuring agency in older persons.

To complement this, we utilise SRT (Kuczynski and De Mol, 2015) – originally formulated by developmental psychologists to study parent–child relationships but now being applied to various disciplines, including social work (Chee et al., 2014), education (Quan-McGimpsey et al., 2013) and health research (Goh and Hsu, 2013) – which provides useful constructs to propel the theorising of agency in gerontological research. SRT is a conceptual framework rooted in the dialectical concept of transactional processes in socialisation

(Kuczynski and De Mol, 2015). In SRT, (older) parents and (adult) children are considered to interact as human agents and components of a culturally embedded social relationship. Older parents and adult children are human agents with inherent capacity to make sense of the environment, initiate change and resist domination by others (Low and Goh, 2015), as agency is viewed as a universal given notion (Kuczynski, 2003). SRT provides clear conceptual definitions of agency to aid us in examining the intricate intergenerational relationship between older parents and their adult children in the context of childcare provision.

While all humans are agents, SRT proposes that they differ in the resources they have to support their actions as agents. Hence, resources constitute power. SRT proposes three sources of power. **Individual resources** include physical strength, control over rewards, expertise and information. **Relational resources** involve access to personal relationships as support for the exercise of agency. **Cultural resources** refer to the rights, entitlements and constraints conveyed to individuals by the laws, customs and practices of a culture (Kuczynski, 2003). SRT thus posits a relational and culturally embedded concept of human agency in the dynamics of relationships between (older) parents and (adult) children. Because of the relational perspective embraced by SRT, this framework considers coexistence of opposing components as inherent in parent–child relationships. (Older) parents and (adult) children are agents, according to SRT, and have separate and potentially conflicting needs, perspectives and goals. They are, however, continually embedded within the unity and interdependence of their shared relationship. Hence, contradictions and ambivalence are integral components of dynamics between (older) parents and (adult) children. In this chapter, we examine the agency of grandmothers through unpacking the rationales for their involvement or non-involvement in childcare, and the goals and meanings they ascribe to their decisions. We view grandparents as agents; that is, capable of setting goals, devising plans and strategies and taking actions to achieve their goals in the relational contexts with their adult children and grandchildren.

Chinese grandmothers in two Asian cities

This chapter interrogates the dominant narratives of 'grandmothers willingly exchange nanny service for assistance from their adult children' and the 'harmonious intergenerational solidarity picture' in Chinese societies by examining two Asian cities: Fuzhou (in the Fujian province of South China) and Singapore. The cultural similarities between these two cities enable comparison. The majority of residents in Fujian speak the Southern Min dialect (known as the *Hokkien* dialect in Singapore). Approximately 75% of Singapore's population is Chinese. Many of the early immigrants who came from China to settle in Singapore were from the Fujian province and spoke the Chinese dialect, *Hokkien*. Hence, many Chinese Singaporeans share similar ancestral roots with residents of Fujian (Goh and Goransson, 2011). These two cities have both experienced rapid economic development and urbanisation and share similar demographic patterns, such as low fertility and an ageing population. In addition, grandmothers are traditionally expected to play active roles in providing childcare in both societies. A survey of Singaporeans' social attitudes found that 85% of respondents felt grandparents should play a role in raising their grandchildren (National Family Council, 2011). Similarly, the China Research Centre for Aging reported that, in 2006, 41.4% of urban older persons and 35.8% of their rural counterparts cared for their grandchildren (Zhang, 2010).

While these two cities share similar Confucian cultural roots, it is noteworthy that their interpretations of Confucian values have evolved differently. In Singapore, the state championed Confucian ethics in the late 1980s and early 1990s to define its national cultural values and instil a sense of identity as a young nation (Velayutham, 2007). Confucian values were used also as a discourse to bring distance from western culture, which was perceived as undesirable (Hill, 2000). On the other hand, Singapore's past as a British colony, and its choice of English as its official language and language of education after independence, means the influence of western values in the society is undeniable.

This contrasts with China, where Confucianism underwent savage assault during the Cultural Revolution between 1966 and 1976. Many of the grandmothers participating in this study in Fuzhou had experienced that social upheaval. In recent years, however, the Chinese government has invoked Confucian values and harmony as the core elements of its governing philosophy (Zhou, 2011). The key research questions that will be addressed in this chapter are:

1. To what extent do their similar yet diverse Confucian roots influence grandmothers in Fuzhou and Singapore in their decisions to provide childcare?
2. What are the sociocultural discourses of grandparenthood in the two cities?
3. Do such discourses constrain or facilitate their sense of agency in decision-making?

Methods

With the aim to foreground the agency of Chinese grandmothers in the issue of childcare provision, we study two groups of grandmothers: childcare providers (Singapore: n=10; Fuzhou: n=10) and non-childcare providers (Singapore: n=10; Fuzhou: n=10). Few studies, if any, examine the intricate rationales for Chinese grandmothers who do *not* provide childcare to grandchildren. It can be assumed that non-childcare providers may have a greater sense of agency as their non-caregiving goes against the grain of societal expectations. By comparing these two groups of grandmothers we hope to illustrate the range of senses of agency expressed by Chinese grandmothers in the two Asian cities.

To access nuanced insights into grandparents' caregiving decisions and experiences, the authors utilised their networks to recruit grandmothers who are engaged in grandchild care and those who are not. The first author is a native of Singapore and the second author is a citizen of Fujian. Recruiting participants through our networks facilitated trust and minimised reservations on the part of the participants. The authors trained three research assistants from both sites (the first author trained those in Singapore and both authors jointly trained those in Fuzhou) before deploying them to conduct the in-depth interviews with grandmothers. As the topic could be sensitive to some grandmothers, we paid attention to creating a safe space for participants to be able to express their range of experiences of providing care, the relationship dynamics with their adult children and grandchildren, their interpretations of family obligations and whether they expected reciprocity on the part of their adult children.

In total, 40 grandmothers were recruited from the two research sites. We avoided recruiting grandmothers who had severe health issues and those who were recipients of financial assistance, as health and financial stressors could confound decisions regarding provision of childcare. For the 20 grandmothers from Singapore, the mean age of grandmothers who cared for grandchildren was 63.7; for non-caregivers, it was 62.3. Among Singaporean grandmothers who did not provide care, six were in paid employment. There was no salient difference in the reported educational backgrounds of these Singaporean grandmothers. In comparison, caregiving grandmothers from Fuzhou were on average 61.2 years old and their non-caregiving counterparts were 64.5 years old. Among the non-caregiving grandmothers from Fuzhou, three reported they were in paid employment. All interviews took place in venues determined by the grandmothers. Most of the interviews were conducted in their homes, with some being carried out on the ground floor of the open-space area in their apartments. Informed consent was sought from the participants and consent for audio recording was obtained before the commencement of the interviews. Participants received a token of approximately US$29 at the end of the interviews. Research ethical approval was granted by the Institute Review Board of the National University of Singapore (NUS–IRB – A-16-375E).

Findings

In this section, we report the findings of our interrogation of the two dominant concepts in literature:

1. With regards to the rationale for grandmothers' agreement or refusal to provide childcare to grandchildren, we attempted to understand the extent to which Chinese **cultural obligation** influences grandmothers' childcare-related decisions.
2. To gain insight into whether Chinese **intergenerational reciprocity** is a significant consideration, we asked the grandmothers whether a belief that providing childcare is a form of 'paying forward for their old-age care' influenced their decisions.

Comparison and analysis of grandmothers who said 'yes' or 'no' to childcare provision across the two sites will be presented.

Grandmothers' perceptions of cultural obligation in caring for grandchildren

Grandmothers who said 'Yes'

Among Singaporean grandmothers who provided informal childcare (n=10), only three reported a sense of cultural obligation and claimed that providing childcare was "a natural option" – alluding to the lack of plans after retirement and therefore caring for grandchildren as the readily available option to occupy themselves. Two, however, explicitly stated that cultural obligation had no influence over their decisions:

> INTERVIEWER: 'Do you think that Chinese culture has affected your decision of whether to take care of your grandchildren?'

GRANDMOTHER: 'No … not Chinese culture. It depends on the person, whether they want to take care [of grandchildren] or not.'

Instead, caregiving grandmothers in Singapore were influenced by a desire to "contribute to the next generation" and because they "enjoyed caregiving". A surprising finding revealed that two of this group were "not interested in being grandmothers", one of whom disclosed that she had to "force" herself to say yes because her adult children persuaded her to accede to the request:

'My immediate thought [when eldest son requested her to care for the grandchild] was that I do not wish to take care of my grandchild. Then he [child's parent] said, "Well it's up to you". But my second and youngest sons persuaded me to help him out since my eldest son is my son after all. Eventually, I thought that I could not possibly bear to see my own child suffer – regardless of the situation, they are still my children and grandchildren. So I just shrugged it [the resistance] off and agreed to take care of the grandchild.'

It is interesting to note that these two "reluctant" grandmothers stated "availability of domestic helpers" as a condition for agreeing so that they could provide "supervision" and not perform direct caring. Rather than cultural obligation, several grandmothers cited the "lack of viable caregiving options" as compelling them to provide care, or as "last resort" of care. For instance, grandmothers cited the need for adult children to work, a grandchild's poor health or grandchildren being unable to adjust to other care options as grounds for agreeing to step in. One finding unique to two Singaporean grandmothers is the explicit consideration of the cost for agreeing to provide childcare before stepping into it – namely, costs to their health (one grandmother has spine problems) – and hesitation about long-term commitment:

'I knew it would be difficult because once I agreed to this, there would be a lot of follow-up action … it is not like working, you cannot possibly resign just because you do not like it. You cannot possibly say, "I do not wish to take care of this grandchild anymore, I give her back to you", because what would my adult children do then? So no

choice … as time goes by and the grandchildren grow up
slowly that will allow me to eventually let go.'

As such, these two grandmothers had to convince themselves and
overcome their reservations before embarking on childcare provision.

More grandmothers from Fuzhou (n=9) than grandmothers in
Singapore cited family obligation (nine out of ten grandmothers) as
the main motivating factor for caregiving. The common expressions
of a sense of cultural obligation included "heaven-given duties"
(*tiānjīngdìyì*; 天经地义), "doing it unquestioningly" (*yīnggāi de*; 应
该的) and "duty" (*yìwu*; 义务). The extent of obligation is so strong
that nine grandmothers said caring for grandchildren was "so natural"
(*shùn qí zìrán*: 顺其自然; *zìrán'érrán*: 自然而然) that no consideration
is needed: "I have never considered whether to provide care, it is our
duty. Even if my daughter-in-law does not have a good relationship
with us, I have the obligation and duty to provide care. If we do not
care for the child, who would?"

Close analysis of data showed that part of the strong obligation
stemmed from the perceived responsibility of paternal grandparents
(n=6): "Such duties [childcare] should be performed by the paternal
family. Maternal grandparents have no obligation because the child
does not carry on our family name." On the other hand, the reverse
is true too. Owing to China's one-child policy, implemented in 1979
and only relaxed recently, most adult daughters are the only children
of their families; hence, maternal grandmothers are keen to care for
the grandchild(ren):

> 'Yes I am willing to do it [care for grandchild] out of the
> love for our own daughter [even when the grandchild does
> not carry on our family line]. I have only one grandchild
> so I am very motivated to care for the child.'

Another reason for the heavy sense of obligation can be attributed
to the cultural perception of other care options. All ten caregiving
grandmothers from Fuzhou deemed both childcare centres and nannies
(*bǎomǔ*; 保姆) to be inferior care options:

> 'Do you think the workers in the childcare centre will
> patiently feed the child? They only do it as a job, unlike
> us the grandparents, we are very patient and careful. The
> safety measures in childcare centres are questionable.'

'Engaging nannies means incurring expenses, besides, trustworthy nannies are hard to come by. When both parents are working and entrust the child to the nanny, you do not know whether she [nanny] will feed "that thing" [drug] to the child to keep [the child] quiet and easy to manage. For us grandparents, they [grandchildren] are our flesh and blood, we will not harm them.'

Grandmothers who 'said no'

Since it is a normative expectation in both societies for grandparents to be actively involved in providing childcare, it is helpful to examine the rationales for non-involvement of the two groups of grandmothers from both sites to illuminate the possible agentic qualities in decision-making that defied expectations. For Singaporean grandmothers who did not provide childcare (n=10), the two main rationales reported were that they were working full time and thus did not have time to be full-time caregivers (n=6), and that other options of care were available – including childcare centres (n=2), the mother (having resigned from work to care for the child) (n=1), domestic helpers (n=1) and the other set of grandparents (n=2). In addition to these two 'socially acceptable reasons for not providing childcare' – that is, their own employment and availability of other care options – Singaporean grandmothers revealed subtle inner struggles that might contribute to their hesitation in proactively providing care, including the "desire to avoid conflict with adult children over care of grandchildren" and the statements that "grandchild care is demanding" and "caregiving is a long-term commitment". It is noteworthy that these non-caregiving grandmothers tended to endorse the alternative care options. For instance, they exalted the other caregiving grandparents as "more competent in caring for children" – one grandmother said that the other grandmother had been a babysitter all along and therefore had more experience. Childcare centres were perceived as a superior option of care by some, as one grandmother explained: "because at the childcare [centre] you [grandchild] can learn more things. Because the child will obey the teacher … there are a lot of activities and the child tends to learn more [as compared to grandparents caring for the child at home]". Although these grandmothers did not provide full-time care to grandchildren, some of them expressed openness to providing supplementary or occasional care when necessary. One grandmother said she told her daughter: "when you need me, I will do my best, but I cannot stay there the entire day to take care of the child". When asked whether they faced pressure from the Chinese sense of obligation for grandmothers to provide childcare, two grandmothers were adamant that caring for grandchildren was not their duty. One said: "You have spent so many years looking after your family, by the time your grandchild comes, your duties are finished", and another asserted: "In my opinion, in this day and age, it is best for the parents to take care [of their children] themselves. Grandmothers tend to 'spoil' them."

As for the grandmothers from Fuzhou, the main reason behind non-caregiving was that the other set of grandparents were caring for the grandchild (all ten non-caregiving grandmothers cited this as the reason). Strictly speaking, most of these grandmothers did not actively 'say no' to the duty of childcare. It is interesting to note that, of these ten grandmothers, six maternal grandmothers reported that the paternal grandparents were the caregivers. This is consistent with the findings from the paternal grandmothers reported earlier, who strongly considered it their duty to preserve the family name by caring for their grandchildren. While paternal grandmothers were deemed more obligated to provide childcare, in this study there was no evidence to suggest that these paternal grandparents absolved from providing childcare when the grandchild was a girl. Only one grandmother stated that grandsons would be preferred, as daughters are "spilled water" (*po chuqu de shui*; 泼出去的水); granddaughters do not carry the family name, and, therefore, are like 'wasted spilled water' that does not add value to the family. In contrast, eight of the ten non-caregiving grandmothers in Fuzhou stated there was no difference in the value of male or female grandchild. Three grandmothers (two maternal and one paternal) did not have a chance to provide childcare because their adult children-in-law were "only children" and therefore the other grandparents wanted the privilege of caring for the only grandchild in their family. Findings from interviews revealed a subtle sense of competition among the older persons to provide childcare:

> 'I think we should just go with the flow (*shùn qí zìrán*; 顺其自然), if there is a need, I will help [with childcare] or if there is no need, I will not fight over it [care for grandchild]. This [if we fight] will cause tension and I tend to avoid tension.'

Since non-caregiving was not their active choice, this might account for the apparent absence of guilt among these grandmothers, considering the strong sense of cultural obligation in Fuzhou for grandmothers to provide childcare. On the contrary, they deemed their decision "not to fight" with the other set of grandparents to be magnanimous. Non-provision of childcare in such cases is not a selfish choice but rather a "selfless decision".

In addition to the dominant reason of care being provided by the other set of grandparents, other reasons cited for non-caregiving included health issues and old age (n=5) and active work life (n=4). Two grandmothers from Fuzhou mentioned that not having to care for grandchildren allowed them to have time and energy to participate in their own hobbies. While defying the dominant Chinese cultural obligation, these grandmothers did contribute to their grandchildren in other ways. Three paternal grandmothers who were still actively working full time and not providing childcare said they gave money to engage a nanny (when the other set of grandparents were not available), paid for insurance policies for their grandchildren and provided financial support to their adult children. One maternal grandmother reported that she contributed 4,000 yuan (approximately US$614) every month towards the expenses of her grandchild. Other support in kind provided by grandmothers included gifts (n=4), buying grandchildren's favourite food (n=2) and paying for groceries for adult children's households (n=3). None of the grandmothers interviewed mentioned or alluded to any relationship difficulties with their adult children or avoidance of the demands of childcare as reasons for their non-caregiving.

Overall, therefore, it is observed that the Chinese cultural sense of obligation to provide childcare to grandchildren is more frequently and strongly expressed by grandmothers from Fuzhou than their counterparts from Singapore. Grandmothers from Fuzhou described their caregiving as "heaven-given duties", thought they "should do it unquestioningly" and saw it as a "duty", particularly for paternal grandparents. Expression of such intense cultural obligation was almost entirely absent among Singaporean grandmothers who cared for grandchildren; milder expressions such as "natural option after retirement" and "individual choice" were motivations behind their choice. It is interesting that Singaporean grandmothers were more vocal about the costs and struggles of being called upon to care for grandchildren. Such ambivalence was not found in the narratives of grandmothers from Fuzhou.

For grandmothers who did not provide childcare, it is noteworthy that the key difference between the participants from these two cities lies in the fact that no grandmothers from Fuzhou *chose* not to provide childcare. Instead, they were "deprived" of the chance of caring, whereas their Singaporean counterparts cited issues of working full time and the availability of other childcare options as relieving them of the responsibility of providing childcare. Non-caregiving grandmothers from Fuzhou felt not only no sense of guilt (despite the strong cultural obligation) but also that giving up the privilege of caring for grandchildren to the other set of grandparents was an act of generosity.

Grandmothers' perceptions of childcare provision and intergenerational reciprocity

Grandmothers who provided childcare

When asked whether they considered providing childcare as part of a cycle of reciprocity with their adult children, particularly as 'advance payment for their own old age care', eight out of ten grandmothers from Singapore disagreed. One grandmother likened expecting reciprocity to expecting a river to flow upstream rather than downstream (*shuǐ shì shùnzhe liú, méiyǒu dàoliú de*; 水是顺着流，没有倒流的) and regarded such a notion "impossible". Three grandmothers who also disagreed with the reciprocity concept were less extreme in their stance – instead of "expectation", they said they had "hope":

> 'I would say it [intergenerational reciprocity] is a great idea but it will not work out. And I don't want to expect. I will love [for them] to [do so], but I don't want to have that expectation. I don't want to be disappointed. I have friends who had expectations but it did not work out. I think the most ideal [situation] is for all our families stay near one another and the children will be able to drop by and look after us.'

It seemed that the grandmothers calibrated their "hope" because they did not want to burden their adult children by becoming another stressor to them. They empathised with them, especially those who struggled to make ends meet: "He needs to take care of his family, pay for electricity and water bills, mortgage loan … I won't request money, I don't request anything much."

There are hints that some Singaporean grandmothers who were actively caring for grandchildren did not rely on reciprocity from adult children but instead formulated contingency plans regarding their own old-age care. Financially, one grandmother planned to encash her public housing to support herself in old age: "Ten years down the road, if they [adult children] really don't take care of me, I [will] encash this flat back to the government to obtain a monthly payment for living expenses". Although nursing homes are still largely seen as carrying a social stigma, a few grandmothers alluded to being open to the option: "I don't want to be a burden to her [adult daughter] … I think it is not fair for the younger people to be burdened with the old folks. I say … just put me in a nursing home, I think I am prepared to accept it".

A small number (n=2) of Singaporean caregiving grandmothers agreed with the notion of intergenerational reciprocity. Of the two, only one had a strong belief in this: "Yes, I agree with this point. I would agree. When you're [referring to daughter] young and I look after you, when you're [referring to daughter] old, you'll look after me ah!" The other grandmother preferred to be independent and saw reciprocity as a last resort: "If like [when I am] really sick then I need to depend on the children. But if [I] can do things without them that is the best."

Compared to their Singaporean counterparts, more caregiving grandmothers in Fuzhou subscribed to the belief of intergenerational reciprocity: half of these caregivers (n=5) agreed with this notion, of whom two were very confident that reciprocity was the way of life: "This [reciprocity] is for sure, my granddaughter is much older now, I am growing older while caring for her. So when I am old, she will take care of me. This is the deal of being a grandmother, right?" This grandmother seemed to have an unwavering faith in intergenerational reciprocity. The other three who agreed were tentative in their stance, as illustrated here:

'If you are sick and confused, of course you hope that your children will care for you. They do have the duty (*yìbùróngcí*; 义不容辞) to care for the ageing parents but whether they care with patience and attentiveness, it makes a big difference; no one can tell how it will unfold.'

This quotation suggests that grandmothers do not doubt that their adult children will care for them when they are frail and weak, but they are uncertain of the quality of care.

The other five caregiving grandmothers in Fuzhou did not agree with the notion of providing childcare as a form of advance payment for their old-age care. They claimed their care for grandchildren stemmed from altruistic motivation without expectations:

'I disagree. I am doing my duty to care for the next generation because I have the ability to care. It has never crossed my mind when I care for them that they have to reciprocate. This is a wrong concept. Perhaps she [daughter] may be incapable of caring for me because of some circumstances – she may be extremely busy or have health problems. Do I stop caring for the grandchild if I know my own daughter will not or cannot care for me in the future? This is wrong.'

All five grandmothers who disagreed claimed that the care they extended to their adult children by providing childcare did not come with strings attached.

Grandmothers who did not provide childcare

Since grandmothers who did not care for grandchildren defied the Chinese cultural expectation that caregiving is a social obligation, it is logical to deduce that these grandmothers may not give intergenerational reciprocity a high status. Indeed, all the grandmothers from Singapore and Fuzhou, with the exception of one, disagreed with the notion of provision of childcare in exchange for old-age care. Two grandmothers from Singapore who did not provide childcare strongly asserted that reciprocity is a wrong motivation. One of the two explained that the right motivation should be love:

'You're driving them away [if you are thinking about reciprocity]. If you're looking after them with love, love always repays. Let love work. Because the pressure [of expecting reciprocity] is terrible. You think they don't know? They are not stupid! Your children are smarter than you anytime and when you're doing that, you're not doing it out of love. If you do things not out of love, it is very soon forgotten [spoken in *Hokkien*]. Do everything with love, love itself will look after you. Your mind, your own mindset has to be correct as a grandparent. I disagree with that [reciprocity]. Totally.'

Adding to the reasons for grandmothers' disagreement with the notion of intergenerational reciprocity, one grandmother remarked that adult children should not be overly dependent on their ageing parents and vice versa:

> 'If suddenly you go [die] now, they [adult children] will
> feel like they have lost something. Like, [they feel that they]
> cannot depend on you too much. Grandparents should also
> not depend too much on their children because they got
> their own family to look after.'

The sentiment of disagreement with intergenerational reciprocity was
equally intense among the non-caregiving grandmothers from Fuzhou
(nine out of ten disagreed). It is interesting to note that, despite their
disagreement with this Chinese cultural notion, two of them reported
being confident that their children would be filial and would take care
of them in old age, even though they did not provide childcare to the
grandchildren:

> 'I don't agree with this concept [of reciprocity]. Let nature
> take its course (*shùn qí zìrán*; 顺其自然). Those who will
> take care of you [when you are old] will do it. Those who
> would not [provide elder care] even if you care for their
> children now, they will not do it. But for my daughter and
> son-in-law, I know they will care for me. They are filial.'

Three of these nine grandmothers were prepared to move into a
nursing home when the time came because they empathised with the
pressure faced by the only children:

> 'They have to care for the pair of old folks from the other
> side plus two of us [herself and her husband], four old folks
> in addition to their child, can you imagine their pressure?
> I tell myself, I will be self-reliant until such a day when I
> am unable [to care for myself], nursing home is a possible
> option – just be open minded. I have never had the concept
> of reciprocity.'

In addition to considering a nursing home for old-age care, one
grandmother said that those who are financially able to do so should
consider engaging domestic helpers to care for them: "In my view if
one has the financial means, engaging a domestic helper to provide
assistance is a viable and wise option." Another grandmother claimed
she prayed regularly to God to let her die without major disease
and to have good quality of life. To achieve good health, self-
reliance and quality of life, she invested in healthy food and diet
supplements:

'I am reluctant to be a burden to my child, so I have been eating health care products (*chī hǎoduō de bǎojiàn pǐn*; 吃好多的保健品). My idea is to pass on without disease. My child leads a very hectic life and I do not have the heart to see her suffer for me.'

In summary, therefore, with regard to childcare provision as part of intergenerational reciprocity, grandmothers from the two cities were qualitatively similar; that is, the majority of grandmothers did not link childcare provision with the notion of reciprocity. Yet, there were differences in intensity of views. Grandmothers from both cities, regardless of whether they were providing childcare, thought treating childcare provision as an advance payment for one's elder care was wrong and "unnatural". Singaporean grandmothers who were actively providing childcare said they would "hope" but not "expect" their adult children to care for them when they were frail. Even the few caregiving grandmothers from Fuzhou who had unwavering faith in intergenerational reciprocity and were confident their adult children would care for them when they were frail were uncertain about the quality of elder care they would receive. Based on Confucian values, Chinese grandmothers who provided childcare could have rightfully expected reciprocity. Counter to this, the participants in this research tended to empathise with the pressure their adult children faced and did not want to be a burden to them. The grandmothers who did not provide childcare seemed to be proactive in planning for their own old-age care, including prolonging their good health, eating supplements, encashing their flats for an income during their old age and even considering a nursing home as a viable option when the time comes.

Grandmothers' agency within Chinese cultural obligation

This chapter provides empirical evidence to interrogate and enrich the construct of 'cultural obligation' commonly used in research to explain Chinese grandparents' involvement in providing childcare. We believe this construct tends to gloss over the experiences, voices and agency of Chinese grandparents. To highlight the agency of Chinese grandmothers in their decision-making processes regarding whether to provide childcare, we have illustrated the way in which they exercise agency in interpreting the notion of 'cultural obligation'. While both groups of grandmothers from Singapore and Fuzhou were Chinese, they expressed a range of agentic qualities. Grandmothers in Singapore were readier to voice their struggles in taking up grandchild care. The lack of expressed ambivalence in the decisions of grandmothers from Fuzhou to provide childcare should not be construed as an absence of agency; instead, in a context of heavy cultural expectations, Fuzhou grandmothers have less access to cultural resources to express their agency compared to their counterparts in Singapore, where individual choice is deemed more acceptable. On the other hand, a surprising finding about non-caregiving grandmothers in Fuzhou illuminates a reverse logic of agency for grandmothers who were deprived of the chance to provide care. Their agency can be seen in the way they fulfilled their desire to contribute to providing childcare, despite the lack of opportunities, through 'indirect care' such as giving money to adult children, buying gifts for grandchildren and paying for insurance policies for grandchildren. We propose, therefore, that a more nuanced understanding of the agentic expression of Chinese grandmothers in relation to their role as childcare providers will enhance researchers' investigation into their lived experience.

Intergenerational reciprocity re-examined

Despite the widespread notion of intergenerational reciprocity – childcare as advance payment for one's elder care – that is commonly used to understand Chinese grandparents and their adult children, it is noteworthy that a clear majority of grandmothers from both cities in this study considered this notion "wrong". Even those grandmothers who subscribed to the notion of intergenerational reciprocity expressed caution and reservation about it; they preferred to "hope for" than to "expect" elder care. This may signal to researchers that we should attune to the shifting ideation of elder-care options among Chinese grandmothers. Explicit plans to care for themselves and to consider a nursing home as an option, and the desire to be independent for as long as possible, are possible hints of emerging shifts in Chinese older adults' agency in planning for their old-age care. Researchers may profit from paying attention to these nuances emerging for new older generations in Chinese societies rather than taking expectations of intergenerational reciprocity as a given.

Acknowledgements

We are grateful to the participants in this study for illuminating to us their agentic qualities. This study was funded by the National University of Singapore HDRSS funds (Heads & Deanery Research Support Scheme R-134-000-093-101).

References

Chee, L.P., Goh, E.C.L. and Kuczynski, L. (2014) 'Oversized loads: Child parentification in low-income families and underlying parent–child dynamics', *Families in Society*, 95(3): 204–212.

Chen, C. (2006) 'A household-based convoy and the reciprocity of support exchange between adult children and noncoresiding parents', *Journal of Family Issues*, 27(8): 1100–1136.

Chen, F., Liu, G. and Mair, C. A. (2011) 'Intergenerational ties in context: Grandparents caring for grandchildren in China', *Social forces: A scientific medium of social study and interpretation*, 90(2): 571–594.

Connidis, I., and McMullin, J. (2002) 'Sociological ambivalence and family ties: A critical perspective', *Journal of Marriage and Family*, 64(3): 558–567.

Fei, X. (1982) 'Changes in Chinese family structure', *China Reconstruction*, July: 23–26.

Fei, X. (1992) 'From the soil: The foundation of Chinese society', G. Hamilton and W. Zheng (trans), Berkeley, CA: University of California Press.

Goh, E.C.L. (2009) 'Grandparents as childcare providers: An in-depth analysis of the case of Xiamen, China', *Journal of Aging Studies*, 23(1): 60–68.

Goh, E.C.L and Goransson, K. (2011) 'Doing ethnographic research in Chinese families: Reflections on methodological concerns from two Asian cities', *International Journal of Qualitative Methods*, 10(3): 265–281.

Goh, E.C.L. and Hsu, H-Y (2013) 'Bilateral parent–child interactions in school-age children's tooth-brushing behaviours', *Pediatric Dentistry*, 35(1): E1–13.

Goh, E.C.L., Tsang, B.Y.P. and Chokkanathan, S. (2016) 'Intergenerational reciprocity reconsidered: The honour and burden of grandparenting in urban China', *Intersections: Gender and Sexuality in Asia and the Pacific*, 39. Available at: http://intersections.anu.edu.au/issue39/goh.pdf.

Guo, B., Pickard, J. and Huang, J. (2008) 'A cultural perspective on health outcomes of caregiving grandparents: Evidence from China', *Journal of Intergenerational Relationships*, 5(4): 25–40.

Hill, M. (2000) '"Asian values" as reverse Orientalism: Singapore', *Asia Pacific Viewpoint*, 41(2): 177–190.

Hwang, K.K. (1999) 'Filial piety and loyalty: Two types of social identification in Confucianism', *Asian Journal of Social Psychology*, 2(1): 163–183.

Kuczynski, L. (2003) 'Beyond bidirectionality: Bilateral conceptual frameworks for understanding dynamics', in L. Kuczynski (ed), *Handbook of dynamics in parent–child relations*, US: Sage, pp 1–24.

Kuczynski, L., and De Mol, J. (2015) 'Dialectical models of socialization', in W.F. Overton and P.C.M. Molenaar (eds), *Theory and method, volume 1: Handbook of Child Psychology and Developmental Science* (7th edn). Hoboken, NJ: Wiley.

Low, S.S.H. and Goh, E.C.L. (2015) 'Granny as nanny: Positive outcomes for grandparents providing childcare for dual-income families. Fact or myth?', *Journal of Intergenerational Relationships*, 13(4): 302–319.

National Family Council. (2011) *State of the family report 2011: Singapore*. Available at: http://www.nfc.org.sg/ResearchPublication/Requestor_SOFR%202011%20Cicada%20v8%20Final.pdf.

Pierce, M. and Timonen, V. (2010) *A discussion paper on theories of ageing and approaches to welfare in Ireland, north and south*, Belfast and Dublin: Centre for Ageing Research and Development in Ireland.

Quan-McGimpsey, S., Kuczynski, L. and Brophy, K. (2013) 'Tensions between the personal and the professional in close teacher–child relationships', *Journal of Research in Childhood Education*, 27(1): 111–126.

Teo, P., Mehta, K., Thang, L.L. and Chan, A. (2006) '*Ageing in Singapore: Service needs and the state*', Routledge.

Timonen, V. and Doyle, M. (2012) 'Grandparental agency after adult children's divorce', in S. Arber and V. Timonen (eds) *Contemporary grandparenting: Changing family relationships in global contexts*, Bristol: Policy Press, pp 159–180.

Velayutham, S. (2007) *Responding to globalization: Nation, culture and identity in Singapore*, Singapore: ISEAS.

Wu, L.L. and Sun, Y.P. (2003) 'Family intergenerational exchange and its impact on mental health of the elder adults', *Journal of Chinese Gerontology*, 23: 803–804 (in Chinese).

Xu, L., Tang, F., Li, L.W., and Dong, X.Q. (2017) 'Grandparent caregiving and psychological well-being among Chinese American older adults: The roles of caregiving burden and pressure', *Journals of Gerontology Series A: Biomedical Sciences and Medical Sciences*, 72(suppl_1): S56–S62.

Zhang, K. (2010) 'Research on social activity and psychological well-being of urban and rural older people in China', Beijing: China Society Press.

Zhou, Z. (2011) *The anti-Confucian campaign during the Cultural Revolution, August 1966–January 1967*, College Park, MD: University of Maryland. Doctoral dissertation.

THIRTEEN

"I am not that type of grandmother": (non)compliance with the grandmother archetype among contemporary Czech grandmothers

Lucie Vidovićová and Lucie Galčanová

Introduction

In many cultures, historical archetypes continue to influence modern understandings of the grandmother role. The lived experience, social structures, institutional framing and cultural images of grandmotherhood are highly relevant for social scientific examination and for understanding the changing and diverse phenomenon of grandparenting. These aspects dynamically overlap, and the overlaps or contrasts they produce have considerable impact on how people perceive themselves and how they co-construct their identity and self-understanding as a grandparent.

We go about our daily lives with omnipresent archetypes. We are in close contact with them from our early childhood; we learn about them from legends and myths, from fairy tales as well as from daily talk. Archetypes live in the stories we tell and form a vivid part of our cultures. As Snowden (2001, p 1) recounts:

> As people tell and retell stories about their environment, their beliefs and values as expressed through the characters within those stories gradually become more and more extreme, until each character individually represents one aspect of that culture, and collectively the characters and the stories that reveal those characters provide a profound set of cultural indicators.

The nature of archetypes also points to their relative durability in time – they transmit values, social norms and cultural codes within and between generations via written and narrated accounts. In many cultures, the historical archetype of the grandmother continues to influence modern understandings of the grandparent role (Meier, 2017; Troyansky, 2016).

In this chapter, we introduce the Grandmother, a true archetype: heroine and saint; symbol of cherishing love, kindness and tenderness, and of national pride. A person, an inspiration, a legend, a cultural legacy; this is the Grandmother[1] portrayed in the Czech book written in 1855 by the female author Božena Němcová. There are few books from that era that would still be on obligatory school reading lists today, and even fewer fictional characters of that time would be visible in our modern culture. But the Grandmother figure seems to reappear persistently, reintroduced by socialisation processes, educational systems, cultural artefacts, public media channels and, last but not least, by various accounts of lay actors in the Czech Republic. We cannot claim she is also a part of everyday conversations, for which we do not have data, but we are able to follow her presence in the research context in interviews conducted on the later life roles of 'young-old' women and men in conjunction with our multimethod project, 'Role overload: Grandparenting in the era of active ageing', which will be outlined shortly.

In this chapter we argue that the Grandmother, as portrayed in the aforementioned book, has become so deeply embedded in Czech culture that it has transformed from being a fictional character into an **archetype** in the sociological meaning of the word: a typified picture and frame of reference employed when talking about how the social role of a grandmother should be performed. We argue that when the young-old in the Czech context talk about their grandparenting experience and claim "I am not *that type* of grandmother", they not only assume a general understanding of what 'that type' represents but also relate 'that type' and its characteristics to Božena Němcová's Grandmother, as a personification of the ideal type, with the intention of framing and (re)positioning (their own) grandparental role performance – either as adhering/compliant or as nonstandard grandmothering.

Our analysis has two goals. The first is to show how cultural artefacts can shape narratives about grandmotherhood and how they may be used to position one's own social role. Second, we aim to add new knowledge on typologies of grandparenthood, because the 'ideal type' (or 'that type') – as the representative of a tacit, cultural archetype – remains poorly understood. By 'ideal', we mean not only a purely theoretical concept but also the norm: the best-fitting or best-performing role holder. Especially in the latter meanings, the 'ideal' reflects dynamic action categories such as caring versus entertaining, active versus passive; that is, dualities of grandparenthood typologies imbued with putative action and role-performance contents and strategies (Bengtson, 1985).

This chapter is structured as follows. First, we provide a description of *The Grandmother: A story of country life in Bohemia* (hereafter *The Grandmother*), its author and relevant contextual information. We then move to eclectic accounts of the reappearances of the Grandmother figure in present-day culture and public arenas to show how the figure is gaining momentum and is made available, or even offered, to today's grandmothers as a relational role model. Following an outline of our empirical data collection process, we move on to illustrate how this ideal type is being 'picked up' by young-old grandparents in the Czech Republic. We will elaborate the process of translation of this cultural epitome of grandmotherhood into self-accentuation, showing how it is reflected in the construction of narrative images of grandmotherhood, from the point of view of not only a grandmother but also an adult grandchild and parent (that is to say, with reference to the earlier parts of the research participants' life course).

With the help of our interview data, we illustrate the ideal type as defined not only by the (more widely discussed) emotional features (kindness, closeness, tenderness, availability, affection) but also by the possession and employment of specific knowledge, which we label as **ruling over materiality**. We find these features especially in references to food preparation and baking. In the conclusion, we discuss how the 'typical' grandmother concept can help enhance existing typologies (or taxonomies) of grandparental roles (cf. Arber and Timonen 2012; Keeling, 2012) and how the normativity of the ideal is being deployed in accounts of today's older persons (cf. Hasmanová Marhánková, 2015).

The Grandmother phenomenon: the author, the book and the story

We draw on both the Czech language original version (1979 edition) and a modernised English translation (2011) of *The Grandmother* for the analysis of the text and quotes used in this chapter. We have consulted diverse secondary literature on the story and the author, such as book reviews and academic texts. What we have found particularly stimulating for our analysis here are readers' online book reviews (their quotes here are attributed to their online usernames) on three platforms: DatabazeKnig.cz (*The Book* database, Czech only, www.databazeknih.cz), Goodreads (www.goodreads.com) and Amazon.com (www.amazon.com). The last two cover a relatively long period of time and are geographically dispersed, featuring input from not only Czechs in English but also foreign readers and expatriates. We also performed a full-text search in the Czech language of online search engines, looking specifically for mentions of The Grandmother in news pieces. Further, thanks to our sensitisation to the topic, we could easily spot several instances of the Grandmother presence in the physical environment and public spaces, and will briefly describe these as well.

Božena Němcová (1820–62), the author, was born in Vienna to a German-speaking father and a Czech mother. Her father was an officer in the royal household of Katharina, Princess of Sagan, wife of Count Schulenberg. Later on, Němcová's mother was also employed by the princess and a great deal of the household management was transferred to Magdalena Novotná, the author's maternal grandmother (cf. Chan and Elder, 2000, on matrilineal grandparenting). The family followed the employer to various destinations within the Empire, so Božena was very mobile and had access to education. The stories about her life never neglect to mention not only her beauty and popularity among men but also the tragic story of her deceased son and unhappy marriage with Josef Němec (in 1837, when she was 17 years old), 'an ardent Czech nationalist but way below his wife's intellectual standard' (Eben, 2011, p 333).

The Grandmother, written by Němcová in 1855, is a story of a grandmother who is invited by one of her three children to join her household after their seasonal move to a nearby village. After initial hesitation, the Grandmother moves in and meets with her daughter, three grandchildren, two dogs, son-in-law and many local characters in the neighbourhood. What follows are 'snapshots' of various events from the life of the family and wider community – including the Princess, for whom the Grandmother's son-in-law worked. The Grandmother is the pivotal character of the book, and its contents relay either events occurring to her (or in her presence) or stories told by or for her.

As the background of the story very closely resembles the childhood experiences of the author, it is believed that the book is autobiographical and that Němcová – present in her story as the main child character, Barunka – is drawing on memories of her own grandmother, Magdalena. Besides the biographical similarities, the introductory lines support this notion and are written from a perspective of deep grief:

It was long, long ago, when last I gazed on that dear face, kissed those pale, wrinkled cheeks, and tried to fathom the depths of those blue eyes, in which were hidden so much goodness and love. Long ago it was when, for the last time, those aged hands blessed me. Our Grandmother is no more; for many a year now she has slept beneath the cold earth. But to me she is not dead. (Němcová, 2011, p 9)

Němcová often travelled and was a skilful collector of folk stories and traditions; it is therefore highly plausible that the book is based on (at least mostly) her folk tale collections rather than solely her autobiography. The text consists of vaguely related events from the Grandmother's life along a fluid chronological timeline, starting when she receives the invitation from her daughter and ending at her own funeral. Particular events, such as visits to different neighbours, are used as a matrix for detailed descriptions of folk wisdom, traditions, proverbs, beliefs and practices, conserving and transferring history, norms, religious/spiritual practices and values of the time (Lotman, 1990, in Málek, 2013).

Several online reviewers compare *The Grandmother* to Louisa May Alcott's *Little Women* (1868). As Lynne Cantwell from the Goodreads online community puts it: 'Alcott's tale about Meg, Jo, Beth, and Amy went a long way towards forming my ideas about fairness, kindness, and how to get along in life. *The Grandmother* serves the same purpose in the Czech Republic'. Indeed, rather than a novel the book is a catalogue of folk and religious wisdom and practices. Almost every page features one or two moral principles or codes of conduct, presented in the form of a story. That is why it is not possible to simply synopsise the plot; describing the sequence of the events will not do the book justice.

The readership: appraisal and critique

Němcová's work is introduced to young children in the Czech Republic in kindergartens and primary schools in the form of her fairy-tale collection. Second graders are assigned *The Grandmother* as obligatory reading in Czech language and literature courses and it is a frequent topic for the secondary school leaving exam (*maturita*), which institutionalises its importance in the course of early socialisation. The fact that Němcová was a successful female author in the 19th century is appealing to modern readership as a representation of gendered agency against the odds of the historical and individual circumstances.

The international online community of reviewers ranges from fans – 'Anyone who grew up with a Bubbi ['grandmother' in Yiddish] should love this book. It is like a page out of their history' (Christa A. Elliot, Amazon.com; cf. Mestheneos and Svensson-Dianellou, 2004) – to those who suggest: 'do NOT read it … EVER … Only if you want to be … bored to death' (Jan Ryšavý, Goodreads, emphasis in original).

Part of the criticism of the book can be ascribed to false expectations fed by the aforementioned general belief that *The Grandmother* is a biographical account, so the absence of a general plot or story may come as a surprise to many. On the other hand, some commentators mention the importance of 'growing into it' and the need to have some developmental capacity to appraise it in its fullness. This reveals two points relevant for our discussion here. First, even when this book 'is known to literally every Czech child' (Fraňková, 2007), it is not always the most valued and generally accepted reading so the ideal of kindness and unconditional love and acceptance comes under scrutiny. Second, knowledge of the actual content of the book varies and is subject to factors such as when it is read, by whom, in which version (original, modernised, abbreviated, seen at the movies and so on) and underlying values and norms related to not only literature but also intergenerational relationships, particularly one's own family ties. What we witness in the public, semantic realm is not always a 'true' picture of the story as it has been written but rather a superstructure of interpretations and memories embedded in social structures.

The Grandmother as a cultural phenomenon

At 14 Na Příkopech Street (one of the most expensive streets in Prague), amid the shop windows filled with global fashion brands you will find a bust of Němcová, with a dedication 'to the maker of *The Grandmother*', installed by the Central Fellowship of Czech Women. This house, in which Němcová died in 1862, is today a three-storey toyshop. If you drive through Polná, a city of 5,000 inhabitants, you can find a statue of Němcová erected in 2017 at the expense of a private 'businessman with family' to commemorate the 177th anniversary of Němcová's move to Polná, where she lived for two years. If you open an issue of the daily paper *Metro*, you see a large picture of the life-sized sculptures of the literary heroine, her grandchildren and two dogs in the green meadow 'Grandmother's Valley' – part of an advertisement for 'the 53 most beautiful places to see in the Czech Republic'. If you ride the 'readers' tram' in the city of Brno, which covered in pictures of books advertising the local library, *The Grandmother* would be there. She also features in online discussions of older people's sex lives:

> Our perception of grandfathers and grandmothers is traditionally asexual – we associate them with wisdom, contemplation, or dullness, but we reluctantly admit their loving desires. 'Can you imagine how the grandmother of Božena Němcová ... masturbates at night?', queries the famous sexologist Petr Weiss. 'For most people, such an idea is not very comfortable. But it is likely that she masturbated – she was fifty-three and lived without a partner.' (Třešňák, 2014)

Partridge's (1999) book review represents an outsider's look at the legacy of Němcová and her writings in Czech culture by summarising *The Grandmother* as 'perhaps the best known and best loved work in all of Czech literature' and claiming its importance 'can hardly be exaggerated' (p 2). He continues:

> The book has appeared in countless editions, there are several film versions ... and *Babiccino udoli* (Grandmother's Valley), not far from the town of Nachod, is a national literary and historical monument. ... In fact, the book is so much a part of the *national consciousness* that almost *every portrayal* of a grandmother in film, on stage or in a book is influenced, and to some extent overshadowed, by Nemcova's heroine. (p 2; emphasis added).

The book has been published in nearly 350 editions and been the subject of dozens of theatre productions and several film adaptations (Málek, 2013).

In 2007, for the first time ever, an adaptation of *The Grandmother* reached the stage of the Czech National Theatre. On this occasion, two accounts of the Grandmother personification were offered in media coverage of the event (Fraňková, 2007). The first came from the scriptwriter and the second from leading female actor Vlasta Chramostová, for whom this was her last active role in the theatre:

> We concentrated on the character of the grandmother. We see her as a woman who struggled for her whole life and who always defended her own opinions. This theme is often hidden behind the idyllic interpretation of the

grandmother. Another important theme is the religious life and the joys of everyday life typical for the Biedermeier period. And lastly, we discovered the theme of women's destiny that intersects the whole book. How the world of women is confronted with the male world and the world of politics. (Lenka Kolihová-Havlíková (scriptwriter), in Fraňková, 2007)

Babicka [The Grandmother] has always represented a source of special emotion for me ... The book has always helped us through difficult times. ... I want to remove some of the pathos because the Grandmother was essentially a working woman, very strong and full of wisdom. There is an Arabic proverb saying that eyes that have cried a lot see a lot. I think that applies to the Grandmother and to Bozena Nemcova as well. (Vlasta Chramostova, actor, in Fraňková, 2007)

In these two excerpts we can see how the notion of the Grandmother is developed; some features are stressed while others are intentionally suppressed. One intriguing point expressed here is the need to deal with the 'idealisation' of the epitome of grandmotherhood – filled with pathos and efforts to overcome the 'typical' – and the difficulty of doing so. This supports the argument concerning the sacred qualities of the text, which therefore should not (and could not) be taken lightly or without the proper respect. This interpretation is supported by the call for help from Němcová in tough times, for both the individual and the nation ('us'), as something close to the practice of prayer. In this view, the Grandmother is more than the personification of familial norms; she represents wider societal and national ideals (Sedmidubský, 1991, in Málek, 2013). In our cultural data from the online book reviews, this sacralisation is reflected in recommendations to read *The Grandmother* by or for Czech migrants who have lost the ability to speak Czech or for/from their children, who long for Czech national identity or simply recognise their cultural roots in the country.

Němcová was the product of her era and milieu and was well known for her nationalist activism in the Czech National Revival cultural movement. This is highly visible in the majority of her stories and novels and also manifests in the story of the Grandmother. František Halas, in his book *Our Lady Božena Němcová* (1940), even draws a parallel between the unfortunate destiny of Němcová and the unfortunate history of the Czech nation. In many ways, this comparison reflects the expectations inherent in the symbolic grandparental roles of historian, teacher and keeper of wisdom, helping future generations re-engage with the past (Bengtson, 1985; Block, 2000; Wilton and Davey, 2006).

The lived phenomenon: the Grandmother in contemporary grandparenting identity

We now turn to interrogating how the 'ideal type' or archetypal grandmother is used by young-old women and men in the interviews for our research project, 'Role overload: Grandparenting in the era of active ageing'. We undertook secondary analysis of data consisting of 30 semistructured qualitative interviews, conducted with 32 grandparents in 2013 and 2014 in the Czech Republic. The sample includes 21 women and 11 men, aged 56 to 82 years, with a mean age of 65. Most participants can be called 'third agers', as the original project's purposeful sampling focused on people who were combining several social roles (such as grandparenting, care for older people, paid and unpaid work, leisure and civic activities) and dealt with the question of how people cope with the potential risks of conflicting demands on their time and role overload. During the interviews, participants described their everyday practices in relation to and beyond their grandparenting experience, with a focus on the personal meaning of these practices. The semistructured interviews also included questions inviting participants to compare their own grandparenting role performance to those of their spouses, parents and grandparents. This approach gave us particularly fruitful insights into perceptions of the grandparent role in dynamic relation to historical-institutional structures and cultural images our participants could relate to – or wished to distance themselves from.

To portray and relate to the various figures of grandparents, participants often used terms that were close to the aforementioned archetypal language and portrayals. The idea of addressing these terms analytically as archetypes was also supported by the fact that some of them appeared in the interviews repeatedly – primarily the 'typical grandmother' – and were used as a narrative shortcut; a tool to strengthen mutual understanding within the interview situation. Participants relied on these figures as something intersubjectively shared and comprehensible. For the purpose of this chapter, we have thus used the technique of focused coding (Charmaz, 2006) and looked closer at those parts of the data in which particular persons were described and characterised as grandmothers, paying attention to what adjectives were used in connection to grandmothering and what meanings could be derived from the wider context of the interview.

The Grandmother from Němcová's book was spontaneously mentioned twice; in both cases, the reference was used to depict the difference between the archetypal literary figure of the Grandmother and the real-life person, especially in terms of the image of old age it portrayed:

> 'Well, my mother, she was, not such a typical little old lady. She looked quite young and she had a good sense of humour. When she died, I was arranging the funeral and I had to change it [the funeral service speech], because it opened with the citation from the Grandmother by Božena Němcová, as it starts with: "It was long, long ago, when last I gazed on that wrinkled face", so, no, no, that cannot stay there, it's really dull [it is not her].' (Mrs Nikola, 74)

> 'For example, that complaint that babysitting grandmothers do not exist anymore ... we have them in the fitness centres; they look after themselves. Božena Němcová's Grandmother, supposedly she was fifty when she came to Bělidlo [to live with her daughter]; well today in their fifties, women are at their best age.' (Mrs Dana, 62)

The literary character of the Grandmother serves in both of these cases to show what a third person (not the interviewee herself) does *not* represent; to depict the strong difference from the generally accepted ideal image of a woman with a "wrinkled face". In the second quote, the image of the Grandmother helps Mrs Dana to describe the changing relation between chronological age and expected appearance, but also to point out that being 50 means dramatically different things nowadays than at the time of Božena Němcová. More importantly, not only are the women not 'really' old but also they are at their "best age"; however, they do not participate in caring for grandchildren in the same way, as they have chosen to work on the personal project of the Self (pursuing fitness and taking care of themselves and their appearance).

The interpretation of this noncompliance with the imagined older version of grandmotherhood that emanates from the interviews is twofold: there is both the morality of performing 'young', even at ages that used to be seen as 'old', and the immorality of not being available for babysitting, which seen as a traditional feature of grandparental performance. However, as we see from the book, the Grandmother was not babysitting – she was co-residing with the children and helping to take care of the house in her own autonomous, almost managerial way. Their time together wasn't arranged as some special 'sitting' time but was incorporated into early-modern rural everydayness in a differently structured way. As many of the stories described in the book involve visits to neighbours and other outdoor activities *together* with the grandchildren, we could even see the Grandmother performing the grandparenthood not as *opposition to* but as *part of* her active ageing, similarly to today's grandparents (Vidovićová et al., 2015). However, because the Grandmother serves as a counterpoint to contemporary grandmothers in the interviews, she appears there as physically and visually old: she has a wrinkled face and is fragile, ascetic and austere.

The second quotation also links the archetypal grandmother to her contemporary counterpart in its complaint that the babysitting grandmother is extinct. Not everyone agrees that all grandmothers have moved from the kitchen to the fitness centre, as the quotation exaggeratedly suggests; however, many make the same point about generational differences, as the same chronological age now has tremendously different connotations – those in their fifties and sixties are now seen (oxymoronically) as 'young-old' people, which enables them to care more intensively for their grandchildren (if they already have some), the older generation or their partners, as well as to dedicate their time to various other activities. As Hasmanová Marhánková (2010) has shown in her research, the 'active grandmother' might stand in symbolic opposition to the 'typical grandmother', connecting activity almost exclusively with self-development, public involvement and leisure rather than with caring for others and activities connected with domesticity.

Like Mrs Dana, Mr Gregor also values his mother as a grandmother for her difference from the narrative figure of "women today", as she performs almost the living ideal – higher age connects with wisdom, indulgence and a caring attitude towards others. She is almost "disappearing" due to her old age; thus, she can be compared to the archetypal grandmother, essentialised in the expression "a grandmother is simply a grandmother". Her performance is also highly gendered, in Mr Gregor's view – while being a caring grandfather (divorced and actively spending time with his six grandchildren), he still performs his role in tandem with her:

'She [my mother] is such an interesting person, she remains very wise until an advanced age, very hospitable, praised by everyone; a grandmother is simply a grandmother. She is disappearing, but she is that type of grandmother. ... [She manages to cook for children,] on top of that, she [also] makes buns for them. It is interesting, the women today, I don't say they don't cook enough, but ... the simple quark cakes or pie, the kids love it and it is way better than pizza or something like that.' (Mr Gregor, 67)

Ideal-typical grandmotherhood is tightly knit with not only specific practices, including transformation of the materiality of food, but also a certain level of frugality and caring for kids and family, as well as for mundane objects:

'My old grandmother ... she was going to church; she was really kind, for family. I always say, we came there, she was standing at the doorstep and wherever you looked, there were cakes, [and] an abundant lunch. She was typical [grandmother]. I am not like that anymore.' (Mrs Doubravka, 62)

'These things that are expected from grandmothers, I haven't developed them ... like, grandmother bakes buns ... and repairs socks, I don't know, these qualities. She cooks the best meals in the world. I mean, I am a good cook, but ... I cook more these fast meals, not the grandmotherly sirloin cream sauce, right? Something based on my fantasy or oriental food ... I am not that typical grandmother in terms of cooking.' (Mrs Alžběta, 59)

We can see that the complex practices of food preparation serve as a reference point for the expression of contemporary grandmothers' identities: "I am not that kind of grandmother anymore". The archetypal grandmother belongs to the past. She is a person close to the interviewee in her familiarity, and her characteristics are positively valued, but she also represents a distant ideal that interviewees do not – and, importantly, do not *wish* to – comply with. As in the book, food plays a highly symbolic role in the narratives. While Mr Gregor uses the example of cooking and baking to appraise his mother and differentiate the image of her he portrays from his critical representation of contemporary grandmothers, Mrs Doubravka and Mrs Alžběta also use the example of cooking and baking to positively evaluate someone else as a "typical" grandmother – but actively dissociate themselves from this archetypal performance. They bake and cook as well, but the difference lies in *how* the food is prepared, its *centrality* for the grandmothering role and how it is perceived both personally and retrospectively.

In Božena Němcová's book, the baking of bread plays a key role in the story and serves as a marker of generations and eras: a time of tradition (as represented by the grandmother) and modernity (represented by the daughter's family life). The Grandmother teaches the children how to handle bread: 'Don't you know that if one steps upon a crumb, the souls in purgatory weep?' (p 18). The baking of bread or sweets, an example of grandmotherly ruling over materiality, is a point at which tradition and modernity meet; at which the mundane matter of food is placed in the sacred context of wider cosmology and the grandmother introduces children to tradition and everyday 'mystique' (or vice versa – makes them see the mystical in the everyday).

In the interviews, the 'right', positively valued care performance is usually represented by women's 'traditional' preparation of time-consuming, complex, nationalised cuisine. As Mintz and Bois (2002) point out: 'Like all culturally defined material substances used in the creation and maintenance of social relationships, food serves both to solidify group membership and to set groups apart' (p 109). Thus, it cannot be a "pizza" but must be *buchty* (a special kind of local sweet yeast bun filled with poppy seeds, quark or plum butter) or the national Czech dish *svíčková* (beef tenderloin in cream sauce). Mrs Alžběta also reflects how "typical grandmothering" is not only connected with tradition but also manifests in the form of the perceived social norm of doing those "things that are expected from the grandmothers". In her negation, however, we can also feel a certain level of pride; her noncompliance with ideal-typical features does not threaten her personal identity – she does not identify with that ideal – rather, she uses it as a meaningful departure point for her personal grandmotherhood narrative, which is constructed around the realms of occupation and personal creativity.

Conclusions

We have sketched a portrait of a 160-year-old cultural artefact that is still alive today in various public discourses and spaces, school curricula, media coverage and, last but not least, lay actors' self-perceptions and identities. We have shown how the artefact emerged from a specific historical context and how it is kept alive and transformed through a variety of discursive channels. Šindar (2009), in his TV documentary that artistically maps the discrepancies between the Grandmother and older women of today, talks about "a perfect national myth", "a romantic model", "a mythological figure in realistic shape and configuration", "a national grandmother" and "a prototype". Together, these features may provide a somewhat false feeling that *The Grandmother* has the quality of a cult. That is not the case. Yet, we have found this approach very fruitful in identifying both obvious and unspoken features of ideal grandmotherhood, which is, of course, 'too good' to be real, but which still hangs above the heads of present-day grandmothers in the Czech Republic.

Over the course of gerontology's longstanding interest in grandparenting, and grandmotherhood particularly, many typologies and categorisations have been produced to describe various patterns of grandparenting, the different roles grandparents play in contemporary families and the diversity of meanings attached to this role, by grandparents themselves or by others, in relation to particular societal, cultural and historical contexts. Timonen and Arber (2012) have traced 'types' or 'styles' of grandparenting back to the 1960s (referencing Cherlin and Furstenberg, 1985; Neugarten and Weinstein, 1964) and critically appraised them: '[T]hese categorisations are not well suited to examining possible differences in how a grandparent relates to different grandchildren, and also overlook the possibility that grandchildren may exert an influence on the nature of the relationship' (Timonen and Arber, 2012, p 7).

The problem with typologies is that they tend to reify particular perspectives by creating conceptual boundaries around practices and meanings that in lived social reality are usually permeable, interchangeable and far more fluid. Nonetheless, simplifications and taxonomic approaches are at the very heart of both scientific and lay thinking; they enable us to communicate, organise and share complex ideas. Furthermore, as we have tried to show in this chapter, they are also a vivid part of thinking and talking about grandparenting in the form of archetypes based on shared cultural images. The aim here is not to create another category, solidifying the patterns of grandparental role performances, but to show how contemporary Czech grandmothers relate to the existing cultural image of the Grandmother and idealised grandmotherhood, actively using its features to delineate their own understandings of the grandparenting role, as well as to outline its embeddedness in local social and historical contexts.

We have shown that the 'purity' and the 'sacredness' of the grandmother archetype make it available for positive evaluation of other women's grandmothering performance, but also make it difficult to comply with the ideal – and possible to distance oneself from it. Noncompliance plays an ambivalent role in the narratives. On the one hand, the ideal serves as a reference point that is expected to be part of shared structures of meaning, as it is interwoven with one of the major national narratives of the Czech imagined community. Both men and women use the 'typical grandmother' to portray an image they expect the audience/interviewer to understand; it represents everything that ought to, but cannot, be reached. On the other hand, older women use this idealised form as a departure point for framing grandmothering practices that may be far from 'the ideal' but generally reflect their positive self-image as modern grandmothers.

Acknowledgement
This chapter was supported by The Czech Science Foundation grant, 'Role overload: Grandparenting in the era of active ageing' (13-34958S).

Note
[1] In this chapter, we use the capitalised noun 'Grandmother' for the instances in which we are referring to the literary heroine, to distinguish it from 'grandmother' as a social and family role and related meanings.

References
Alcott, L.M. (1868) *Little Women*, Boston: Roberts Brothers.

Amazon.com (n.d.) *The Grandmother: A story of country life in Bohemia*. Reviews. Available at: https://www.amazon.com/Grandmother-Story-Country-Life-Bohemia/dp/1112463240.

Arber, S. and Timonen, V. (eds) (2012) *Contemporary grandparenting: Changing family relationships in global contexts*, Bristol; Chicago, IL: Policy Press.

Bengtson, V.L. (1985) 'Diversity and symbolism in grandparental roles', in V.L. Bengtson and J.F. Robertson (eds) *Grandparenthood*, Beverly Hills, CA: Sage, pp 11–25.

Block, C.E. (2000) 'Dyadic and gender differences in perceptions of the grandparent–grandchild relationship', *International Journal of Aging and Human Development*, 52(2): 85–104.

Chan, Ch. G. and Elder, G.H. (2000) 'Matrilineal advantage in grandchild-grandparent relations', *The Gerontologist*, 40(2): 179–90.

Charmaz, K. (2006) *Constructing grounded theory*, London: Sage.

Cherlin, A. and Furstenberg, F.A. (1985) 'Styles and strategies of grandparenting', in V.L. Bengtson and J.F. Robertson (eds) *Grandparenthood*, Beverly Hills, CA: Sage, pp 97–116.

Eben, K. (2011) 'About Božena Němcová', in B. Němcová, *The Grandmother (Babička)*, Praha: Vitalis Verlag, pp 333–335.

Fraňková, R. (2007) 'Bozena Nemcova's Babicka at National Theatre for the first time'. Available at: http://www.radio.cz/en/section/curraffrs/bozena-nemcovas-babicka-at-national-theatre-for-the-first-time.

Goodreads.com (n.d.) *The Grandmother*. Reviews. Available at: https://www.goodreads.com/book/show/1478958.The_Grandmother?from_search=true.

Halas, F. (1940) *Naše paní Božena Němcová* [Our Lady Božena Němcová], Praha: Fr. Borový.

Hasmanová Marhánková, J. (2010) 'Konstruování představ aktivního stárnutí v centrech pro seniory' [The Construction of Active Ageing idea in the Centres for Seniors], *Sociologický časopis / Czech Sociological Review*, 46(2): 211–324.

Hasmanová Marhánková, J. (2015) '"Být dobrou babičkou" Normativní očekávání spojená s rolí babičky v současné české rodině' ['"Being a good grandmother": the normative expectations attached to the role of grandmother in Czech families today'], *Sociologický časopis/Czech Sociological Review*, 51(5): 737–760.

Keeling, S. (2012) 'Grandchildren's perspectives on grandparents in rural New Zealand', *Journal of Rural Studies*, 28(4): 371–379.

Lotman, M.J. (1990) *Štruktúra umeleckého textu* [The structure of artistic text], Bratislava: Tatran.

Málek, P. (2013) 'Babička Boženy Němcové: od idyly k elegii. K některým aspektům adaptace klasické literatury' ['*The Grandmother* by Božena Němcová: From idyll to elegy. Adaptations of classical literature — some aspects'], *Česká literatura* [Czech Literature], 2: 183–217. Available at: https://www.ceeol.com/search/article-detail?id=259255.

Meier, I. (2017) *Grandparents: Archetypal and clinical perspectives on grandparent–grandchild relationships*, Oxon; New York: Routledge.

Mestheneos, E. and Svensson-Dianellou, A. (2004) 'Naming grandparents', *Generations Review*, 14(3): 10–13.

Mintz, S. W. and Bois, C.M.D. (2002) 'The anthropology of food and eating', *Annual Review of Anthropology*, 31: 99–119.

Němcová, B. (1979). *Babička. [The Grandmother]*, Praha: Československý spisovatel.

Němcová, B. (2011) *The Grandmother*, Praha: Vitalis.

Neugarten, B.L. and Weinstein, K.K. (1964) 'The changing American grandparent', *Journal of Marriage and Family*, 26(2): 199–204.

Partridge, J. (1999) 'Book review: *The Grandmother*', *Central Europe Review*, 1(7). Available at: http://www.ce-review.org/99/7/books7_partridge.html.

Sedmidubský, M. (1991) 'Das Idyllische im Spannungsfeld zwischen Kultur und Natur: Božena Němcovás »Babička«' ['The idyllic in the field of tension between culture and nature: Božena Němcová's Babička'], in A. Guski (ed) *Zur Poetik und Rezeption von Božena Němcovás „Babička"* [*On Poetics and Reception of Božena Němcová's "Babička"*], Wiesbaden: Otto Harrasowitz, pp 27–79.

Šindar, J. (2009) 'Kam se poděla (národní) babička?' ['Where has the (national) grandmother gone?'], *The Czech Television*. Available at: http://www.ceskatelevize.cz/porady/10213536631-kam-se-podela-narodni-babicka/30929434013.

Snowden, D. (2001) 'From storytelling to narrative: Archetypes as an instrument of narrative patterning', *Knowledge Management*, 5(4): 1–5. Available at: http://www.anecdote.com.au/papers/Snowden2001Archetypes.pdf.

Timonen, V. and Arber, S. (2012) 'A new look at grandparenting', in S. Arber and V. Timonen (eds) *Contemporary grandparenting: Changing family relationships in global contexts*, Bristol; Chicago, IL: Policy Press, pp 1–21.

Třešňák, P. 2014. 'Horké chvilky seniorů' [Hot moments of seniors], *Respekt 2014/38*. Available at: https://www.respekt.cz/tydenik/2014/38/horke-chvilky-senioru.

Troyansky, D.G. (2016) *Aging in world history*, New York; London: Routledge.

Vidovićová, L., Galčanová, L. and Petrová Kafková, M. (2015) 'Význam a obsah prarodičovské role u mladých českých seniorů a seniorek', ['The meaning and performance of the grandparenting role among young-old Czechs'] *Sociologický časopis / Czech Sociological Review*, 51(5): 761–782.

Wilton, V. and Davey, J. (2006) 'Grandfathers: Their changing family roles and contributions', *Families Commission Blue Skies Report*. Available at: http://www.superu.govt.nz/sites/default/files/BS-grandfathers.pdf.

FOURTEEN

Conclusions: the grandparents' century?

Virpi Timonen

The chapters in this book have examined the cultural and welfare state contexts of grandparenting. The focus on gender, welfare states, economic development and grandparental agency binds together the diverse contributions to the volume. It is now time to take stock of the contents by sketching out the main lines of argumentation and contributions to the literature contained in the chapters. In other words, this is an opportunity to formulate some key take-home messages and to indicate promising avenues for future research. A notion I will reflect on throughout this chapter is the idea that the 21st century could perhaps be called the 'grandparents' century'. This is a reference to the prediction that by the middle of this century, for the first time in human history, there will be relatively more 'old' people (60 and over) than children (aged 15 and under) in the global population. As the majority of older adults are grandparents, the global population in the 21st century is indeed characterised by the presence of unprecedented numbers of grandparents. The deeper meanings of this demographic transformation, however, remain to be teased out and cannot be taken for granted.

In Chapter Two, Margolis and Arpino presented a broad overview of the demographic changes not only driving the generally increasing prevalence and importance of grandparenthood but also leading, in some parts of the world, to increases in the age when people typically become grandparents. They demonstrate striking differences in the proportion of older adults who are grandparents, varying (among countries included in their analysis) from just under half in Switzerland to nearly nine in ten in the United States. Rising numbers of childless adults translate into a growing share of the older population who do not become grandparents. In some parts of the world, the growing share of older adults who will not become grandparents translates, at the micro level, into inability to enter a role that many older adults find gratifying and socially important, and that might be beneficial for their health and wellbeing. Postponement of parenthood in the cohorts currently of 'reproductive age' translates into later entry into the grandparent role among their parents. As a result of this postponement and increases in longevity, tomorrow's grandparent populations will be older than today's – but the implications of this pattern depend very much on the evolving health and employment status, as well as lifestyle choices, of older adults.

Those who do become grandparents are likely to have fewer grandchildren. This in turn will result, overall, in increased investment of time and other resources per grandchild, but with considerable variability arising from the time and health resources of grandparents. The 'time resource' is also influenced by pressures towards later retirement; where older workers become grandparents well before their retirement, time available for young grandchildren might be limited. Data on labour market participation rates presented in Chapter Two showed that these vary greatly between countries; this in turn suggests a possible conflict between the roles of childcare provider and worker among grandparents in contexts with high older worker participation rates. Relating to this concern, in Chapter Three Price and co-authors marshalled an argument for taking a two-generational approach to making sense of how childcare policy is organised and shaped in different welfare states. Price and colleagues conceptualised policies as impacting on families in two generations – both on employment opportunities and care requirements, and as embedded in gendered and generational cultures. They argued that we should reposition childcare in policy analysis as two-generational, relating primarily to collaboration between mothers and grandmothers. Chapter Three conveyed the strong message that, to understand grandparental childcare across countries, we must include not only a family policy regime framework but also analysis of labour market structures, cultural indicators of availability to provide childcare and normative expectations around care. Importantly, Price and co-authors alert us to the fact that, where grandmothers are providing childcare in the absence of (adequate) formal provision, this can lead to complacency about whether formal childcare provision is needed.

Chapters Two and Three therefore opened up the 'macro scene' of grandparenting and highlighted the increasing importance of engaging in comparative research to make sense of variations in how grandparenting is shaped by demographic and welfare state developments. Economic development, often accompanied by new societal challenges, is another major structural force that impacts on grandparents and their family practices. In Chapter Four, Knodel and

Teerawichitchainan readily acknowledged the importance of cultural factors in shaping grandparenting practices, but their chapter aims first and foremost to highlight the often-ignored aspect of economic development as a force that also influences grandparenting. Knodel and Teerawichitchainan compared three South Asian countries, which share important cultural underpinnings but contrast markedly in their level of economic development – a factor that helps to account for a large part of the intercountry differences in grandparenting practices. While the proportions of older adults co-residing with adult children appear high from the perspective of many other economically developed contexts, they still vary considerably; in the case of the countries discussed in this chapter, from 77% in Myanmar to 57% in Thailand. Compared to some western countries, very high proportions of people aged 60 and over have at least one grandchild; for example, as 93% of older people in Vietnam are grandparents, it is currently a widespread status in this region.

Co-residence with grandchildren is also very common in developing economies; as Knodel and Teerawichitchainan pointed out, about half of elders in Myanmar and Vietnam reside with at least one grandchild of any age. One in ten Thai elders live in skip-generation households with one or more grandchildren, largely as a consequence of economic development and work-related migration of their adult children. Urban versus rural dweller status matters, too; the odds of grandchild care are considerably higher for rural than urban dwellers in Thailand, especially in care of grandchildren whose parents are absent (again reflecting the likelihood of parents moving to locations where employment is available). On the basis of the low proportions of grandparents stating that they experience grandchild care as a burden, Knodel and Teerawichitchainan conjectured that Asian grandparents often gain satisfaction from carrying out a culturally valued family role, or find it gives meaning to their lives. In light of this analysis, the 'grandparents' century' may be an era of enhanced life satisfaction for large numbers of older adults who find grandparenting gratifying and socially valued.

A contrasting picture emerged in Chapter Five, where Hoffman explored grandparenting in (South) Africa. Hoffman identified a descending pattern of care, as older persons are increasingly looked upon as continuous providers of family support, with rising uncertainty about the reciprocal nature of such support. The terms Hoffman uses to characterise African grandmothers' position ('obligatory contribution', 'entrapped responsibility') paint a stark picture of seemingly never-ending family obligations and vulnerability – something that is unfortunately (and unintentionally) entrenched by pensions provision to older adults, who become sources of 'cash and care' to their younger family members. The search for 'a life of their own', evident from the more recent data collected by Hoffman, offers an indication that grandmothers might not always be prepared to accept their position of entrenched vulnerability as the lynchpin of meeting their extended families' needs.

Many grandparents now develop and sustain relationships with their grandchildren in a context where they live in different countries. In Chapter Six, Zhou directed our attention to the decisions and choices made by Chinese grandparents who travel to Canada for varying lengths of time to support their adult children, who are first-generation immigrants and require support with childcare. Chapter Seven, by Vildaite, analysed the experiences of grandmothers who remained in Lithuania when their children emigrated to Ireland, and the experiences of the grandchildren who moved with those parents. These two chapters constitute an opportunity to compare and contrast situations where grandparents engage in extensive circular migration to offer assistance to younger family generations (here, the China–Canada context) and where the frequency of intergenerational co-residence and intensity of instrumental supports between generations living in different countries are lower (here, the Ireland–Lithuania context).

Discussing the case of transnational grandparenting prompted by their (skilled, educated) adult children's migration to Canada, Zhou explored in Chapter Six how migration brings about profound changes in grandparenting as a caregiving practice and a generational relation. Moving abroad for long periods of time to provide grandchild care positions Chinese grandparents in Canada as agents of change in transforming a culture of intergenerational reciprocity. By demonstrating the impact of transnationalism and translocality, Zhou illustrated the limits of overreliance on culturalist approaches, which leave little scope for understanding how grandparenting practices are evolving in important ways.

The transnational family practices outlined by Zhou are reminiscent of Baker and Silverstein's (2012) notion of 'family maximisers' in the Chinese context. It is striking that none of the grandparents in Zhou's study considered *not* responding to the request to provide grandchild care, even though that meant (temporarily) relocating abroad (to Canada) and in some cases abandoning other obligations at home (for instance, their own ageing parents in China). Immigration controls often forced circular migration and led to some grandparents' decision to apply for permanent residency/naturalisation in Canada, despite concerns about leaving family and friends behind in China. Adult children's emigration therefore prompted a complex response among their parents: on the one hand, almost reflexive intergenerational functional solidarity; on the other hand, challenges of adjusting to three-generational coexistence and worry about one's own old age in a foreign country.

The idea that grandchild care is helpful for children(-in-law) to manage their lives in general – a theme that also featured strongly in Chapter Nine on grandfathers in Finland – is another central finding in Chapter Six. These findings suggest grandparents are responding strongly to structural pressures that arise for working parents in late modern societies and economies. However, it is interesting to note that many grandparents –in both Zhou's study and another study of Chinese grandmothers in this book (Chapter Twelve by Goh and Wang) – stated they do not expect (or anticipate) their children to reciprocate the care provision when care needs occur in old age. In Chapter Six, data extracts feature talk that has parallels with the process of 'breaking the chain of obligation' (outlined in Conlon et al., 2014) – grandparents stating they do not expect reciprocity (care in later old age in return for their efforts in caring for grandchildren). Instead of hands-on care, several of the transnational grandparents in Zhou's study referred to expectations of love and concern; in other words, their expectations had shifted away from adult children 'caring for' and towards 'caring about' them in their old age. Witnessing the younger generations flourish in their new homeland was also construed as a form of 'payback': if their children and grandchildren have happy, secure lives and good livelihood, these will constitute a 'new' form of filial 'repayment' that does not extend to direct care provision.

In Chapter Seven, Lithuania presented a particularly apposite case for the study of the impact of family migration on older adults, as a country that has experienced very heavy emigration of working-age adults and their children since joining the European Union in 2004. Under these circumstances, the high proportion of older adults in the population is partly the result of many younger Lithuanians' relocation abroad – a situation that presents challenges for the maintenance of intergenerational relations. It is important to note that, despite the geographical distance, about half of both the youth and grandmother samples in Vildaite's study recounted strong, enduring emotional connections between the grandparent and grandchild generations. In cases where minimal or distant relationships were recounted by the grandchildren, the reason for this was not attributed to migration or distance but rather to other factors. In particular, the quality of the grandmother–grandchild relationships *prior to* migration was shown to be an important influence, especially in cases where the grandmother had been a central caregiver while the child was growing up in Lithuania.

The life course was also thrown into sharp relief in Vildaite's chapter; adolescents turn towards peer groups and prioritise education and exploration of their interests, making it harder to actively keep in touch with grandparents 'back in' the country of origin. All family relationships are continually renegotiated – and it is perhaps particularly challenging to renegotiate relationships over a geographical distance, during short but intensive periods spent coexisting in the older/younger family generation's household while visiting. Notwithstanding the promise of information and communication technologies (ICT) in facilitating easy, cheap and frequent communications across borders, most adolescents' communication with grandparents, while certainly facilitated by ICT, was also mediated by the parents, who acted as the relational bridge between the 'bookend' generations.

The section on gender and intersectionalities began with Chapter Eight by Craig, Hamilton and Brown on the gendered patterning of grandparental childcare in three different contexts. This chapter offers a novel analysis of division of labour between grandmothers and grandfathers and presents a cross-country comparison of these patterns. Chapter Nine by Ojala and Pietilä engaged with the still underresearched topic of grandfathering and developed this field further by offering an analysis of how grandfathering practices vary by social class. In Chapter Ten, Dolbin-MacNab and Few-Demo argued for the importance of applying the intersectional approach to our analyses of grandparenting.

In Chapter Eight, Craig and co-authors made the important point that the *composition* of grandparent childcare time matters. In other words, in addition to the frequency and amount of caregiving we need to understand the types of caregiving tasks that grandmothers and grandfathers are involved in; that is, how the division of labour between different types of grandchild care might be gendered. Craig and co-authors point out that mothers' and fathers' childcare tasks evince deeply gendered patterns, with the time-critical, physical care tasks falling predominantly on mothers and the more talk-based, social care time being more in fathers' domain. This raises the question of whether these gendered patterns are replicated among grandmothers and grandfathers or altered; for instance, as a result of greater availability of time when both grandparents are retired. The composition of caregiving is likely to affect grandparents' enjoyment of childcare, its impact on their health and wellbeing and the extent to which they can fit these tasks around their work, leisure and other interests and commitments. For instance, supervising children at play is likely to be less demanding than bathing and feeding them.

Australia, Italy, France and Korea were chosen for comparison by Craig and colleagues because these countries have contrasting patterns of employment participation, gender norms and policy constellations. The data analysis by Craig and colleagues revealed that a higher proportion of total physical care is performed by grandmothers than grandfathers in all four countries. The distribution of time spent on physical care tasks was unequal in all four countries, with considerable variation, ranging from grandmothers providing 90% of physical care in Italy to grandfathers contributing 41% of such care in France. Nonetheless, across all countries, men's care included relatively less physical care than women's care. The distribution of the other three forms of care – accompanying, talking and minding – was more equal by gender. In all countries except Italy, grandfathers reported that talk-based care took up the greatest proportion of their time. In Italy and Korea, the countries with low rates of part-time work and poor access to childcare, grandparents play a more 'intensive' role; that is, they are undertaking more routine care (physical and accompanying) as a proportion of their overall childcare. They also undertake more physical care as a proportion of their own overall childcare compared with grandparents in France, where a strong public childcare system means grandparents are more likely to provide 'occasional' childcare, and Australia, where grandparents play a 'middling role'.

It therefore appears that, while there is considerable intercountry variation, gender norms in the distribution of care tasks persist into grandparenthood. Institutional contexts shape the types of childcare tasks that grandparents undertake and contribute to reproducing gendered patterns of childcare across generations. Where policies support mothers to combine work and care (in this case, Australia and France), grandmothers do less routine care as a proportion of their overall childcare. Where there is little support for mothers to combine work and care, and grandparents are likely to assume more 'intensive' childcare responsibilities, grandmothers are spending much more of their childcare time in routine care, especially physical care tasks. Viewed through this perspective, the 'grandparents' century' perhaps has rather onerous implications for the subgroup of grandmothers who are involved in extensive physical care provision. The findings presented in Chapter Two are of obvious complementarity to the findings by Craig and colleagues.

In Chapter Nine, Ojala and Pietilä demonstrated how grandfathering practices in Finland are shaped by not only social class positions but also, importantly, the grandchild's age. In the case of young grandchildren, Ojala and Pietilä showed that both working- and middle-class men tend to take a gendered division of labour for granted; that is, to assume that care of young grandchildren is grandmothers' domain. This manifested in the inability of the grandfathers in their Finnish sample to give detailed descriptions of how time was spent with young grandchildren. In contrast, in the case of older grandchildren men were able to give accounts of shared activities, evincing their growing involvement as the grandchildren passed the early childhood stage. With the older grandchildren, social class manifests in the Finnish context in the focus of working-class grandfathers on imparting practical skills such as car repairs, construction and cooking. This differs from the more 'abstract' instruction that middle-class grandfathers try to impart; for instance, regarding the importance of getting schoolwork done and creating networks to advance one's career. This unveiling of socioeconomic differences is an overdue contribution in a literature that has tended to side-line the impact of social class.

Ojala and Pietilä also unpacked the 'family saver' concept by showing it is primarily middle-class grandfathers (and grandmothers) who fulfil this function, as their adult children tend to be pulled towards working long and irregular hours, in contrast to the working-class families, where work is more neatly delineated to regular hours covered by the public day-care system. While the Nordic welfare state is functioning well in enabling mothers to work through universal provision of childcare, the 'reserve army' of grandparents is still needed for the emergencies that can occur when a child falls ill or a parent has to work late. Interestingly, Ojala and Pietilä point out that it is middle-class parents in time-intensive, globally networked jobs that benefit from this 'family saver' function of grandparents more than their counterparts who work in lower-remunerated, manual and locally based occupations.

Chapter Ten, by Dolbin-MacNab and Few-Demo, built on the extensive literature on custodial grandparenting in the United States by highlighting the intersectional approach that is sensitive to how gender, class and ethnicity shape entry into custodial grandparenthood and outcomes for grandfamilies (families where grandparents are raising the grandchildren). Grandparents raising grandchildren in the US are disproportionately more likely to be women, living in poverty, single, members of minority ethnic groups, younger and less educated than grandparents who do not live with their grandchildren. Approximately one in five of all grandparents raising grandchildren have incomes below the poverty line. In short, a significant proportion of grandparents raising grandchildren experience cumulative disadvantage.

Dolbin-McNab and Few-Demo alerted us to the dangers of 'glorifying' the self-sacrificing grandparent, a viewpoint that they point out fails to account for grandparental resilience, families with cultural traditions of multigenerational households and expectations of women as family caregivers. In actuality, some grandparents raising grandchildren might be resentful of the responsibility and others might not think twice about what they are doing for their families; there is diversity in approaches and experiences. Grandparents raising grandchildren are viewed more negatively when the reasons for raising their grandchildren are deemed socially unacceptable or stigmatised – for instance, drug use. Assumptions that these grandparents have somehow failed as parents, and will continue poor parenting practices, are also common. Grandparents raising grandchildren are often viewed through cultural narratives imbued with ageism, classism, sexism and racism. The accumulation of these disempowering narratives across multiple social identities often marginalises custodial grandparents and compromises their wellbeing.

The 'last resort' nature of many of the services and supports available to grandparents in the US means the majority of grandparents raising grandchildren are effectively barred from using them. The persisting emphasis on relative placements in the US can be viewed as reducing the burden on the child welfare system by shifting the burden of care to individuals and families. The best way to address the cumulative disadvantages of grandfamilies calls for long-term, effective strategies to combat the social and economic forces that generate those disadvantages for women, minority ethnic groups and those who struggle economically. Here lies a major challenge for 'the grandparents' century': how do we ensure greater equality in access to the grandparent role, on terms that do not make enormous demands on groups of grandparents who might already be struggling under economic stress and other forms of disadvantage?

In *Contemporary grandparenting*, we pointed out that grandparents themselves exert an influence on how they 'perform' their role, leading to changes in the practices and perceptions of grandparenting. However, this angle remained relatively underexplored in the first book and has come more into focus in the volume at hand. This will be of interest to diverse audiences who are interested in gaining a more nuanced understanding of what goes on inside the grandparent population, still often erroneously perceived as a homogeneous group.

In Chapter Eleven, Bengtson and Silverstein presented their analysis of religious continuity and discontinuity across family generations and developed the concept of intergenerational momentum of influence over time. In addition to revealing a perhaps surprising degree of intergenerational transmission of religiosity, they also illuminated situations where this intergenerational momentum is broken. It seems likely that many religious grandparents will continue to vigorously and ultimately successfully transmit their values across generations, while others will accept or indeed encourage younger family generations following the trend towards secularism.

In their investigation of grandparenting in two Asian cities in Chapter Twelve, Goh and Wang interrogated the scope of Chinese grandparents for 'saying no' in the face of family expectations, with a focus on the use of agency by grandparents. They used social relational theory to unpick the possible differences between grandmothers who are providing grandchild care and those who are not. The authors' starting point was that those who do not provide childcare may have a greater sense of agency, as their non-caregiving goes against traditional societal expectations that have centered around cultural obligations to help with childcare and the norm of reciprocity in intergenerational provision of care. Significant differences in motivation emerged between the caregiving grandmothers in the two contexts (Singapore and Fuzhou). Whereas the Fuzhou grandmothers overwhelmingly cited a strong sense of family obligation as their chief (almost 'automatic') motive, the Singapore grandmothers recounted a wider range of personal reasons, including enjoyment of caregiving on one end of the spectrum and, at the other end, a reluctant agreement on the condition that additional (domestic) help would be available alongside their involvement to make the caregiving manageable.

Among the non-caregiving grandmothers in Singapore, most reasoned either that they had to work, and therefore could not act as main caregivers, or that the alternatives (such as the other set of grandparents or a crèche) were preferable. The analysis by Goh and Wang gives some interesting insights into the reasoning offered by these grandmothers, whereby they portray the alternative to their own involvement as somehow superior; the better caregiving skills of the other grandmother, for instance. However, a minority of grandmothers also flatly rejected the idea that caring for their grandchild was in any sense a duty, stating that rearing their own children had been a sufficient contribution and that no more could be expected from them. In contrast, in Fuzhou the chief reason for non-involvement was that the other set of grandparents had been engaged as the primary carers, often simply on the grounds of being the paternal grandparents. This in turn meant that non-caregivers were able to frame their decisions not to 'fight' over who cares for the grandchild as a selfless act, as looking after a grandchild in Fuzhou was considered something of a privilege. As an alternative manifestation of solidarity, the working grandmothers in Fuzhou reported significant financial and practical support for their grandchild(ren)'s upbringing, including payment of care fees and other expenses.

Somewhat similarly to the middle-class Finnish grandfathers portrayed in Chapter Nine by Ojala and Pietilä, the grandmothers in Singapore expressed strong solidarity towards the work-related stress of their adult children, signaling that this prevented them from expecting or asking for much from their adult child. Rather, the overwhelming emphasis was on downward generational solidarity, supporting the younger generations without any explicit demand for that support to be reciprocated. While hoping for a measure of help in their old(er) age, the grandmothers in Singapore still preferred to formulate their own strategies, such as being prepared to cash in the value of their dwelling to finance care. This is perhaps in line with broader trends in other advanced developed countries, where expectations regarding 'hands-on' care inputs from adult children are waning. By and large, expectations of care in Fuzhou were much stronger, evincing the continuation of a more traditional set of ideas around intergenerational obligations, although a 'no strings attached' approach did also feature among some Fuzhou grandmothers. Indeed, the Fuzhou grandmothers empathised with the position of their only children, faced with the prospect of possibly having to care for four elders: their own and their spouse's parents.

The continuing use and significance of grandparent archetypes was explored in Chapter Thirteen by Vidovićová and Galčanová, who argued that grandparent 'types' can provide a useful guide for understanding how grandparents socially construct their roles. They point out that (useful) simplifications are central components of both scientific and lay thinking as they enable us to communicate complex ideas. In the Czech case that Chapter Thirteen addresses, the vivid archetype of 'the Grandmother' has clearly generated a panoply of cultural images that are used in the everyday talk and portrayals of grandparents. Contemporary Czech grandmothers relate to the existing cultural image of the Grandmother and idealised grandmotherhood, and, importantly, actively use its features to delineate their own understandings of the grandparent role. The grandmother archetype is not only available for positive evaluation of (one's own or other women's) grandmothering performance but also makes it possible to distance oneself from it. The archetype is used by grandmothers as a departure point for framing their own practices, which may be far from 'the ideal' but fundamentally reflect their positive self-image as modern grandmothers who have the option of departing from stereotypes.

The 21st century will be 'the grandparents' century' on the strength of the growing numbers of grandparents globally. However, as I have sought to demonstrate above, how this century pans out will vary between cultures, welfare states and subgroups of grandparents. Grandparents will be increasingly old, and many of them will enjoy good health. In some cases, they might even compete over the opportunity to spend time with and care for one or two grandchildren. We have witnessed the rise and impact of 'intensive parenting' or 'concerted cultivation' (Lareau, 2011) of middle-class children in many societies – might we next detect 'intensive grandparenting', as the older family generation invests heavily in concerted cultivation of the youngest? Higher proportions of the younger grandparents will be working, if the plans to extend working lives succeed, but they will share such long spans of life with their grandchildren that they might have a better opportunity to bond when the latter are teenagers or young adults. Indeed, grandparents (rather than parents) might become important sources of direct material transfers to their grandchildren as the latter struggle with, for instance, the costs of education or housing, while their parents are still paying off student loans and mortgages. But many older adults will not become grandparents, as their children do not wish to or cannot become parents. Whether and when people become grandparents, and how this varies across contexts and cohorts, is set to define a new type of inequality: access to, or inability to enter, the grandparent role. What are the experiences of those who never become grandparents, especially where they harboured strong expectations of grandparenthood and witness others engage in intensive grandparenting?

With reference to those who *do* become grandparents and their practices, important questions remain unanswered yet are growing in importance, many of them of broad relevance for social gerontology and other disciplines such as epidemiology and public health. Are improvements in physical and cognitive health keeping up with lengthening life spans? What are the main lines of inequality in healthy life expectancy, and how are these reflected in grandparenting practices and in grandparents' health and wellbeing? Among future grandparents, the distribution of intergenerational duties will vary considerably, both by choice and by pressure of circumstances (for instance, where adult children cannot afford or do not trust formal childcare). Chapters in this book suggest that this variance will continue to be shaped by gender, social class and location in terms of culture and welfare state.

As a result of longer shared lifespans, interacting with one's grandchildren will increasingly mean interacting with them in their adulthood. Research (including chapters in this book) has, to date, overwhelmingly focused on interaction with young grandchildren. What kind of sociologically interesting changes will we start to see when we have the opportunity to study grandparents who have coexisted with their grandchildren through the latter's infancy, childhood, youth, early and even middle adulthood? In some parts of the world, we will witness growing numbers of older adults who also enter the great-grandparent role and hence become members of four- or even five-generation families: what are the future dynamics in these 'extreme' beanpole families? For instance, will we have more grandparents caring for grandchildren but also caring for their own very old parents? The future of grandparenting is impossible to foresee, but it is reasonable to expect great individual and societal enrichment as the scope for intergenerational coexistence and interaction increases, and as this works primarily – I strongly predict – to the benefit of the grandchildren but also – I hope – the grandparents.

References

Baker, L. and Silverstein, M. (2012) 'The well-being of grandparents caring for grandchildren in China and the United States', in S. Arber and V. Timonen (eds) *Grandparenting: Changing family relationships and global contexts*, Bristol: Policy Press, pp 51–70.

Conlon, C., Timonen, V., Carney, G. and Scharf, T. (2014) 'Women (re-)negotiating care across family generations: Intersections of gender and socioeconomic status', *Gender & Society*, 28(5): 729–751.

Lareau, A. (2011) *Unequal childhoods: Class, race, and family life*, Berkeley and Los Angeles, CA: University of California Press.

Index

Page references for notes are followed by n

V

W

Y

Lightning Source UK Ltd.
Milton Keynes UK
UKHW020915030320
359674UK00005B/361